# IT'S ALL ABOUT

# TIME
## - Corporate Transformation -

How a Deliberate Approach to a Chain of Reforms
Produced Double-digit Growth
Over Nearly Two Decades

## TADASHI SAEGUSA

DJ Publications Inc.

CC: Legal Dept

1475 E. Woodfield Rd., Ste. 1300

Schaumburg, IL 60173

Limitation of Liability/Disclaimer of Warranty:

While the publisher and author have used their best efforts in preparing this book, they make no representations or warranties with respect to the accuracy or completeness of the contents of this book and specifically disclaim any implied warranties of merchantability or fitness for a particular purpose. Neither the publisher nor author shall be liable for any loss of profit or any other commercial damages, including but not limited to special, incidental, or consequential damages, based on your response to this book.

ISBN: 978-0-578-76325-5 (Hardcover)

Library of Congress Control Number: 2020918845

Translator/Editor: Glen K. Anderson

Printed by: LSC Communications, in the United States of America
First printing, 2021.

# IT'S ALL ABOUT TIME
## - Corporate Transformation -

# TABLE OF Contents

# Prologue

# Taking up the Gauntlet of Corporate Transformation

## A Chance Encounter at a Crossroads

"Mr. Saegusa, how would you like to take over for me as CEO of Misumi?"

The question from Mr. Hiroshi Taguchi, founder of Misumi (now MISUMI Group Inc.) caught me completely flat-footed. After all, I had only become involved with the company three months earlier as an outside director and was there to attend what was just my fourth board of directors meeting. Meanwhile, he was contemplating retirement and looking for someone to replace him.

At the time, I had my own company, Saegusa International Co., Ltd. I was a corporate turnaround specialist helping revive Japanese companies struggling in the aftermath of the economic bubble's collapse. I had launched a career in corporate turnarounds at a time when the concept was unknown in Japan. To survive in this new profession, I needed to develop the necessary skills and experience through trial and error.

When I was approached about joining Misumi's board as an outside director, I was already working for Mr. Satoru Anzaki, then CEO of Komatsu, the second largest construction-equipment manufacturer in the world after Caterpillar. I had been retained to turn around one of the company's loss-making businesses. About two years had passed since the turnaround project launched, and with the toughest of the reforms behind us, success was within reach. (My book *Turnaround Task Force* depicts that reform effort.) As a result, I had enough time to spare for an outside directorship. Working as chief executive, however, would be an entirely different kettle of fish.

During my 16 years as a turnaround specialist, I had been offered three different CEO positions. But I turned them all down because their businesses didn't excite me.

Nevertheless, I was in my mid-50s, nearing the home stretch of my career, and restless for a new challenge. I had a feeling Misumi might be just what I was looking for. It was a big step for the founder to cede control of his company, to be sure, but I was grappling with an even more weighty decision: Did I want this post?

I explained to Mr. Taguchi that taking over the reins at his company would mean I would have to close my own turnaround business of 16 years.

He looked at me knowingly, with a subtle smile. Perhaps he felt a sense of relief that I hadn't rejected his offer out of hand. Months later, at a press conference called to announce his retirement and my succession, he declared, "I knew by September that no one but Mr. Saegusa would do."

By September, I was only three months into my position as outside director on the board. I couldn't think of anything that would have made me stand out in Mr. Taguchi's eyes. Maybe he had heard reviews of my turnaround work. Or perhaps he had read my books, and my thoughts on strategic management had resonated with him.

We had travelled different paths to this juncture. But here we were, nevertheless, after a chance encounter at a crossroads.

By any standard, Misumi looked like an unconventional company. Yet I wondered whether there was enough there for me to make the leap—to close my own business and commit to spending the rest of my career at someone else's company. It would require marshalling the management skills, strategic techniques and leadership styles I had accumulated over my career and applying them to this final mission. I needed time to think it over before I could make up my mind.

## Running Businesses in My 30s

Eventually, of course, I accepted the offer, and ended up leading a series of reforms. Each stirred up a whole host of issues. In the end, during my 16 years there—12 as CEO and another 4 as Chairman—what we accomplished amounted to nothing less than a complete corporate transformation.

Of course, reform efforts can entail great risk. A misstep in method or strategy can drive a company into *Death Valley*. The success of reforms and business turnarounds hinge on whether you can assemble a suitable plan and develop a workable strategy. To do so, you need to accurately diagnose what ails the business and identify the root causes of those ailments.

Readers of the Poirot or Colombo detective stories are never let in on their failures—the times when they overlooked important evidence or arrested the wrong person. But neither of them could have achieved greatness without such stumbles.

The same applies to business. In the fog of *chaos*, you need to look reality directly in the face, shrewdly *solve riddles* and capture the true essence of the problems. These abilities don't develop overnight. They take years of experience to cultivate, through setbacks and failures.

Not everyone is cut out to be chief executive of a large corporation. So why me?

Throughout my career, as far back as my 20s, I have continually taken on risk in conservative Japan, making forays into professions 10 to 20 years ahead of the times. Of course, I've had my share of failures. I originally embarked on a conventional career path. After college graduation, I joined Mitsui Petrochemical Industries (now Mitsui Chemicals) but left in less than three years. Back then, Japanese employers took a dim view of anyone who left one company to join another. So, leaving a large, reputable firm like Mitsui after such a short stint was practically unheard of.

Before long, I was hired by the Boston Consulting Group as its first locally hired consultant in Japan. I worked in Tokyo and Boston. At the time, BCG had barely begun to make a name for itself in the US, but from my first day on the job I was impressed with the top-tier talent there. In the 1970s, BCG spearheaded a global trend in *strategic management.*

My experience at BCG inspired the logic and strategic orientation I have applied to management ever since. I also learned volumes about how to conduct myself professionally.

While at BCG, I developed an itch to become a *business leader* myself. After getting my MBA from Stanford Business School, I had the good fortune to head three companies while still in my 30s.

The first was a joint venture between Sumitomo Chemical and a US outfit. At the age of 32, I joined as managing executive officer and took charge of the entire company a year later. In my late 30s, I worked on the turnaround of a troubled venture that Otsuka Pharmaceutical was trying to salvage. And at age 39, I launched and ran a $60 million venture capital fund as its President. I had landed many opportunities that ordinarily would never have come my way in Japan's conservative business environment.

By my own volition, I chose the path of an outcast shunned by the establishment. During my journey, however, I encountered other independent-minded businessmen. Together, we formed an inconspicuous network, one that led to a series of leadership opportunities early on in my career.

In my early 30s I had already accomplished my dream of becoming a top executive. Of the many obstacles I met, it was the people issues, not the strategic ones, that I found most vexing. But in the end, I found the more trouble I encountered, the more I learned. Those who seek shall gain the greatest learnings.

## Becoming a Turnaround Specialist in my 40s

By the time I turned 40, I had accumulated experience as a strategy consultant and as president of two businesses and one venture capital fund--an unconventional career path at the time, to say the least. (I suppose that would also hold true today.)

At the age of 41, I decided to start my own company, Saegusa International. The move was reported by *Nikkei Sangyo Shimbun*, one of Japan's major industrial newspapers.

Friends and family worried that I would not be able to make a living, but I proved their misgivings wrong. Working to hone my management skills, I eventually set my sights on becoming a *professional CEO*. After Japan's bubble economy burst in the 1990s, major corporations began to hire me to turn around their loss-making businesses.

Japan embraces a Confucian respect for elders. Publicly traded companies enjoy elevated status in society. By extension, those who eventually rise to the ranks of upper management in these companies are treated with reverence, based on both their age and position. Yet there I was, an independent consultant perhaps 20 years their junior, telling them how to fix their problems. Awkward, to say the least. More importantly, was this a viable occupation?

At the time, *corporate turnaround* was an unfamiliar concept in Japan. More than a decade would pass before the Industrial Revitalization Corporation of Japan—a public turnaround fund— would emerge. So, there was no guarantee then that I could make a career out of managing corporate turnarounds.

I may have been the first to be called a *turnaround specialist* in Japan. It wasn't just a novel job; it was an entirely new profession. Without a mentor to guide me, I had no choice but to learn the ropes on my own, through trial and error.

That led to the next turning point in my career.

The top executive of a publicly traded company had heard of me through the grapevine and decided to retain me to help with his firm's struggling business. The company had grown by leaps and bounds during Japan's post-war economic miracle, but it had become hidebound and fallen into a sorry state. Its employees had lost their drive, and it was rudderless, saddled with a lackluster salaryman culture and uninspired leadership.

*Salaryman* is a term you will come across often here. It describes a certain mindset fostered by the seniority-based system of pay and promotions common in Japan over the half-century following World War II. Under this system, companies awarded their employees age-based promotions and pay raises, regardless of job performance.

A salaryman would never get rich but could look forward to pay-raises and promotions just for showing up to work. Many grew complacent, happy to collect a paycheck that afforded them a stable lifestyle and security for their families. The term salaryman was coined to describe this phenomenon. Many salarymen believed and behaved as if their jobs were secure as long as they followed orders, so they saw no need to take on new challenges. Over the last half century, the ranks of unambitious salarymen have swelled, while ambitious leaders willing to take risks have thinned out, sapping companies of their vitality.

Nevertheless, there are CEOs who sincerely want to exercise inspiring leadership, to revitalize their companies. I wanted to help them, and that served as a decisive factor in choosing which clients to work with.

When I was retained to turn around an ailing company, I would typically take on a title like executive vice-president or division director and use the authority the post gave me to drive needed reform. In other words, rather than working from the outside like a consultant or mere adviser, I would insert myself into the heart of the company's leadership to propel change from within. I leveraged my position to *sever ties* with old management habits, halt negative trends and return the company to a healthier path of growth.

### Riddle-solving for Business Leaders (1): Severing Ties

*Sever* as I use it here does not imply laying people off. Rather, what you should sever is entrenched *management practices* to point the company in a new direction and drive it forward. Businesses develop kinks. First, get to the heart of the problem and deconstruct it. Then establish a new strategy, win buy-in from *the incumbent players* and take them in a new direction.

Simply put, my goal was to save companies whose leadership had repeatedly failed to implement reform. In order to succeed, I needed to exhibit greater management skills than current and past CEOs. I had to roll up my sleeves, get my hands dirty and find the breakthrough strategy that would rescue it from the thralls of *Death Valley*.

Invariably, I would encounter chaotic situations. As I led a company through what might be its last chance for survival, there were some senior managers who either refused to cooperate or failed to pull their weight. Sometimes, it pushed me to my mental limits.

After a long day with the client, I would return to my own office usually by 10:00 pm. Its smart interior design and soothing sound system helped me to unwind. By then, my secretary would have long since gone home, allowing me some solitude. I would put on my favorite classical music, sink into the sofa, and immediately fall into a deep slumber.

Eventually, I would awaken and bathe in the soft sounds of the music in the background.

Those drowsy moments brought a real sense of contentment, but when the clock passed 11:00, I knew it was time to go home to sleep. This little ritual restored my energy for the next day.

On every turnaround I led, there would be a period of deep chaos that made it hard to see the light at the end of the tunnel, obscuring the path out of *Death Valley*.

How did I stay motivated to work so hard for the sake of what was, after all, someone else's company? While most businesspeople encounter chaos at some point in their careers, I've probably had 10 times the experience at 10 times the intensity. It goes with the territory, but each episode only helped to burnish my professional skills—and that's what kept me engaged.

### Riddle-solving for Business Leaders (2): Battlefield Chaos

I look at chaos as a form of severe dysfunction that can easily spin out of control. It can drive you into a corner where you're pinned down by people interested only in protecting themselves. The chaos has less to do with logic (*Is it right?*) and more to do with emotion (*Do I like it?*). A flawed strategy may be at the core of the problem, but it is exacerbated by personal and political factors.

My work allowed me to gather a wealth of management literacy and experience exceeding the average businessperson's by far. Eventually, grappling with corporate contingencies came to feel routine. Often, I would realize, "I've seen this before" and I've

xvi    IT'S ALL ABOUT TIME

used these insights to achieve differentiation in my management *frameworks* (I will define frameworks in detail in Saegusa's Management Note 1: What is a Management Framework?). Without a doubt, Poirot and Colombo went through their own learning curves.

## A Final Change of Direction in My Late 50s

The management skills I developed as a turnaround specialist fall into three broad categories.

1. **Strategy:** The ability to instill strategy throughout the organization and inspire enthusiasm.
   Strategy is not a tool reserved exclusively for the C suite. Strategy needs to be explained in easily understood terms to the entire organization, from top to bottom. That strategy needs to be outward-looking and cognizant of the competition. It cannot get bogged down in intractable internal conflicts that hamper progress. The leader needs to communicate the strategy effectively to inspire enthusiasm.

2. **Organization:** The ability to move an organization that's stuck in the mud.
   As a turnaround specialist, you need your own *organizational theory*, learned through a series of painful experiences managing people and organizations. If key players are spending too much time building consensus or playing political games, the organization should be dismantled and rebuilt from the ground up. Think of yourself as an architect. Call it an organization, or a business process. Either way, the end product encourages personnel to be creative, entrepreneurial and competitive in the marketplace.

3. **People:** The ability to discern talent.
   Visit a company on the brink of failure and you may be surprised to find how insouciant and uncooperative people

can be. Even executives and senior managers may feign support for transformation but drag their heels when it's time to do their part. Others may keep their disgruntlement to themselves, then vent once they're out of earshot. In the US, such people would be promptly fired, but Japanese companies tend to be reluctant to make quick, bold decisions, thereby undermining their progress. Choose the wrong people to push reform, and that effort is destined to fail. The chaos that is part and parcel of quick-moving reform efforts acts like a UV light that quickly exposes the fakers.

Fortunately, my hard-won experience in corporate renewal served me well in the later stages of my career. By my early 50s my leadership skills had improved considerably.

## What Does It Mean to Be a Professional CEO?

By my 30s, I had decided that I wanted to become a *professional CEO*. It was a risky ambition because it implied breaking the mold established by Japan's seniority-based personnel systems. In contrast to the managers these systems elevated from within, I had accumulated a great deal of experience in different companies and businesses. Nevertheless, I didn't feel for a long time that I was quite ready to be called a professional CEO, as I define it here.

1. Someone who can quickly get to the bottom of things. Problems manifest themselves on the surface in many different ways.
2. Someone who can explain the issue concisely in *easily understandable terms*.
3. Someone who can leverage the above two attributes to *unite* executives and the rank and file to move the organization forward.
4. And, of course, someone who can ultimately produce *results*.

Even iconic business leaders may not be cut out for this role. If they only have experience at one company, they are just *the CEO of that company*. Their management style may only work there, and nowhere else.

5.  Professional CEOs possess *versatile* management skills, strategic capabilities and an entrepreneurial mindset that transcend differences in industry, company size, and organizational culture. These attributes can be applied wherever they go.
6.  They have gathered *solid management experience*, including tackling chaotic situations. They draw on that experience to address challenging situations with a level head.
    Another characteristic of professional CEOs is that they earn more than their peers. Moreover, taking the helm at a different company requires adaptability and battle-readiness. Similarly, professional athletes who can change teams and play well from day-one are valued more.
7.  Naturally, professionals will be richly compensated *commensurate with their skills*.

The top post is not for everyone. Honing your skills as a specialist in a specific area, such as sales or development, is a perfectly respectable career choice. However, many Japanese assume that their work in specific functions will automatically translate into improved leadership skills and lead to a role in senior management down the road. Often, it doesn't work out that way. This misconception stems from the seniority-based practices that have pervaded Japanese corporations.

If you strive to lead a company, appreciate that business leadership is a distinct profession in itself. This is the advice I often give Japanese aspiring to become CEO: No later than your mid-30s start to focus your energy and time on acquiring top-management skills that will open doors for you.

## Riding the Wave of the International Megatrend in Business Innovations

This book is not simply a grab bag of random and isolated reform stories. An historic avalanche of business innovations swept across the world in the early 1990s. The fallout would change the global industrial map for decades to come. Its effects even linger today.

The 1990s saw the emergence of concepts such as *time-based s trategy, reengineering,* and *supply chains,* and operational innovations that led to Industries 4.0 in Europe and the rise of Amazon and other e-commerce platforms in the US. I address this in depth in the section titled Saegusa Management Note (5): The International Megatrend in Business Innovations.

In short, the US leveraged these trends to regain industrial strength, while Japanese companies failed to give chase, bogged down by the burst of the bubble economy in the 1990s.

If we trace the history all the way back, though, we find that these trends were originally inspired by Japanese management systems such as the Toyota Production System (TPS). While Japan failed to harness TPS more broadly to drive innovation in other corporate activities and business management, Western players saw a chance to leverage it to do something new. The obsession with time that lies at the heart of TPS was the secret sauce that enabled corporate rejuvenation in the West from the 1990s onward.

Japanese companies found themselves knocked by these upstarts off the comfortable perch from which they had dominated the international market because they had fallen behind the curve in applying the megatrend in business innovations to their operations. It was an ignominious defeat for the Japanese management style.

Even today, many Japanese are not fully aware of these trends. But Misumi was different. After I took over in 2002, we immediately began to implement various reforms. Despite setbacks, we were able to revamp its business strategy and the foundations undergirding it. Each of our reforms interlocked with the others, like links in a chain, to strengthen not only the individual units but also the business model as an integrated whole. These concepts and the staff's relentless efforts are what underpinned the transformation and *rebirth* of Misumi.

It was not an easy process. In the first half of each chapter, I describe our failures, where the reform projects did not proceed as planned. In the second half, I outline how we overcame the challenges we encountered and forged breakthroughs that enabled success. All of the stories I introduce are true, and the *frameworks* I introduce throughout are versatile and general enough to be applied to a range of situations.

Like my previous books—*Professional Strategist, A Crisis in Japanese Corporate Management*, and *Turnaround Task Force* (currently only available in Japanese)—I eschewed a stuffy textbook on business theory. I wanted to outline a *logical* and *strategic* approach to management through a vivid description of events as they unfolded, in a style similar to live news coverage from the scene.

Each of my past books tells the story of *short-term showdowns* of turning around struggling companies or businesses within two to three years. In these pages, I describe the story of a *transformation—a chain of reforms*—that we implemented at Misumi. I share the story of how we turned a domestic-focused trading company with a headcount of just 340 into an internationally competitive e-commerce company specializing in industrial mechanical components with 25 of its own production sites and a workforce of more than 10,000 globally.

While each of my past books resembles traversing a treacherous ravine, here we are out on a plain, undertaking a massive and back-breaking endeavor to redirect the flow of a wide river. In each chapter, I describe a number of the dangerous pitfalls we encountered in each stage of the transformational project. Not until all of the pieces of the puzzle had been snapped into place to form a coherent whole—an effort that spanned more than a decade—could we consider our work done.

## To Those Who Strive to Become Business Leaders

None of the reforms I describe in these pages occurred spontaneously. They were all *consciously* instilled by Misumi's leadership, who appear as characters in this story. Each of our reforms ran up against people who could have stifled them through sheer incompetence or poor decisions. Against this backdrop, I shine a spotlight on the true reformers who quickly overcame these and other barriers to change.

In implementing these reforms, I would sometimes sit back and take a bird's eye view of the situation. At other times I would swoop down to ground level to take command. This book does more than serve up a collection of discrete, unrelated episodes. By the time you read the last page, you will understand the chain of reforms that transformed Misumi into a completely different company.

I have referred to Misumi by name throughout the book, and I am the protagonist of this tale. Since the events described here played out, I have moved into a new capacity, serving as Senior Chairman.

I have also used Mr. Taguchi's real name rather than employing a pseudonym, as it is public knowledge that he was Misumi's founder. Throughout my time there, I have been careful not to publicly criticize him or dismiss his policies, but in this book, I give an honest account of the rationale underlying the decisions I made.

For this book to have any meaning at all, it must frankly address why I needed to make such drastic reforms immediately after taking over. My actions belied the image Misumi enjoyed as a successful enterprise. I delve into my concerns and the situations I sought to avoid.

I provided a copy of the manuscript to Mr. Taguchi before submitting it to the publisher. He expressed satisfaction that it was a true account of events and did not request a single revision.

While parts of this book may appear to criticize Mr. Taguchi's leadership, I do not in any way wish to belittle his achievements as the company's founder. He is an ingenious entrepreneur, and the 40-year history of the company that he built provided a solid base that was indispensable for moving the company forward.

## This Story is Not Unique to Misumi

I've given pseudonyms to all of the characters in this book except for myself and Mr. Taguchi. Most characters are based on an actual person, while some are an amalgamation of multiple players.

In preparing to write this book, I asked about 30 of Misumi's current senior managers to share their recollections of our reform efforts and my management style. I also asked mid-level personnel to write down their reflections on cards. Their responses used some 500 cards in all.

There is plenty of documentation to back up the facts described in this book. On the other hand, there is no accurate record of conversations I had, nor was I privy to most people's internal thoughts. Some are my personal observations and therefore subjective. I have taken the liberty to augment and revise some of the testimonials I received, based on my memory of the events. Responsibility for the content therefore lies entirely with me.

Finally, I have a request for you, the reader. Understand that the lessons shared here are broadly applicable beyond Misumi. While the events unfolded there, the business circumstances, people's actions and emotions, and the logic behind the strategies described have wide applicability to almost any situation. If you keep that in mind, you will gain much more from this book.

If I had turned down the job at Misumi to become CEO elsewhere, I most likely would have implemented reforms there as well. Perhaps I would have published a book about those experiences after moving on, just as I have done here. But I imagine that most of the important lessons of one story would overlap with the other. Business and its strategy have a *generality* that can be applied at any company. Developing a wealth of flexible, adaptable frameworks to draw from will enhance your effectiveness.

I hope that this book will be enjoyed by those who aspire to become future business leaders and CEOs. If even one person finds something of value in these pages, the effort that went into to writing it will not have been in vain.

Now, this is where I stop writing as I, and start the story of how Tadashi Saegusa took on the challenge of *transforming a company*.

# Chapter 1

# Uncovering Strengths and Weaknesses

After 40 years in business and an initial public offering, Misumi's sales had reached $500 million. During the next four years, Saegusa doubled that figure. Then he navigated the global financial crisis and pushed sales past $2 billion during his 12 years as CEO. By the time he retired as Chairman of the Board four years later, in total serving for Misumi for 16 years, sales had surpassed $3 billion. What kind of riddle-solving enabled this corporate transformation?

## Section 1:
# Drawing Up the Business Model

## Only Four Months Left

"Mr. Saegusa, how would you like to take over for me as CEO?"

It was September. At the time, Tadashi Saegusa was serving as an outside director on Misumi's board. The offer came as a surprise, and of course Saegusa did not answer on the spot. Accepting the role would not only represent a dramatic change of direction, most likely, the position would be the last of his career.

Saegusa figured he had until January to make a final decision, which left only four months. In that time, he would need to uncover Misumi's strengths and weaknesses and determine whether the business would be enough of a challenge to stir his passion. He would need to move quickly.

Saegusa had been in this kind of situation before. Every time he first set foot in a company he was tasked with turning around, he felt as though he had been dropped into a maze to wander aimlessly without a map. From past experience, he knew that briefing materials prepared by the company for him would be useless, reflecting only weak analysis, misguided strategy and poor leadership. No one was going to bring him the answers. He had to seek them out himself.

### Riddle-solving for Business Leaders (3):
### *Death Valley*
Any leader trying to point a company in a new direction will inevitably stumble upon some form of a *Death Valley*. You can't avoid it, but if you know it's coming and you're prepared, you'll boost your chances of safely reaching the other side. The key to success here is to show both a high degree of management literacy and passionate leadership.

For 16 years, Saegusa had been working as a turnaround specialist. On his first visit to a new client's office, wary employees saw him as an interloper. He paid that no mind and quickly set about getting familiar with the place.

Walk around and observe the people there—officers and staffers alike. There are moments that provide glimpses into the problems. The signs lie in their inadvertent comments and jokes, in the subtle changes in their facial expressions. It's as if a window opened, revealing a landscape, only to shut again right away. That momentary glimpse could reveal the absence of something that should be there, or the presence of something that should not. Either way, it feels off.

You may doubt your intuition. Maybe you're over-thinking it. To know for sure, you need to open that window again and take a better look.

If you sense something amiss, venture out into the workplace and get a close-up look to measure the essence of the problem. You are there as CEO and you can make any move as you like. Ask around. Once you're satisfied nothing is awry, you can take your leave. It's a hands-on approach that strong business leaders employ every day.

## The Key to Misumi's Strength

As a trading company in the obscure B2B world of supplying industrial mechanical components, Misumi sells parts used to make production machinery like automation equipment, robots, dies and molds. It does NOT sell parts that go into automobiles, personal computers and other products that end up in a consumer's hands.

For those who enjoy the B2C world, the industrial components business may be boring, without much marketing involved and little need for strategy. But they don't know what they are missing.

From experience, Saegusa knew that B2B involves many dynamics, from strategy to marketing and more.

Historically, Misumi had delivered outstanding performance. Its sales of $500 million made it small compared to its peers in Japan, but it boasted a gross margin of 35% to 40% and an operating margin of 10%. Even as Japan's economy shrank, Misumi continued to post strong earnings. Its margins were unusually high for a trading company, a business model that typically generated thin margins on large volumes. It would be inconceivable for major trading houses like Mitsubishi Corporation or Mitsui & Co., Ltd. to enjoy anything close to Misumi's margins.

So, what makes Misumi's business unique?

Someone who knows the company (and not many do) would say it sells mechanical components through a catalog.

You might be surprised to see the catalog. At 1,200 pages, it is thicker than a phone book and too heavy to comfortably carry around in one hand. Flip through the pages and you may be disappointed: There are no beautiful models or color illustrations. Just numbers and symbols. Nothing fancy. (Saegusa would quickly move this business online, sharply reducing the need for paper catalogs and telephone and fax orders.)

He walked around Misumi's offices, asking people what makes their company unique. Everyone gave the same answer: "We provide customers with standardized components through our catalog. Many engineers find the catalog as convenient as a dictionary."

At first, he wasn't sure what to make of that. What did they mean by *standardized*?

In fact, the word *standardized* embodied an amazing business innovation.

When Misumi was founded half a century before, it only handled die and mold parts. Dies and molds are the workhorses of manufacturing. They're used to produce many of the products around us, from automobiles and electronic products to personal computers and mobile phones. They're what make plastic products such as buckets and toys possible.

For example, think of an autoparts maker using a press machine to manufacture automotive components. To produce the component as designed, the press machine is fitted with one or more dies. If the product design or specifications are changed even slightly, the dies must be swapped out. Each die is made up of multiple parts. That's where Misumi saw its chance.

### *Testimonial from M. Aragaki (Age 53. Director on the board)*

*Long ago, we regularly visited all our customers—the die makers—to take their orders for die parts. We passed those orders to parts makers. When the parts were ready, we delivered the products to the die maker.*

*When the die maker's designer created a new die, a detailed blueprint was drawn up for every component used to build the die. We instructed parts makers to build each part exactly as specified in the blueprint.*

*It used to take about two to three weeks from order to delivery of the product. But if the part delivered didn't conform exactly to the specification, it would have to be remade, which of course took extra time.*

*The buying process took time and effort, such as blueprint reviews and receiving inspections, where incoming parts were checked to ensure they conformed exactly to the blueprint. These factors made die parts more expensive.*

## Misumi's Innovation

That was standard procedure in the industry at the time. However, the founder Mr. Taguchi devised a revolutionary solution. After 15 years in business, the company published the first-ever catalog of die components.

The catalog featured myriad parts tables. Each part table accommodated dimensional differences down to the micron. The catalog was all numbers and symbols. But eliminating the need for die designers to draw up blueprints was a truly groundbreaking development.

- Rather than fussing with blueprints, designers could select the desired part and dimensions using the numbers and symbols provided in the catalog's part tables.
- Misumi used the numbers and symbols as the part number for ordering purposes. The designer could convey that part number to Misumi's customer center via phone or fax.
- Misumi would then forward that part number on to a contract manufacturer, whose employees knew exactly what to do because the necessary information was included in the part number.
- The contract manufacturer could produce a high-precision component with micron-level accuracy in just one day. The parts were shipped overnight from the manufacturer to Misumi's distribution center, then sent out the door on the third day. (By the time this book was first published, Misumi had further shortened the process by a day, from three days to two days.) For an extra fee, the customer could place a rush order that would ship in one day.
- The catalog lists product prices, eliminating the customary estimate and price-negotiation steps.

Before this innovation, customers would draw up a blueprint for every part, meaning that each was essentially a special-order part. With the catalog, they could be handled as standardized parts. The implications were enormous.

The system provided convenience, saving the die maker's designers a tremendous amount of work. Misumi set rigid standards for quality, which won the customer's trust.

Orders started coming in from all over Japan, and growth skyrocketed from there.

It is valuable to consider this innovation from an historical perspective. By the late 1970s, Misumi had already launched its catalog-based business for micron-level precision industrial components based on made-to-order single-piece production, with no minimum quantity requirements and quick delivery to the customer's door. It was a revolutionary development akin to the changes retail giants like Amazon would bring to their industries decades later.

## Drawing Up the Business Model

After observing the company with his own eyes, Saegusa began to wonder. "There must be something more to this standardization touted by the people here." Yet no one could explain it fully.

Was standardization the sole source of Misumi's strength? Or was there more to it?

### Riddle-solving for Business Leaders (4): Identifying and Sharing the Business Model

Even a superlative business model could become obscured if you have not identified and expressed it in clear terms. Failure to define the business model risks missing opportunities to devise comprehensive strategies to strengthen that model. If your rivals recognize the model's value and emulate it, they may encroach on your competitive advantage.

**Key Turning Points: Riddle-solving and Decision-making for Business Leaders**

- Through his experiences turning around businesses, Saegusa found that employees gave short shrift to the business model. This is symptomatic of weakness, a herd mentality, and an inclination to copy others.
- However, Misumi was not weak—it had continued to post strong growth and earnings. Nevertheless, the Misumi Business Model needed to be depicted in a structured way that captured all the elements identified as discrete strengths.
- Taking the helm without fully understanding the business model could lead to missteps. So, Saegusa sought to draw up the business model himself.

It's not easy to explain a business model. You need to pick out the essential elements from a complex web of confounding factors like internal systems and the competitive landscape, then paint those key elements into a simple picture.

After many attempts over several days, Saegusa finally had that picture in mind. Surely, this would offer a fresh perspective for the company's people. A lot of creative work went into drawing up this model, so it would be his personal framework. He dubbed it the Misumi QCT Model.

1. The strength of any company's product rests on three elements: quality, cost and time. A product of high quality (Q) offered at the lowest cost (C) and delivered in the shortest time (T) will be most popular with customers, absent some other compelling factor.
2. Consider the customer-facing side of the business to be the *front end*. Misumi made history by introducing catalog sales and fundamentally transforming the distribution channel in a segment of the industrial mechanical components market. The catalog was the *detonator* that blew up traditional distribution channels and triggered explosive growth for the business.

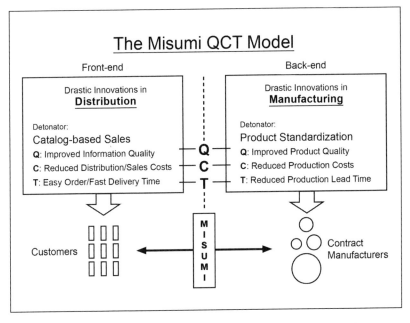

The Misumi QCT Model

Q: The information contained in the catalogs was far more comprehensive than what local die-parts shops provided. Ending dependence on sales representatives dramatically improved the quality of the information delivered to the customer.

C: The introduction of a catalog and direct order by fax (later online) eliminated the need for sales representatives entirely. Direct sales cut out the middleman's margins. Distribution costs dropped substantially.

T: Standard orders that used to take two to three weeks now shipped within three days.

3. Consider the contract manufacturers to comprise the *back end*. The company's transformative product standardization was the *detonator* on this side of the model.

   Q: Production volumes at contract manufacturers grew dramatically as compared with the traditional order-made single-piece production, and standardization facilitated improvements in production technology, which in turn drove quality enhancements.

C: Increased production volumes improved econo-
mies of scale dramatically. Additionally, product
standardization facilitated specialization and the
accumulation of expertise, which in turn drove up yields.
Amazingly, costs fell by two-thirds. Even after slashing sales
prices, there was still plenty of room for comfortable
profit margins.

T: Contract manufacturers implemented a single-piece
production method, an important concept in the Toyota
Production System (TPS), and substantially shortened
production lead times. This significantly cut total lead
times—from order to shipment —which met customers'
strong needs for quick and on time delivery.

## Riddle-solving for Business Leaders (5): A Detonator in the Business Model

Merely tweaking the business model for incremental
improvements can't come close to the dramatic change
that successful fundamental reform delivers. An innovative business model contains something—whether it
be a technology or an idea—that alters the competitive
dynamics of the market or rewrites the landscape
in one fell swoop. Saegusa called that "something" a
*detonator*. A strong business model incorporates at least
one detonator. As he depicted the MISUMI QCT Model,
Saegusa found two detonators, making it a truly powerful
business model.

Actually, throughout Saegusa's management career, *time* had always
been a decisive strategic factor. Aspiring business leaders need to
have a *time-based strategy*.

## Riddle-solving for Business Leaders (6): Time-based Strategy

In the early 1990s, observers in the US realized that the Toyota Production System (TPS) was more than just a means for improving production activities; it also served as a *time-based strategy*. This game-changing insight, once implemented, helped push the scope of improvement from the production floor out to the business as a whole and revolutionized the approach to re-engineering, supply chain and ERP. Most recently, it's been employed in Europe, for Industry 4.0. To be more competitive, incorporate the benefits of a time-based strategy into internal work processes. (For more on this, see Saegusa's Management Note 5.)

Indeed, Misumi's catalog had set off a blast that shattered the norms of distribution in this segment of industrial mechanical components. Pleased with his depiction of the Misumi QCT Model, Saegusa wondered, would this business model ever become outmoded? Could a competitor copy the model or displace Misumi as the driver of innovation?

Furthermore, what does it mean that its people do not clearly recognize the business model? Had the superiority of the business they and their predecessors built bred complacency? Is it a sign that they lack the initiative to continue innovating?

Therein lies the strength of a framework—it triggers questions like this. Saegusa needed to test his diagram of the Misumi QCT Model with the people there to confirm that it was on the mark.

*Testimonial from M. Aragaki*

*About half a year after Saegusa joined the company, he invited me to a local sushi restaurant for dinner and drinks. We were having a good time. Suddenly, he picked up the discarded paper envelope from his disposable chopsticks and began to draw something on it.*

*"This captures the essence of Misumi's business, right?"*

*I was taken aback. He was supposed to be new to the company. Yet he was able to sum it up in a concise diagram that allowed me to see it from a different angle.*

*Of course, at that time I had no clue he would become our CEO. I figured it would always be Mr. Taguchi's company to run.*

## The Pillar Undergirding Strong Earnings and Growth

Saegusa continued his survey of the company. He learned Misumi had taken various steps to bolster the business infrastructure underlying its die-parts business. It had upgraded the customer-care and distribution centers, and the IT backbone that made it all possible. Its infrastructure functions adhered to the motto, *deliver on time*. Officers even boasted that this spirit was written into the company's DNA.

He made an interesting discovery. The infrastructure undergirding the company's first business—the die and mold parts unit—had, thanks to regular upgrades, become so sophisticated that it could be leveraged to sell other products and drive new growth.

That led to product diversification, just as the outlook for growth in metal-press die parts began to level off.

First, the company moved into mold parts used in plastic molding. Then it expanded into parts used in factory automation equipment. Before long, it was selling electronics components and wiring parts, jigs and fixtures used in broader manufacturing settings, and much more. Leveraging its business infrastructure as a platform, it launched forays into other product categories. If it had limited itself to die parts, its robust earnings and growth would have long since slowed.

His research had been going well so far. He came to the conclusion that the machinery driving its remarkable corporate performance was part of what made it unique.

Was there enough there to justify accepting the CEO offer? To distinguish this final chapter of his career, he wanted to take a homegrown Japanese company led by managers he had trained out into the world beyond Japan's shores. Was Misumi ready to make that leap?

He found out that no one overseas was implementing anything like Misumi's model. Japanese companies were ceding their competitive edge to international rivals, but Misumi might just be in a position to make a splash overseas. Things were getting interesting.

By now, about four weeks had passed, and the end of October was approaching.

## SAEGUSA'S MANAGEMENT NOTE 1
# WHAT IS A MANAGEMENT FRAMEWORK?

### The Volume and Quality of Frameworks Determine a Leader's Capabilities

I use the word *framework* often in this book. A framework is a structure that captures the essence or makeup of something and explains it in clear and simple terms, and it is the paucity or abundance of these frameworks that determines a leader's capabilities.

When a capable leader notices something is wrong, an alarm sounds internally. Others pass on by without sensing anything amiss.

Those who realize something is off have an idea of how things should look, and that serves as a point of reference. They compare their observations against these reference points to spot potential problems.

This applies to our daily lives as well. We judge situations and take action based on how things look vis-a-vis how they should look. Animals do the same. If an animal grows up instilled with a fear of humans, it will shy away from them. Animals without that sense of fear don't go out of their way avoid people.

Engineers have many reference points for technology, strategists have theirs for strategy and high-level executives have their own for high-level management. I refer to the ideas and viewpoints included in these reference points as *frameworks*.

These frameworks don't have to be some complex chart or concept developed by a consultant or academic. They can be something much simpler—a way of thinking, a point of view. For example, if you believe that a certain situation requires an end goal to motivate people, you must have some belief or experience tied to setting goals and motivating people that you have internalized as a framework.

Capable leaders have many frameworks from which to choose and then employ as each situation requires. That is what leaders do.

## Freeze, Defrost, and Use

We learn much from experience and study. To commit these learnings to memory, rather than memorizing every detail of a complex idea, you select a few simple words that capture its essence, and store them in a refrigerator in your mind. I call this *freezing*. You do it for things you feel are important, that you want to preserve for future use. You don't know when you will use it again. You might even forget you have it stored in your freezer.

We store many frameworks in our mind's freezers. Some are covered in frost and past their expiration dates. But when confronted with a new situation that you struggle to process, there comes a moment when you draw a connection to something you have stored in your freezer. So, you open up that freezer, brush off the frost and thaw it out. And that triggers memories and knowledge from the past that are relevant to your current situation.

That idea you defrosted may be a theory you read in an academic's book long ago, or it may be something you heard that made an impression. I call these *borrowed frameworks*. They may come from someone else, but in the beginning, you shouldn't hesitate to borrow other people's ideas. I often say, "steal as many as you can."

These borrowed frameworks rarely—actually, never—make a perfect fit for the situation you're facing. Adjust the idea or how it is applied to make it work for you. Making even a minor adjustment means that you have developed your own new logic, what I call a *self-made framework*.

Collecting these borrowed and self-made frameworks empowers you to root out the essence of problems before others do. Thus, to enhance your capabilities, you need to go through the process of preserving your learnings and experiences in accessible pieces and storing them in your freezer.

Consider a situation where you experience a complex problem or feel angry or vexed about something. If you want to store lessons learned as a framework for the future, you have to remove the emotional elements, discard the pronouns and distill it into an abstraction. This process is essential if you want to apply that lesson down the road in a different situation. Generalize the idea before you store it in your freezer.

Avoid storing these memories as long threads weighed down by excess trivia. Think of it as good pasta—best kept simple. Our freezers have limited capacity and fill quickly.

Generate your self-made frameworks, collect them in your freezer and apply them to the situations you encounter. This process is essential to developing leadership capabilities.

## Section 2:
# Withdrawing from New Businesses

### Encountering a Problem on Day One

Saegusa came to understand the strength of the Misumi QCT Model. But thereafter a different side of its business came into focus. The company appeared in the media often. The attention made him apprehensive, and now he knew why: For many years the company had been making forays into different businesses instead of focusing on its core business.

At the general meeting of shareholders where Saegusa was first elected to Misumi's board, Taguchi presented the company's plan for new businesses. Here is the gist.

Last year the company had 12 small business teams, including those in industrial mechanical components. This year, there are 17.

Five years from now there will be 20 or more new business teams.

Saegusa asked around. What exactly do these small internal ventures do? The answers surprised him.

"It costs a lot to repair foreign-made cars in Japan. Our new business will import after-market replacement parts and sell them to foreign-automobile repair shops."

"Storefront signs take too long to make and cost too much. This new business will make signs on short lead times at an affordable price."

"Built-in home furniture is very expensive. This new business will design, fabricate and install low-cost built-in furniture on short lead times."

"Local pubs are small with limited menus. This new business would deliver to pubs semi-prepared foods that they can microwave and serve on the spot."

After completing his rounds, Saegusa had made up his mind. "These new businesses are doomed to fail."

Why look to shutter nearly 10 years' worth of new businesses after a day of interviews?

In his late 30s, he had served as chief executive of a $60 million venture capital firm. There, he had developed a nose for promising business ideas and learned that even auspicious businesses could be run into the ground by poor management. He had felt the stinging pain of seeing an investment vanish before his very eyes.

Talk of the new business ideas set off sirens in his mind. What was the concern?

## Jack of All Trades, Strategy in None

It was as if Misumi's people had dropped their core business for a trip to the moon. There were no synergies, no matter how you looked at it.

Based on his experience, Saegusa had a framework to elucidate the problem. The new businesses reminded him of the forays into meaningless ventures that Nippon Steel and other smokestack-industry companies had attempted in the mid-1980s. (For more, see Chapter 1 of *A Crisis in Japanese Corporate Management*.)

Amusement parks, sports clubs, resorts, training, publishing, staffing, copying services, restaurants, mushroom farms, super-sized mazes, and so on. These are just some of the examples of diversified business forays reported in the press. But not a single one could save these lumbering old companies from business downturns.

Saegusa called that a *Jack of all trades, strategy in none*. He had met many of the people pushing those efforts. They possessed no true entrepreneurial spirit. It was typical salaryman behavior.

Within three years, the hype had faded. That's how much time and money it took for major corporations to realize that nothing would come of their diversified businesses.

He lamented the lack of managerial prowess exhibited by these Japanese companies. He called it a "crisis in Japanese corporate management" and later published a book bearing the same name to warn the Japanese business community.

Twenty years later, Misumi appeared poised to follow in their tracks. The company risked becoming a Jack of all trades with a strategy in none. It turns out, the push into new businesses—and away from the core business—had accelerated over the past three to four years.

### Riddle-solving for Business Leaders (7): Business Synergies

Here are some of the factors essential to realizing synergies: 1) a connection between the businesses and/or products; 2) leveraging of common technologies; 3) overlap between markets or customers; 4) overlap in sales channels; 5) the potential to leverage existing brand power; 6) strategic cohesiveness because the competitors are the same; 7) the important competitive factors leading to victory are the same and you are accustomed to that fight; and 8) the required internal organization is the same and can be leveraged.

Misumi's new businesses didn't benefit from any of these eight synergies. Not only were there no synergies with its core business, there were no synergies among the new ventures themselves. Truly random.

Clearly, this random collection of ventures was the result of a lack of central control. Likely, the company lacked an overarching strategy. A glaring error in management.

## The Key to Success

Typically, once a venture gets an influx of cash, the people involved get bullish and the future looks bright. But the Achilles' heel of a venture is not cash, it is strategy.

People with little management literacy don't see a crisis coming until it is upon them. Once they get an influx of cash, they are on fire and work feverishly. (Nothing like a salaryman.) They seem to glow. But money and effort are not enough. Eventually, fatigue sets in. Finally, when cash and energy run out, so does the business.

Hard work is very important—it may lift you over the first hurdle. But it won't be enough to secure true victory over the long haul. What you need is structural strength rooted in a business strategy.

Without strategy, the venture hits a ceiling. Once it reaches a certain size, growth slows to a halt. Everyone's hard slog keeps it going for a while. But there is a timing to success in business. Once that time is past, the business is doomed to wither away. The competition pushes ahead, and the venture's ability to compete evaporates.

Therefore, a leader has to always watch whether the company is on the winning track. If not, the strategy must be quickly adjusted. A weak company should have a strategy accurately reflecting its weaknesses and limitations.

The people in Misumi's business teams were obviously passionate. They were hard workers—young, with limitless energy and a sparkle in their eyes.

Having worked on turning around many old Japanese companies, Saegusa was impressed by the energized work environment at Misumi. Unfortunately, however, its people lacked advanced strategic capabilities and management literacy. They needed to step up their game to reach the major leagues.

*Testimonial from Y. Nishi (At 37, the youngest corporate officer)*
*I was hired straight out of college. Back then, the headquarters office was nothing more than a prefabricated two-story house. That gave me pause, but once I understood the company's unique business, my misgivings disappeared, and I grew excited to start working here.*

*Mr. Taguchi built an overwhelming edge in the die-parts business by pioneering standardized products and revolutionizing the distribution of production components.*

*Eventually, the die-parts business matured, and growth rates slowed. Then, Mr. Taguchi approved the launch of the Factory Automation (FA) components business. But it did not grow much in its early stage. There were no other businesses that appeared poised to grow. Mr. Taguchi worried about the company's future and committed to changing its trajectory. He accelerated the launch of a series of new businesses unrelated to our core competencies.*

*Immediately after Mr. Saegusa moved in, he brought Misumi back to its core businesses, and the FA business achieved booming growth under his direction. It became a pillar of our global business and eventually replaced die parts as the primary earnings driver.*

## Strategic Literacy

During the first week of December, an annual review meeting was held. It was attended by the board and open to about 100 core managers. Called the Vision Presentation Meeting, it was a crucial management review of business plans for the following year. It also served as the venue for their reappointment to a one-year term as corporate officer. The officers were tense as they gave their presentations, anxious to secure approval for their plans.

For some reason, many presentations included unrealistically large numbers for the potential size of the target market. Saegusa suspected many of them believed that the larger potential market they could show, the better chance their plans would be approved.

As an outside director, he had chosen to remain quiet at first. But after seeing the pattern play out a few times, he could not stand it anymore. Finally, he raised his hand to ask a question. Now, many of those in attendance glanced at him, wondering who he was and what he planned to say.

"You said your target market is worth $3 billion. What did you say was your sales target after five years?"

It was $10 million after five years. A drop in the bucket for a company with sales of nearly $500 million. Presenting such a plan at a forum like this was real minor-league stuff. But that was not the point Saegusa wanted to make.

"So, you foresee sales of $10 million in a $3 billion market? You call that a new business proposal?"

The presenter did not understand the question. Perplexed, he looked around for help.

Saegusa rephrased, "Five years from now, who will have the other $2.99 billion?"

The presenter finally understood the question. But he had no good answer and stood there speechless. The plan failed to consider the competition, one of the building blocks of a sound strategy.

"Your plan looks like a little bubble waiting to pop. You need to be the number one player, even if the market you define is small." Therein lies the key to success.

The officer nodded his head. The room seemed to agree.

## Where Growing Ventures Hit a Wall

At the time, corporate officers led multiple business units playing in different industries. To Saegusa, they looked like sole proprietorships.

Another officer stood up and gave a presentation on extending the mechanical-components business into the US market. But the company's business scale in the US was small and the officer's plan lacked ambition.

Later, the same officer rose to the podium to speak again. This time it was to talk about a food-product business under his supervision. His plan was to sell takoyaki to pubs in Japan. (Takoyaki are ball-shaped pancakes containing small pieces of octopus made in a customized frying pan.)

Taken aback, Saegusa suppressed his reluctance to speak out and raised his hand to ask another question.

"Earlier you presented your US strategy. Now, you're talking about takoyaki? Which one is your highest priority?"

A loud burst of laughter rose from the audience. Struggling to answer, the officer joined in. So did Saegusa, but he knew this was no laughing matter.

Without hesitation, the answer should have been that the US business was more important than takoyaki. This episode exposed the lack of clarity across the company on the relative strategic importance of each business.

For just a moment the window had opened, revealing a typical scene—either the absence of something that should be there, or the presence of something that should not.

### Riddle-solving for Business Leaders (8): Internal Ventures' Weak Spots

In the case of internal ventures, the checks that should be executed at each gateway—from *exploration* to *experimentation*, *selection* and *commercialization*—tend to be weaker than if executed by external pros. So, people working in the business pass through the checkpoints never learning the agony that is part and parcel of fundraising. Some may talk the talk, but at the end of the day, they are no more than salarymen putting in face time. Calling it a venture risks inviting short cuts in strategy and talent development.

## Not a Single Winner

How can a company justify funding such businesses? No venture capitalist would fund a single one of them. That much Saegusa knew, having been one himself.

Even businesses that had grown to relative scale within the company had peaked out at sales of a quarter-billion dollars. And they were still losing money. Many ventures hit their first wall at that size in revenues and never transcended it. The same thing was happening here.

Let's jump ahead in our story for a moment. After accepting the chief executive position, Saegusa had his people calculate the total loss accumulated in its new business ventures over the preceding 10 years. It came to $50 million, or over $70 million if you include consultancy fees, headquarters costs, officer personnel expenses and other difficult-to-capture costs. That is quite a sum, considering the fact that at the start of that 10-year period the company's annual profits amounted to $20 million to $30 million. That might have bankrupted the company, if not for the rich profit margins its core business delivered.

Saegusa was ready for a clean break. Those were all sunk costs anyway.

> ### Riddle-solving for Business Leaders (9): Moving on from Sunk Costs
> Sunk costs are losses that have already been incurred, costs from the past that are no longer relevant to deciding the best course forward. (For more, see Chapter 1 of A *Crisis in Japanese Corporate Management*.)

Saegusa was becoming increasingly aware of a problem more critical than sunk costs: lost profits.

As new businesses boomed, the core business of industrial mechanical components faded into obscurity. As new businesses grabbed the spotlight, some people in the core business started to feel left behind.

Ambitious people transferred to new businesses, leaving existing businesses with skeleton crews. Industrial-components catalogs were issued less frequently. Some products lost share as price competition from new rivals went unaddressed for too long.

These were not sunk costs if the company's market position and profitability were still shrinking but its heart was still beating.

## A Turning Point for New Businesses

The Board of Directors meeting took place on December 19, a week after the Vision Presentations. The board would decide on each officer's business plan and appointment to another term.

As expected, the debate got off to an inauspicious start. Surprisingly, it seemed as if a business still losing money in its eighth year could be approved without any substantive debate.

If allowed to pass now, there would be no check for another year. It seemed as if these businesses were getting carte blanche not for one year, but for eight.

Misumi advocates *freedom and self-responsibility* and *responsibility for results*. But this process seemed devoid of both results and responsibility. In his capacity as outside director, Saegusa felt compelled to speak up. Fortunately, support for his views was beginning to solidify.

In part, this was thanks to a full-day strategic training seminar for all officers he had given the previous month at the request of Mr. Taguchi. The company's officers were developing a common language on strategy.

Saegusa spoke to the board. "We should decide the merits of a business logically, based on strategic theory."

Those words sparked a change among the directors. The bar for determining the merits of new businesses suddenly rose.

There was one more change. Mr. Taguchi expressed no resistance to how things were developing. Directors felt free to speak more openly.

"This business doesn't have the strength or growth potential its advocates claim."

"This business cannot seem to make it out of the red."

Similar comments followed. There were questions about many of the new businesses. Finally—and surprisingly—the decision was made to fold or shelve most of them.

## Withdrawal from Seven Businesses

At the time, Misumi had a certain air about it, as if there were a constant life-or-death struggle, but almost like a game. It motivated people, and there was a lot of drama.

Those days would soon be over. To some, it came like a thunderbolt from a clear sky. The board of directors decided to withdraw from or shelve seven businesses. The decision severed ties with past management habits. (See Riddle-solving for Business Leaders 1.)

- Liquidate and withdraw from three existing low-potential businesses.
- Cancel plans to launch four new businesses and disband those teams.
- Disband the affected teams within three months and re-assign personnel to other parts of the company.

Shock waves reverberated throughout the company. People who for years had enjoyed venture-like fervor saw their businesses disappear before their eyes as if by magic.

Only three businesses were allowed to continue. Each had revenues of about $20 million to $30 million. They were losing money, but the losses had narrowed. Now each would be spun off to facilitate a future public offering, disposition or liquidation, as Saegusa had advocated.

What eventually happened to these three businesses? None made it to an initial public offering. Each was sold to another company within a few years, though none at a price that covered its cumulative losses. In fact, they were lucky to fetch any price at all.

Saegusa was happy with the decision to halt the seven businesses, convinced the company should focus on its one core business—industrial mechanical components—and go global.

## Psychological Dilemma at the Top

Back to where we left off. At this point, Saegusa had not yet decided whether to accept the CEO post.

For Mr. Taguchi, who had led a diversified strategy into new ventures for a decade, the decision to change direction could not have come easily. Yet he made no objection to the board's decision. Presumably, he was prepared to change course.

There are significant psychological limitations at play when management makes a drastic change to its strategic direction.

At the time, the mass media and the stock markets lavished attention on the company, making it quite well known considering its size. Mr. Taguchi had published multiple books and ran the company with flair. The company was even taken up as a case study at Keio University's business school, a textbook example of a unique company that MBA students could learn from. Many professors from top-notch schools made a point to refer to the company. It appeared in newspapers and magazines as well. Mostly, the coverage lauded the company's uniqueness.

On the outside, the company garnered attention for its uniqueness, but on the inside, the business felt increasingly stagnant.

You may be aware of the psychological dilemma that takes hold when a company's image restrains management from making decisive changes. If you have experienced this, you understand how painful it can be. Saegusa had experienced it in his 30s, and the unforgettable lesson remained with him vividly, as a framework.

## Section 3:
# Presenting a Reform Scenario (Sheet 1)

### A Renewed Request

Before Saegusa came to a decision on the CEO offer, Mr. Taguchi wanted to discuss a compensation package. It turned out to be a far more generous package than chief-executive remuneration typically provided in Japan.

Once the compensation bit was complete, Saegusa took the opportunity to broach a subject far more important to him than pay. "Mr. Taguchi, I just want to be sure. Do you truly intend to retire?"

Saegusa preferred to handle matters like this with straight talk.

All too often a founder who cedes the chief executive position will continue to exert influence behind the scenes, creating a dual-leadership regime within the company. Over time, the founder ages, grows increasingly suspicious and seeks out a scapegoat. He had seen this scenario play out too many times.

As Misumi's founder, Mr. Taguchi had been revered like a god. If an outsider CEO were brought in only to lock horns with Mr. Taguchi, the company would most certainly devolve into political morass.

Saegusa's intent was unmistakable. No matter the company, no matter the pay, if he were not afforded the leeway to execute strategy as he saw fit, his answer would be, "No, thanks."

Mr. Taguchi gazed at Saegusa intently. Clearly, he had already given this thought. "Mr. Saegusa, if I step down as chief executive, I am prepared to relinquish representative rights and executive authority. I'm happy to act as a non-executive director and advisor.

What I want is for you to really grow this company. Change what you want."

There are not many founders who would say and mean something like that.

Mr. Taguchi seemed weary after so many years at the helm. Saegusa believed he truly was ready to retire. This resolved his greatest concern about taking over and marked an important turning point in reaching a decision.

## Accepting the CEO Position

Saegusa continued his survey of the company for another month, focusing next on the infrastructure departments.

Recall that the strengthening of the infrastructure functions paved the way for shortening lead times, improving product quality, introducing robust information systems, and so on. He surveyed operations in customer centers, logistics, IT systems and sales to determine whether these infrastructure functions had maintained their strength.

Surprisingly, he found signs of weakness had developed over the nearly 10 years the company had lost its focus on the industrial component business. Of immediate concern was a bias toward outsourcing that permeated the company. Mr. Taguchi had trumpeted his asset-light model to the press, but Saegusa had his doubts.

Misumi was a trading company, so it had delegated production to contract manufacturers from the outset. The original business model was based on outsourcing. Saegusa learned that everything else had been outsourced, too, from the customer centers' order intake functions to the logistics centers and IT systems. The company had only a few personnel in each of those organizations.

Moreover, accounting had been outsourced, too, leaving only two or three Misumi personnel in that function. The human resources organization had long since been disbanded.

Impressive. Yet concerning.

"So, what remains that could be called Misumi's core competencies?" he wondered.

A company that fails to clearly identify its core competencies struggles to sustain its growth potential and profitability and may be headed toward an ignominious end.

What the company did itself was plan products and make catalogs. But that did not cover all the elements that drove customer satisfaction. It had done too much outsourcing, leaving too few staffers committed to driving innovation in each support function.

Perhaps the company had become too absorbed in the strength of its business model and neglected to implement forward-looking measures. It might fall behind and devolve into an obsolete enterprise with a high cost structure.

His analyses over the past four months had yielded many insights. He felt there were few people in Japan who could fundamentally transform Misumi and usher it into a new stage of success. This may seem like overconfidence, but he had a track record of taking on challenges where few could succeed. By doing so, he had sought to distinguish himself as an outsider shunned by Japan's established business circles after he left Mitsui in his 20s.

He identified the company's strengths and weaknesses and concluded that if done right, the company had tremendous potential to grow. Indeed, the company was interesting enough that he decided to bet this final stage of his career on it. Finally, he made the decision to become Misumi's next chief executive.

At age 57, Saegusa had chosen a new path fraught with risk. He could continue to run his own business as a turnaround specialist, but he felt drawn to the opportunity to take the company into his own hands, reform it and groom the management talent that would build it into an international player.

Some four months earlier, Saegusa knew virtually nothing about Misumi. He was still engaged in the turnaround of Komatsu's industrial equipment business, visiting Misumi during lulls in that project. He had spent the full-time equivalent of one month at the company, enough to make up his mind.

Some things never change. In his 20s, he had made a practice of challenging himself in uncharted territory. Now in his late 50s, he felt that same spirit pulsing through his veins.

In the middle of January, Saegusa communicated his intent to Mr. Taguchi, who welcomed the news.

"Let's put it to the February 20 board meeting and follow immediately with a press release."

Effective March 1, Saegusa would assume the post of representative director and executive vice president, then ascend to CEO pending approval at the June shareholders meeting. The stage was set for the change in leadership.

## An Inaugural Presentation

Mr. Taguchi had a request for Saegusa before the change was made official. "Would you give an inaugural presentation to our officers before the board meets to approve your appointment?"

It would be tricky to pull off, however. The speech would come two days before the official decision by the board of directors and resulting press release. So, the fact that he would be nominated CEO could not yet be disclosed to the audience. Yet his presentation had to rise to the occasion, so that when the audience reflected on it days later, something would resonate with them.

He agreed to the request. At three or four months into any turn-around project, there came a watershed moment that called for a speech to set a new direction. This time it just came a little earlier than usual.

### Riddle-solving for Business Leaders (10): A Watershed Moment—Presenting "Sheet 1"

The success of a reform hinges on presenting "Sheet 1"—where you look reality directly in the face, capture the true essence of the problems and reflect in a brutally honest fashion. The watershed moment comes just as the reform is about to begin. People can instinctively sense whether "Sheet 1" is on the mark. If "Sheet 1" lacks rigor, "Sheet 2" will also fall flat, and even reforms moved to the implementation phase ("Sheet 3") are unlikely to generate results. (For more, see Saegusa's Management Note 2.)

### Misumi's Eight Weaknesses

At 3 p.m. on February 18, about 120 officers and key managers gathered in a large conference room on the 5th floor of the company's headquarters building. Outside, it threatened to snow. Inside, however, the room was warm.

"At the request of your CEO, Mr. Taguchi, I have spent the past four months as an outside director identifying the company's challenges. Today, I will share my conclusions frankly."

Saegusa launched into a diagram of the Misumi QCT Model. Here, the framework focused on cadence in the cycle of Create→Produce→Sell as the key to business success. The attendees were seeing this diagram—refined since he first sketched it on the back of that chopsticks envelope at the sushi restaurant—for the first time.

### Riddle-solving for Business Leaders (11): Create→Produce→Sell (The Basic Cycle of Business)

As a company swells into a behemoth, the pace of cooperation between development, production and sales decelerates. The feedback loop that disseminates customer demands internally and delivers solutions to the customer also slows. Companies that achieve a higher cadence in their basic cycle of business beat out the competition in the market over time. A company's competitive strength is rooted in its cadence through that cycle. Although they have different historical roots, the Toyota Production System (TPS) and supply chain philosophies share the same concept. (For more, see Chapter 1 of *A Crisis in Japanese Corporate Management*.)

"There are few companies in Japan capable of designing a powerful business model. Yet, you've built an amazing one here, based on the Toyota philosophies." That was all the praise he would offer his audience that day. He went on to present eight concerns, as Mr. Taguchi listened from his seat nearby.

1. Disconnects between the business and sales units
   - There are signs of a slow cadence to the Create→Produce→Sell cycle that makes up the core of the Misumi QCT Model. It is a symptom many ailing companies exhibit.
   - In particular, there are breaks in the ties between the headquarters and local customer contact points such as customer centers and sales teams.
2. Customer Center concerns
   - Surprisingly, the company has 13 customer centers dispersed across Japan. Perhaps this antiquated business

model is a remnant from the days of costly long-distance phone charges. Moreover, each center uses different work processes, leading to inefficiencies.

- Outsourcing is a problem. A company must be positioned to hear customer pain points itself, instead of delegating that work to temporary staffers.

3. Subpar logistics
   - A tour of the company's distribution centers revealed a reliance on outsourcing here, too. Not a single Misumi employee works at the warehouses. So how do you evolve your service organization to keep up with the times?

4. Weak IT systems
   - The company's IT systems appear to be lagging global trends. Here, too, outsourcing is to blame.
   - The headquarters function charged with responding to the spread of the internet is weak. A lack of coordination across the company has allowed overlapping and duplicative investments.

The conference room fell silent. Saegusa summarized his observations of the infrastructure functions. "The company's business platforms are weakening. Over time, we could lose our competitive edge."

It was the first time the attendees had heard such a dire warning, to say nothing of the direct criticism of outsourcing, one of the strategies championed by Mr. Taguchi. Such a refutation of how the company had been run was a bit much from someone who was, after all, nothing more than an outside director.

Nevertheless, the audience didn't stare daggers at him. They did, however, steal glances at Mr. Taguchi, who was seated near the podium, trying to read his reaction.

For his part, Mr. Taguchi remained cool and collected, betraying no emotion at all.

## Applying Pressure

By then, the board of directors' decision to withdraw from or shelve seven businesses had already been announced internally. That decision set the stage for Saegusa's next comments.

5. A questionable pursuit of new businesses
   - Synergies between the new and core businesses were too weak. We might as well be a complete novice starting from scratch. What competitive edge can we expect to gain from the outset?
   - The board's decision to withdraw from businesses indicated a judgement that the strategic story was too weak.
   - New businesses required substantial investments. To date, the company had made only small bets, unable to commit to major investments.

The decision to withdraw from the businesses struck people like a bolt out of the blue. Now, for the first time, they were hearing the rationale explained. The room was tense. No one could have known that two days from now the company would announce the appointment of a new chief executive. Yet this speech could not be dismissed as random opinion.

6. Slow to go overseas
   - The delay in expanding overseas could soon prove life-threatening for the company.
   - To date, the company had made only half-hearted investments to grow overseas.

Over the past 30 years, Saegusa had given many speeches like this. He could tell from people's facial expressions whether his words were resonating. Sometimes, the response was sour. Not today. He had reached them. He had hit the mark.

He moved to wrap up. He wanted to make a few final points to tie things into the forthcoming announcement of his appointment as chief executive.

7. Lacking an everyday sense of urgency
   • Misumi's principle of *freedom and self-responsibility* is a wonderful concept, suited for professionals. But do you all truly appreciate it? Do you all strive to maintain a high level of urgency day-in and day-out?

8. Talent is not being cultivated
   • What is the company doing to cultivate management talent? Japanese companies that fail to nurture management talent end up bloated with listless salarymen when they need to be raising samurai who can wage battle in global markets.
   • Is working at Misumi your dream job? Or just a stepping-stone toward your next move?

This final point was rooted in the company's high employee turnover.

The facial expressions in the audience spoke millions. "Management talent? What's that? Who, me?"

They had put so much energy into running internal ventures apparently unaware they needed to step up into the role of senior management as they pursued these risky ventures. There needed to be more accountability and more leadership.

He concluded his speech with a summary slide titled "Misumi's Eight Weaknesses". No one present could have foreseen that each theme on the slide would sketch out the direction of the drastic reforms that he would lead over the next 12 years.

# Misumi's Eight Weaknesses

1. Sales organization disconnected with division headquarters.

2. Low efficiency and morale at the 13 customer centers.

3. Excessive reliance on outsourcing logistics stymies drive for better services.

4. Excessive reliance on outsourcing IT resulted in insensitivity to new technologies and underdeveloped internal resources.

5. New business pursuits have failed over a decade.

6. Slow to cultivate overseas markets.

7. Little sense of urgency in the face of many challenges.

8. Scant effort to develop management talent.

The speech was over in 40 minutes. The room fell silent. Not a silence of rejection or opposition. Yet there was no applause, either. More precisely, it was as if the room was saying collectively, "I see your point, but I need some time to wrap my head around it." Their minds were spinning, and their perplexed emotional state was palpable.

Misumi's Eight Weaknesses was the centerpiece of his analysis of the company. The quick work he did grasping the reform story in advance laid the stage for speedy action once he was positioned to lead the company.

Of course, he made clear that his findings were tentative. He would have time to confirm his observations after taking the reins. But as it turned out, his initial observations were on the mark and formed the impetus for many reform projects.

Outside consultants would charge a pretty penny for these kinds of observations. Recall the first two of seven criteria for a professional CEO laid out in the Prologue.

1. Someone who can quickly get to the bottom of things. Problems manifest themselves on the surface in many different ways.
2. Someone who can explain the issue concisely in *easily understandable terms.*

On that day, he felt comfortable he had met these criteria. And his confidence seemed to resonate with the audience.

## Announcing a Change of the Guard

Two days later, on February 20, the board met as planned. It formally named Saegusa representative director and executive vice president, effective March 1, and CEO pending approval at the shareholders meeting to be held in June that year.

That evening, a press release was distributed to the Tokyo Stock Exchange and media outlets. Newspapers ran the story the next morning complete with photographs. Saegusa had crossed the Rubicon.

A press briefing was held at Tokyo's prestigious Imperial Hotel, a venue befitting Mr. Taguchi's status as a well-known entrepreneur. Rising to speak, he said, "I have been praised as the antithesis of the traditional Japanese management model for the visionary leadership I have practiced. But perhaps in some ways I may have gone too far in that direction."

*Testimonial from Hiroshi Taguchi, Misumi's founder*
*Three years after I ceded the CEO role, I was interviewed by the Nikkei Sangyo Shimbun. I honestly revealed my reasons for retiring, which were quoted as follows.*
*"Frankly, I resigned because I felt I had reached my limit. My management approach was to do what others don't. Seek out a market*

*where there is no competition and grow there. But that is a strategy for the weak.*

*"Once the company's sales surpassed $500 million, I found myself bumping up against the competition. I needed to be able to win the fight head-on. A global strategy was key, too. That was more than I could do.*

*"I actually preferred to bring in someone like Mr. Saegusa from the outside. It felt risky to promote someone from within the company who knew nothing but Misumi, so I was comfortable giving Mr. Saegusa full control. I intend to spend the rest of my working life doing things that build on my abilities and experience."*

At the press conference, there were questions for Saegusa, too.

"Mr. Saegusa, no outside director has ever been named chief executive of a publicly traded company in Japan. What will your priorities be as CEO?" (At the time, few Japanese governance structures employed outside directors. And, under Japan's lifelong employment system, most executive positions at major companies were filled by talent who climbed the ranks internally or were seconded from affiliates. So, there was little precedent for a move like this.)

He answered, "My top priority is to cultivate strong business leaders."

The reporters looked puzzled. "My second priority is to grow the business," he quickly added. "I want to build Misumi into a new type of Japanese company ready to take on the world." Saegusa's comments were rooted in a painful recognition that for many years Japan had largely failed to develop strong managerial talent who could compete in global markets.

It goes without saying that most people taking the helm of a major company would provide a more conventional answer, that the priority would be first and foremost to grow the business, and then to cultivate talent as a means to that end.

had encountered at old-style Japanese companies. Misumi's people were hardworking, and they overcame fatigue to generate creative solutions and lead reforms through trial and error.

Reforms inevitably entail some failures and setbacks. He believed that if you must admonish your staff, make it a *solid scolding*. If a problem arises, don't leave things unresolved to pop up again further down the road. Fix the problem once and for all.

Sometimes that involved raising his voice. Those who faced his fury directly, or perhaps just heard about it, may have learned to fear him. An unavoidable consequence. What they might not know is that even then he was holding back. You will see in the following chapters just how much restraint he exercised.

In some cases that involved waiting things out when a reform stalled. Common sense holds that a CEO who spends six years on a single reform is a failure. In the US, no doubt, that executive would be unceremoniously fired. Saegusa knew how it worked in the US, but even in Japan, six years is the typical length of a chief executive's tenure at large Japanese corporations. Nevertheless, with patience and faith, he saw the reforms through to completion.

Paradoxically, the staff here are quick to act. They actually move much faster than employees in a typical Japanese company. Many new hires praise the feverish pace of work at Misumi.

With reform and strategy, you don't know how things will turn out until you give them a try. Without exception, strategies are nothing more than hypotheses. Only when you try something out do you identify what needs revising or feel the pain of failure.

That failure or setback may lead to a *solid scolding*. But at the same time, you urge them, "Take your time. Do it right!"

### Riddle-solving for Business Leaders (12): Do it Right!
Even if it takes time, don't compromise. Do the right thing. Keep your eyes on the goal. Direct your staff at the outset to have the courage to stop if need be.

*Do it right!* During his 12-year tenure as CEO, he repeated those words often—in Japan, China, Asia and elsewhere. It has become part of the company lexicon.

After a failure, you redesign, then have another go at it. Get running again, moving faster than anyone else. Usually, success comes on the second try. In the worst-case scenario, you hit another setback. It's a disheartening experience for anyone. But what can you do? Back to *Do it right!* again.

By now, it should be obvious that the six years outlined above were not spent dilly-dallying. With each failure, the officers and staff upped their management abilities another notch. There was no greater reward for their tireless efforts. Nevertheless, Saegusa sometimes rewarded his people in other ways, with a trip to Hawaii, for example, after the team had made its way out of a long tunnel. He also paid out monetary bonuses that exceeded what was common at ordinary Japanese companies.

When a company has been pushed to the precipice, there may be nowhere left to turn besides restructuring. But what of the employees at those Japanese companies who went through the restructuring or sale of the business? After surviving those changes and sticking with the business, are they now energized? Has the business become a driving force for the company? No, you never hear stories like that. Instead, most of the time, the restructuring temporarily stanches the bleeding, but fails to instill any changes in how work gets done there. And the strategy to grow earnings remains on the shelf.

That's why Saegusa maintains that the key to reviving a Japanese company does not lie in reducing headcount. It's about figuring out how to galvanize people.

In his view, people who spend too much time in a poorly performing organization become paralyzed by a mentality of collectivism. However, a clear strategy explicated by a competent leader shows employees how they can join forces and work to that end. Together, they can accomplish three or four times more—as if the organization tripled or quadrupled its workforce. This kind of sea change is something Saegusa experienced turning around businesses.

## The Ensuing Growth Trajectory

After Saegusa took over, the company successfully navigated *Death Valley* and embarked on a tremendous growth trajectory. Here, let's skip ahead to the growth the company achieved during his 16 years there (12 as CEO and another 4 as chairman of the board).

It took Misumi 40 years from its founding to reach $500 million in sales. In just four years, Saegusa doubled that to $1 billion, a compound average annual growth rate of 19.5%. The high rate of growth distinguished it among its peers, which were struggling in Japan's stagnant economy.

For another two years, the company continued to grow, reaching sales of about $1.25 billion in Year 6 of his tenure.

Then the global financial crisis struck. The repercussions were severe. Even Toyota posted an operating loss as profit shrank more than $20 billion from the previous year. Misumi floundered as well, losing four years' worth of sales growth. It booked a monthly operating loss for five consecutive months but managed to eke out a profit for the full year, while many of its peers reported losses.

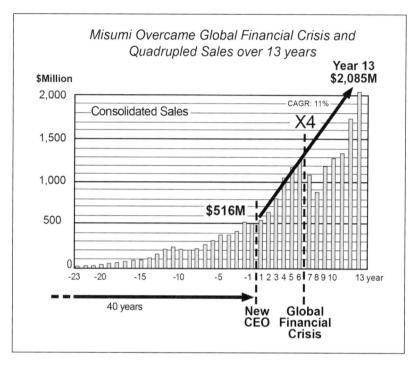

Saegusa saw a silver lining in the financial crisis. "The past six years of strong growth were a strain on the company. Let's get our house in order and position ourselves to push forward." By Year 7, the company had broken free from the malaise of the financial crisis and began to grow again.

Within two years, sales and profit returned to their pre-crisis levels. Sell-side analysts called the company's recovery "the fastest in the industry." That was Year 9 of his tenure.

Winter passed, making way for spring. But the world had changed. China and the rest of Asia were stirring. Before the crisis, the company's Asian competitors had been underwhelming. But they emerged in its aftermath more energetic, forging a path toward growth. While Japanese and Western companies had to hunker down to ride out the crisis, their Chinese and Asian competitors closed the gap.

The company found itself subject to severe cost competition and forced to battle for market share. That battle continues to date.

In Year 12 of his tenure, Misumi acquired two US die-parts makers. The company's growth up to that point had been organic. These acquisitions added $150 million to the topline, and total sales surpassed $1.7 billion that year.

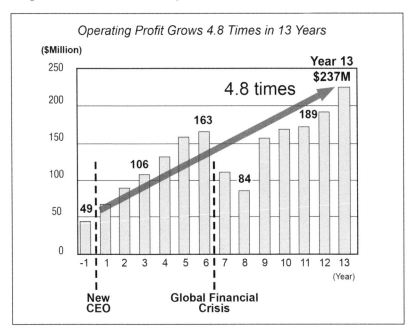

In June of Year 13, he stepped down as CEO. By the end of that year, sales had surpassed $2 billion. In 13 years, sales had quadrupled, profit rose from roughly $49 million to $237 million, and dividends per share grew 4.6 times. When he retired from the Chairman of the Board at the end of Year 16, sales had surpassed $3 billion.

One of the greatest changes during his tenure was the growth in headcount. When he took over, Misumi was purely a trading company and relied heavily on temporary staffers. It had only 340 full-time personnel.

With the acquisition of Suruga (See Chapter 5) in Year 4, employee headcount swelled, as shown in the graph.

Headcount continued to grow as Saegusa pursued the strategy to have Suruga establish manufacturing operations in major industrial regions overseas, and the company made acquisitions in the US in Year 12. When Saegusa retired from the position of the Chairman of the Board in Year 16, there were more than 10,000 employees across the globe.

The phrase, "from 340 to over 10,000" came to symbolize Misumi's growth tale. The expansion vaulted the company into an international player on a completely different scale. For Saegusa, the years passed in a flash. But the graph of employee growth is a gratifying reminder of how far he had come.

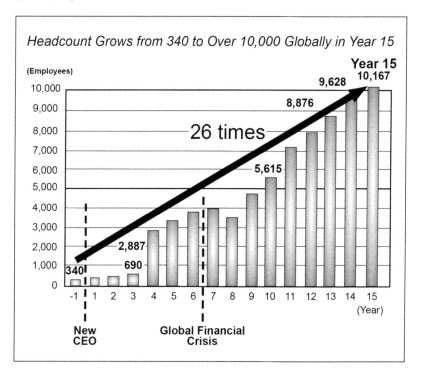

## SAEGUSA'S MANAGEMENT NOTE 2
# RIDDLE-SOLVING MAKES OR BREAKS A BUSINESS LEADER

### Your Work Starts with Riddle-solving

In the Prologue, I pointed to the similarities between how the great detectives Poirot and Columbo honed their skills to how management talent raises its leadership capabilities. The key here is the *ability to solve riddles*.

How did managerial legends like Jack Welch of General Electric acquire their ability to take decisive action?

Imagine that you're faced with a chaotic problem with no obvious solution in sight. That chaos is a convoluted entanglement of many different elements, like yarn tangled up in a bunch.

Consider the situation at Nissan Motors. The officers and employees there had lost sight of what changes were needed to turn the company around. Pull on the wrong string and the knot only tightens. A new management team came in and turned the company around in only two years. How?

I map out a path to turnaround in my framework: *"Sheet 1➔ Sheet 2 ➔ Sheet 3"*. This framework is an important part of the shared lexicon within Misumi, which I taught in a series of lectures at the Misumi Strategy School I established.

Even recent hires come to understand what it means when their leader tells them, "Your Sheet 1 needs work."

### Riddle-solving for Business Leaders (13): "Sheet 1→Sheet 2→Sheet 3"

The sharpness of a leader's ability hinges on how quickly and accurately that leader can prepare a 3-sheet strategy scenario. "Sheet 1" gets to the bottom of things, identifying root problems that can manifest themselves in many different ways on the surface. This is done by directly addressing reality with brutal honesty. "Sheet 2" sets forth strategy, plans, a reform scenario, or countermeasures aimed at resolving the root causes of the problems identified in "Sheet 1". "Sheet 3" is an Action Plan based on "Sheet 2".

## Finding Structure in a Chaotic Reality

Skilled leaders are quick to unravel the tangled knot and understand the inner workings of the reality they face. Their accuracy in solving the riddle and capturing the essence of the problem is spot on. In these situations, what calculations do skilled leaders perform?

First, the leader mentally unravels the tangled knot and reveals the important factors that seem to be interacting with each other amid the mess. I refer to each of the strings untangled as a *causality*, which means the relationship between cause and effect.

Toyota's Kaizen method tells you to do this by reversing the order. Identify the problem as it appears on the surface. Then, seek a causality to uncover the cause. Repeat five times, each time digging deeper, so that you can expose the root cause at its bottom.

Either way—bottom up or surface down—a skilled leader deftly completes this initial disentanglement. If you can do it, that alone is a significant step forward for the organization, but not enough to exhibit leadership ability.

Next, sort the causalities into those generating negative outcomes, those generating positive outcomes, and those that are neutral. Finally, identify which of the negative causalities are at the root of the problem. You exhibit leadership if you get to the point where you can say, "Hunh…, I think this is the core issue we face."

Here, causality is dynamic, changing with time like the melody to music. By definition, a leader shows the way by picking out the important elements and simplifying the problem. If accurate, it clears the fog so that others can nod in agreement, "Oh, now I see what you mean."

A skilled leader, much like the renowned Detective Poirot, solves riddles quickly and accurately. A strong leader does this consistently.

If there is no one in the organization imbued with those abilities, the knotted bunch remains a jumbled mess. If it takes being pushed to the brink for a leader to figure out what needs to be done, that person is doing nothing more than reacting. The person may occupy a managerial position but is not functioning as a leader. In contrast, a skilled leader quickly identifies a path toward resolution. It takes resolve to do so in a situation where many questions remain unanswered.

"Sheet 1" represents this initial process done right.

Imagine you have before you three sheets of blank paper, one on top of the other. At the bottom, "Sheet 1" reflects a variety of causalities that make up the convoluted situation you face today. Highlight with a marker those causalities that lie at the root of the problem, the ones causing the most chaos.

### Riddle-solving for Business Leaders (14): Isolating Causalities

You need to break chaos—that tangled knot of yarn—down into manageable chunks for you to make any sense of it. That requires a hands-on approach—checking the details to make sure for yourself. It is a logical process to identify the important *causalities* driving the chaos. Ironically, prior experience in that company's industry often gets in the way.

## Tell a Simple Story with Passion

Once "Sheet 1" has been filled in, place "Sheet 2" on top of it. You can see "Sheet 1" through the blank sheet of paper, so what needs to be done becomes clearer than when you were looking at the chaos in its entirety. On "Sheet 2", a skilled leader clearly defines a strategy, scenario and countermeasures that address the problems identified on "Sheet 1".

When addressing "Sheet 2", a leader needs to speak with passion. Your team needs not only more clarity on the problems, but also the motivation to follow, stoked by the leader's enthusiasm. A *simple story delivered with passion* brings people together in solidarity to take inspired action.

Next, devise a concrete Action Plan on "Sheet 3", based on the direction and strategy laid out in "Sheet 2". It is an actionable workflow with specific dates identifying what actions should take place in what sequence. "Sheet 2" and "Sheet 3" must be in complete alignment. A skilled leader fosters a unified mindset and enthusiasm and sustains execution. A leader who cannot simplify the problems on "Sheet 1" will allow the chaos to spill over onto "Sheet 2" and "Sheet 3". Without leadership, the situation persists.

A skilled leader does not rush through these three sheets, but instead thinks things through fully before making a move. Then, the leader shares this 3-sheet set with the staff, establishing a task force for that purpose if necessary.

# Chapter 2

# Instilling Strategic Orientation

What is strategy? Here we focus on a troubled team that learned strategy and overcame painful obstacles to develop a strategic scenario and transform a $150 million business unit into a global business with sales of over $1 billion.

## Innovating the Business Model With a Chain of Reforms
### (Competing Against the International Megatrend)

Growth Acceleration

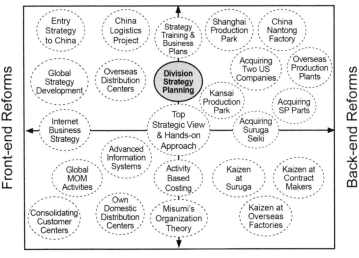

Front-end Reforms

Back-end Reforms

Increasing Quality and Efficiency

## Section 1:
# Lost at the Gate to Strategy

## Where to Begin

Saegusa had set out a clear course of action for reforming the company. Misumi would refocus its attention on its core business and pursue global expansion. He was determined to implement substantial reforms to make that possible.

Industrial machinery components was the core business, but it needed renewed focus. Its high profitability had more than offset the losses from new business forays over the previous decade, but it received no plaudits or recognition. Instead, it was consigned to the shadows while the new businesses stole the spotlight.

What's more, despite its importance to the company, the industrial machinery components business lacked anything you could call a strategy. There was no coherent direction for executives and staff to pursue in their day-to-day work. The situation was as bad here as with the new businesses the company had decided to withdraw from.

To start, the staff clearly lacked the necessary management literacy to discuss strategy. They appeared to be making it up as they went along.

But Saegusa saw an opportunity. The business had achieved outstanding growth and profitability without a strategy. What might happen if he applied a sound strategic concept to it? As a turnaround specialist, when it came to rescuing failed businesses, he never compromised on strategy. Misumi might prove to be the most interesting challenge so far.

For years, the company had maintained solid profits and strong growth, but its financial results for the fiscal year before he took over stumbled, mainly due to a downturn in the economy.

Sales were forecast to drop 8% year-on-year to about $500 million, while operating profit was set to fall by as much as 24% to $50 million.

To many, the sudden decline came as a surprise. Saegusa saw it as a temporary setback, since the company's results had dipped twice in the past decade during economic downturns. Earnings recovered on both occasions, and he was confident that this time would be no different.

Meanwhile, he realized that this was the perfect opportunity to get the ball rolling on reforms—the more people fretted about declining performance, the more open they would be to new possibilities. He wanted to start with the industrial machinery components business, but experience told him that it would be folly to try to reform all three of its main businesses at once. Much wiser to mold one of the units into a model case. A success in one could then be rolled out to the others.

### Riddle-solving for Business Leaders (15): Avoiding War on All Fronts

Change can be unsettling for people. Unless the company faces immediate existential risks, reform-minded leaders need to start with a focused scope. Avoid launching a destabilizing war *on all fronts*, which can backfire on you. See one reform through to success, then roll it out across the organization.

So, which of the three business units would he target first?

- **Die Components Division:** Die components was Misumi's original business and delivered the lion's share of sales. It served as the *main stronghold* of the company's business and had generated more than enough cash flow to cover losses from new business forays. But as markets shifted to China, growth in Japan had halted. The division clearly needed reform. Executives and staffers alike were happy with the status quo and seemed *utterly unconcerned* about the trouble looming on the horizon. Saegusa had seen similar insouciance at underperforming businesses he turned around in the past.

- **Factory Automation (FA) Division:** Misumi's current growth driver. Sales were second only to Die Components. It sold components installed in production machinery used on factory lines. The FA business had been operating for 14 years but had grown rapidly in the past 3, ever since K. Nagao (pronounced [Nah-gah-oh], the ao being similar to that in *cacao*) took over as general manager. With a little fine tuning, Nagao might grow into an outstanding business leader, but he didn't show much interest in corporate leadership.
- **Electronics Division:** Launched 11 years before, sales hadn't passed the $50-million mark, but its growth performance was second only to the FA business. It sold electrical and electronic components, such as wires and connectors, used in production machinery. Within the company, the business had a lower profile and its small scale made it an ideal place to start the reform ball rolling quietly.

When planning corporate reforms, a key strategic problem is where to start.

Divisions that have been around for a long time but are sapped of vitality are often rife with people who are *unable* to accept change and resort to playing politics instead. So, it may be best to avoid these divisions at first. Better to aim first for success in a more-obscure organization, then showcase that story to that rest of the company.

Another absolute priority is to ensure that the unit you target has a strong leader who will *take up the cause* of reform.

## Riddle-Solving for Business Leaders (16):
## An Untainted Leader

Reformers brought in from outside the company are not saddled with responsibility for previous errors of management or strategy. They are free to implement reform without having to rationalize what happened in the past. Similarly, a reformer from a peripheral part of the company is not shackled to the company's past and thus enjoys more leeway to take action and implement reforms. Best to choose an untainted leader who can work from a clean slate.

Saegusa put together the following thoughts as he decided where to start the reforms.

### Key Turning Points: Riddle-solving and Decision-making as a Business Leader

- Implementing reforms inevitably causes *organizational instability*. To avoid risk, ensure that the instability remains under your complete control.
- If a business is at the brink of failure, it must be rescued *swiftly*. Misumi could afford more time, thanks to its strong profits. That makes a *decisive difference* in the actions a business leader takes.
- The first target for reform would be the FA Division. It was neither the *main stronghold* nor a *peripheral* organization, but something in between. The main reason was the key players. K. Nagao, the head of the division, showed promise as a business leader. Also, the FA business was growing rapidly and might produce a success story more quickly.
- The reforms would be pursued quietly, without fanfare, and there would be no strict deadlines. This was to give Nagao and his team psychological breathing room if the reforms hit a wall.

Why did Saegusa devote so much thought to the question of where to start the reforms? Readers will soon realize the importance of this choice. Saegusa's decision would have major implications for the company's business over the next decade. More on this at the end of this chapter.

## Where is the Competition?

Without warning, Saegusa called Nagao, the head of the FA Division, and asked him to explain the business. As he hung up the phone, Nagao couldn't realize he was about to embark on a turbulent year. He appeared at the CEO's office with documents in hand.

"Since I was made general manager of the FA Division three years ago," Nagao explained, "I've focused on product development, which has led to the launch of many new products."

As a result, domestic sales grew from $85 million before Nagao took over to $100 million the following year, and $150 million the year after that—up 80% in two years.

Great progress. However, that year—his third leading the division—sales had slumped in the wake of the economic downturn. Sales were now forecast to fall $50 million short of the $184 million target.

"But we're stronger than our competitors," Nagao asserted.

Its competitors were all seeing year-on-year declines of 30 to 40 percent, but Nagao's division would dip only 10 percent. So, its market share would actually increase.

Nagao outlined the future business plan. He quoted aggressive figures—sales would grow from $132 million to $410 million in five years, for instance. It was a bullish plan assuming strong growth at a time when Japan was still grappling with the aftermath of the bubble economy's collapse. According to Nagao's graph, sales would climb steeply.

Saegusa replied simply, "Is this realistic? This graph depicts what we call a hockey stick, with the tail end rising so sharply. So, again, is this realistic?"

Surprised by the reaction, Nagao carefully walked through the plan to add $278 million in sales over five years. But the plan seemed full of holes.

"Do you really expect to triple sales with such a rough plan?" he asked. "How can you win when you haven't even defined your competition in this document? This is no strategy."

As head of the division, Nagao wasn't used to being challenged like this. His logic was being scrutinized with trenchant and forceful questions.

Saegusa was throwing around terms—*competition* and *winning the battle*. But those words were simply not part of Misumi's vocabulary at the time, as Nagao would later confess.

Misumi's founder often said the company's role was to look after the customer by procuring and supplying the items they needed. If it devoted itself to acting as a purchasing agent, the competition would fade away. So, the term *competitor* was anathema.

But within days after Saegusa arrived at Misumi, he had discarded his predecessor's mantra in one fell swoop.

"Let's think realistically," he said. "Every product has a competitor. Show me one customer that has left all purchasing up to Misumi and does none on its own."

Nagao had no answer. The beliefs he had held up as sacred truths were beginning to crumble.

Saegusa declared, "A business plan that fails to address the competitive landscape is nonsense. That's not management."

Nagao understood the point. He had harbored private doubts about the prospects of reaching $410 million in sales within five years. In all honesty, he thought they might make only half that.

"The higher you aim, the greater the risk of failure." Saegusa continued, "So you need to come up with a strategy. That strategy will help you identify pitfalls."

Nagao had sensed their new leader would usher in sweeping changes. But he hadn't expected the wave of reform would strike his FA Division so soon, especially given its strong performance. He'd been watching the reform initiatives from a comfortable distance, expecting that his business would be the last in line.

But Saegusa had different plans for Nagao.

## Strategy Without a Concept

Nagao returned to his desk, then assembled four leaders from the FA Division in a meeting room.

"The new boss says we need to develop a strategy," he announced. "I want each of you to draft a strategy for your product lines."

The four leaders looked confused. This was the first time the word strategy had come up. Nagao had delegated everything to them without truly understanding himself what needed to be done. Unwittingly, Nagao had already made one mistake. Fortunately, he did give his leaders one good hint.

"Last fall, when he was still an outside director, Mr. Saegusa held a strategy training session for all company officers," Nagao said. "I remember he talked about *selection and concentration* and *focus*."

The project launched on March 13. First, the four leaders set out creating numerous charts.

By the end of March, Nagao had selected one of his team's charts and carried it to Saegusa in high spirits.

The chart plotted multiple products with sales growth rate on the vertical axis and operating profit margin on the horizontal axis.

Nagao's enthusiasm was promptly short-circuited.

After a quick glance, Saegusa had one question: "Where does this show whether we beat the competition?"

Nagao was caught off guard. True, the chart didn't address the competition. Just one question reduced two weeks of hard work to nothing. Dejected, he went back to the FA Division and gave his team further instructions. But even then, he failed to lay out a concrete approach or method for analysis.

### Riddle-solving for Business Leaders (17): Management Literacy

Management literacy is the application of textbook knowledge to real-life situations. It gets refined through repeated cycles of failure and success. Today, a leader's strategic creativity determines success. The common problem with chronically underperforming companies is that they fail to discuss issues logically or place importance on the numbers. They tend to get swept up in the old company dynamic. Management literacy is the key to fundamentally strengthening a company.

Nagao and his team pressed on, still unsure of what exactly they should do.

"We need to focus our strategy on key products—those with strong sales, profit margins and growth. From there, we can narrow it down to those that are unique to Misumi. That would be products A, B and C from group one."

Once again, they'd jumped to a conclusion that highlighted products A, B and C. All they did was list up what they had always felt were key products. They'd skipped the step of really *thinking it through*.

Nagao's team made dozens of charts, confident they were doing something they hadn't done before. Just gathering the data involved overcoming challenges; that alone made them believe they were creating a masterpiece.

But Nagao's work elicited the same response from Saegusa again.

"This charts sales growth and profit margins of each product, but again, it doesn't show me whether we beat the competition," Saegusa said. "What problems is your strategy supposed to resolve?"

It wasn't as if Saegusa had left the team completely to their own devices. He'd made sudden appearances and joined in their discussions, even as they worked late into night.

The team would be surprised to see him still at the office despite the late hour and were impressed that he'd gone to the trouble of visiting them at their workplace, something his predecessor never would have done. Such gestures would have been rare at any major company. Although he popped in to offer advice, he didn't give them the answer.

## Why Not Give Them the Answer?

On April 17, a month after the project launched, the team completed a map of what they dubbed the "ultimate new strategy". They were convinced it would pass muster this time. But the new chart had the same axes as the first, which had been rejected in seconds. There was still no hint of where the competition figured in.

"You're chasing your own tail," Saegusa warned them.

He had been keeping a tight lip, but that approach was nearing its limits. Nagao's team had already taken an inordinate amount of time. Saegusa was confounded but impressed that the regular business hadn't suffered while they were immersed in this project away from their normal responsibilities.

He couldn't stand by and let them waste any more time. After foraging in the wild for so long, unable to find food, the team was close to starvation.

But if he had known the answer all along, why hadn't he given the team more specific guidance?

"Before I came here, the company had hired external consultants on a number of occasions," Saegusa commented, looking back on it a few years later. "Each team of consultants came to us from renowned firms. Each had been given more than *million-dollar* budgets. I read all their reports, but Misumi put almost none of their suggestions into practice.

"I decided I couldn't simply give them the tools or the answers. They needed to flounder about on their own for a bit! This was the only way to ensure that a group of people who had never given significant thought to management or strategy would develop the habit of thinking for themselves." Saegusa reflected on his commitment to cultivate management talent at the company.

The process was hard on him, too. On past turnaround projects, typically Saegusa himself generated a course of action within days. But here, he might have to wait as long as a month. Even so, Nagao's team had brought him the wrong answer. He worried he'd have to wait another few weeks.

"But I had committed to groom our next generation of business leaders," he noted. "It was a case of *more haste, less speed.*"

## Back to Basics

Nagao had been leaving all the thinking and heavy lifting up to his team. He wasn't providing guidance on fundamentals like how to consider and implement strategy and how to drive reforms forward. Nagao found himself backed into a corner.

"I finally realized," he recalled, "that until I, as the leader, mastered the approach or tools we needed and used them to guide my team, they would drift aimlessly."

You might wonder what took him so long, but Nagao had at last begun to understand the role he needed to play in devising a strategy. Leaders who don't have a stock of frameworks can't exercise effective leadership. For a rudderless organization to become a strategy-oriented unit, the individuals working there need to change, as Nagao was beginning to.

After that, the team's behavior did begin to change, albeit gradually. Simply put, they had no escape, because the CEO had a habit of turning up where they were working late at night.

## Riddle-solving for Business Leaders (18): Hands-On

Management leaders need to keep the pulse of the workplace, while also viewing problems from a broader perspective than the team has. If the team is spinning its wheels, a leader needs find the right time to give re-direction or a way out of the jam. This entails showing them where they can cut corners so as not to waste time on fruitless work. Being *hands-on* is one of the keys to leadership.

Nagao was stuck. And the team was exhausted from putting in so much overtime day after day. Something needed to be done.

In an attempt to identify what kind of frameworks he needed to acquire, Nagao re-read one of Saegusa's books, *Turnaround Task Force*. One part struck a chord. The book describes how the members of a reform task force had started by directly addressing the realities in front of them. The whole team spent several days off-site brainstorming all the factors that had led to their defeat, and then used this to develop a logical explanation based on thorough reflection. The observations served as a starting point for their reforms. Nagao realized that, unlike the team in the book, his FA Division was blaming its poor performance entirely on the economy. They had neglected to root out the real problems in the business.

"This was a turning point for me," Nagao said. "I realized that I'd skipped that step and made the mistake of jumping straight into playing around with figures and graphs."

He had thought that studying the basics of manage-ment was meaningless, but he decided to give it another try. Combining his experience with his studies, he hit upon something significant: the benefits of *management literacy* and *frameworks*. He gathered his team to go back to the drawing board and root out the problems.

## Getting to the Core

It was Saturday, April 27, six weeks into the project and the first day of Golden Week, one of Japan's biggest national holiday seasons.

"Let's start by writing out what we don't know", Nagao announced to his team. "I'll offer some broad categories". They were: *customers, the company, cost, competition, product development* and *contract manufacturers*.

As the ideas trickled out, Nagao wrote each on the whiteboard. Eventually, they had a list of questions and problems. He'd thought they would finish that evening, but the brainstorming continued until nearly midnight.

The next morning, they gathered in the same meeting room. Merely listing the problems hadn't revealed the true essence of those problems. Nagao and his team re-organized their problems into six categories: *product development, contract manufacturers, new customer acquisition, profitability by product, market and growth* and *supply chain*.

On his way home, Nagao pondered their next move. The next day was a public holiday. At home, Nagao continued to mull it over. He had a nagging suspicion that they had not yet uncovered a more fundamental problem.

Suddenly, he realized, "All of these problems have occurred because we have been acting without a goal."

You might think he made some leap in logic. But a leader who cuts to the root of a problem, who simplifies and abstracts the chaos, will make such leaps to a realization that helps them move forward. (See Saegusa Management Note 2: Riddle-solving Makes or Breaks a Business Leader.)

Nagao realized they had historically targeted only two perfor-mance metrics: overall sales and overall profit. That was based on the belief there were too many products to set individual targets. Similarly, Nagao's plan for the FA business targeted only total sales of $410 million.

There was no clear strategy for each individual product, and therefore nothing to guide the actions of the product managers. The competitive landscape and customer base differed by product and, therefore, should merit different actions, but the business plan failed to address these elements.

"We've always been content to discuss the business as whole on a macro level," he realized, "and thought that was enough to run it."

Here is a copy of the actual slide Nagao presented at the Misumi Management Forum conference forthcoming in Section 2 of this Chapter.

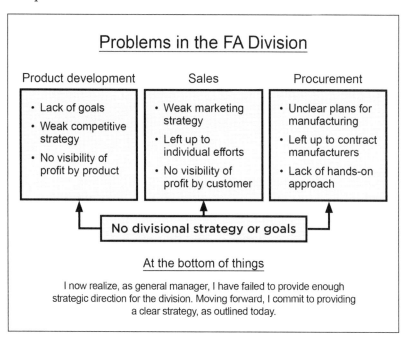

Note that he says, "I now realize, as general manager, I have failed to provide enough strategic direction for the division."

Nagao was a corporate officer and division general manager at the time. Would you believe that someone in such a senior position could address the entire company with such humility? His words made a profound impact on the audience.

Perhaps Nagao was inspired to take such a humble approach by Saegusa's framework, a *Brutally Honest Reflection* (Management Note 8: The Four Forces Driving a Passionate Organization). It marked an inflection point in the path toward success for the FA division's reform effort and the explosive growth that would follow in the years to come.

He learned one more thing. Saegusa often talked about *isolating individual issues*, and now Nagao understood. He had often been asked to define a *good product* or a *bad product* and a *good customer* or a *bad customer*. But he couldn't answer because he hadn't known the profitability of each product.

Of course, he could access sales and gross margin information broken down by product. Any company would have these figures. But a high gross margin doesn't automatically make a good product. Often a product could ultimately lose money as various expenses mount, or because of customer complaints.

You need to have a clear view of profitability to distinguish the *good* from the *bad*. Without that distinction, you won't know what actions need to be taken.

Finally, Nagao thought he saw what needed to be done.

## Riddle-solving for Business Leaders (19): Isolating the Individual Issues

To identify root causes on "Sheet 1" of the planning process "Sheet 1→Sheet 2→Sheet 3", break down the problems into pieces you can understand and manage. You isolate the issues, whether it be for product, customer, employee or activity. That puts you in a position to do a deep dive. Ask "why" again and again, relentlessly, until you have identified the root cause and solved the riddle.

## Redefining the Project

Nagao finally understood you can't develop a strategy without knowing individual product profitability. He realized he couldn't pick key products blindly, that he needed a clear view of profitability.

"We should go back and calculate net profit by product," he told Saegusa, expecting to be taken to task for it.

Instead, Saegusa said, "Good. You're on the right track. But how will you calculate profitability for each product?"

With the CEO, the simplest questions were the most vexing.

"It's not easy to calculate net profit by product." Saegusa explained how common methods of allocating expenses in proportion to sales or cost of goods could invite misguided strategic decisions. Nagao hadn't thought that far ahead. Once again, Nagao had neglected to consider the *concepts* and *methods* that lie at the heart of the work he was proposing.

Saegusa offered him a helping hand. "Why don't you try Activity Based Costing? ABC is a cost accounting method."

He went on to give a simple explanation. Employees were involved in a range of activities, including processing orders, issuing orders to the contract manufacturers, gathering products at the warehouse, packaging and shipping, logistics, and handling of complaints. The true costs of these activities differed depending on the product or customer. ABC elucidates how such indirect costs accrue. It can help calculate the cost of goods and profitability of each product more accurately than conventional methods.

"I see. We'll try ABC then," Nagao replied, without realizing this rash decision would send him hurtling toward another hopeless mess.

Saegusa knew the *hell of ABC*. Meanwhile, Nagao's team smiled in relief, thinking the day's meeting had gone well.

People who try to create something new rather than simply follow another have to carve out an unfamiliar path. This is true both for developing technology and pursuing management innovation alike. To hone your management skills, you must endure trial and error, overcome the unsettling emotions that accompany it, and engage in a great deal of intellectual labor. It requires intelligence as well as discipline and physical stamina. People who possess these attributes are what Saegusa calls intellectual athletes. Japan's university sports clubs produce this type of person. The clubs are known for their grueling physical regimens and rigid hierarchical structures, a culture that carries over into the work environment in Japan.

Nagao and his team commenced their ABC analysis.

In this book, the strategy of using ABC analysis is the focus of Saegusa's Management Note 4: How Costing is Critical for Strategy and the following chapter. Readers who want to know what Nagao and his team had to tackle to introduce ABC should skip ahead to that section and the next chapter before reading on.

## SAEGUSA'S MANAGEMENT NOTE 3
# HOW PPM BECAME THE MISUMI-SAURUS

### How PPM Became the *Misumi-saurus*

The results of the ABC analysis provided unprecedented clarity on the problems the FA Division faced, thanks to a strategy concept I will explain here, before moving on with the story.

The theory of Product Portfolio Management (PPM) was originally devised by Bruce Henderson, the Boston Consulting Group (BCG) founder. It gained such wide popularity that the 1970s were known as the *era of strategy*. As a classic theory, it had a tremendous presence, like a giant dinosaur, in the early days of strategic management.

However, in subsequent years PPM was rarely adopted in real-life management scenarios. Why? There are various criticisms of PPM, but my explanation is simple.

PPM seeks to explain the immense complexities that determine a company's success, failure or competitive edge using only two mechanisms: *growth rate* and *market share*. PPM fell out of favor because many found the explanation too simple, *too narrow* for a strategy concept.

In the 1980s, consultants and academics attempted to transcend PPM's simplicity. That led to a succession of new strategic-management theories exploring what *competitive edge* is in the first place or investigating how companies gain a competitive advantage. The most renowned of these theories is Professor Michael E. Porter's Five Forces model. It explains the mechanisms behind competitive edge on many different levels.

One after another, new strategic-management theories would garner attention, only to fade away. Businesspeople would grasp at these new theories, try them out, cast them aside, and move on to the next. Through this churn, interest in PPM rapidly cooled.

Yet, I recognized that PPM was a valuable concept and continued to use it in real-life management scenarios. I would like to think that among the world's business leaders—or even among the more than 10,000 people said to have worked at BCG—no one continued to advocate the value of PPM and employ it to the extent that I have over the past 40 years.

Here is a list of the steps involved in formulating strategy. PPM plays a definitive role in these steps.
1. Narrow down the *key business* for company-wide strategy
2. Narrow down the *key product group* within the key business
3. Narrow down one *key product* from within the key product group

Then follow five more steps.
4. *Define strategic segmentation* in the key product's target market
5. Identify a *mix of sales approaches* for the target segments
6. Efficiently manage *salesforce activities* across that mix
7. Manage the progress of the resulting *sales by customer*
8. Initiate the *feedback loop*, i.e., review results and communicate feedback to the key business in step one

## The Effectiveness of PPM

I mentioned PPM was criticized for being too simple and too narrow to explain competitive forces. I disagree. True, it is simple, but this simplicity makes PPM even more valuable in practical use.

Can a business leader solidify their thoughts on strategy without considering: 1) growth potential; 2) profitability; and 3) whether the business is winning today or will continue to win tomorrow? Of course not.

Its simplicity is what makes PPM such a strong theory and provides utility even today. PPM draws from only a narrow set of the many elements of strategy. But the elements it does leverage are incredibly important.

Decades later, there is still no other theory that achieves an equivalent level of insight on strategy regarding the dynamic relationship between the three key elements of competition identified by Henderson. In this respect, PPM is unmatched in terms of clarity and practical applicability.

And although it has been criticized, no one has yet developed a better practical-strategy tool. There are many factors to consider when developing strategy. But no one has devised a strategic management theory that encapsulates *all* those factors. That's how complex corporate activities are.

I like to use PPM as the *starting point* in solidifying a strategy. PPM is most incisive when used as a tool to expand your perspective. Then, compare the interpretation PPM provides you with other concepts. Finally, check for inconsistencies or inhibiting factors.

In some quarters, PPM is an outdated theory only discussed in business-school settings. But far from being extinct, at Misumi PPM is *alive and well* and has generated truly positive results over the years. Here, the dinosaur that is PPM has become our *Misumi-saurus*, which casually ambles around the company.

I brought the Misumi-saurus here. But it was Nagao and others on the task forces who gave it the food and water to keep it alive.

The keyword is the *ground level*. Rather than reserving PPM as a tool for top management, make sure that mid-level staff in the business lines completely understand it and leverage it as a tool for raising their own business performance.

## Route 1: The Path to Glory

Within the PPM model I gave names to the routes to success. *Route 1* represents the path from launch to growth, culminating in the box labelled *Glory*. Meanwhile, *Route 3* represents the path to defeat. In between them is Route 2. This path is more of a mixed bag.

Again, this is a true story. Nagao allowed his team to aimlessly carry on without a framework. Upon further review, Nagao uncovered something surprising—the fundamentals of stage-based product strategy. I reinforced this framework often at my internal strategy training courses.

Start by plotting your products on a PPM chart. That helps you establish the appropriate approach for each product.

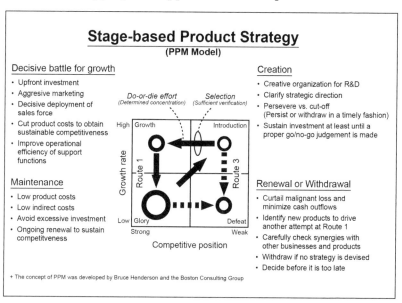

### Stage-based Product Strategy
#### (PPM Model)

**Decisive battle for growth**

- Upfront investment
- Aggresive marketing
- Decisive deployment of sales force
- Cut product costs to obtain sustainable competitiveness
- Improve operational efficiency of support functions

**Maintenance**

- Low product costs
- Low indirect costs
- Avoid excessive investment
- Ongoing renewal to sustain competitveness

*Do-or-die effort*
*(Determined concentration)*

*Selection*
*(Sufficient verification)*

High | Growth | Introduction

Growth rate

Route 1 | Route 3

Low | Glory | Defeat

Strong | Weak

Competitive position

**Creation**

- Creative organization for R&D
- Clarify strategic direction
- Persevere vs. cut-off (Persist or withdraw in a timely fashion)
- Sustain investment at least until a proper go/no-go judgement is made

**Renewal or Withdrawal**

- Curtail malignant loss and minimize cash outflows
- Identify new products to drive another attempt at Route 1
- Carefully check synergies with other businesses and products
- Withdraw if no strategy is devised
- Decide before it is too late

+ The concept of PPM was developed by Bruce Henderson and the Boston Consulting Group

## Section 2:
# Strategizing to Compete

## Back to Formulating Strategy

Nagao and his team successfully completed the arduous ABC project (See Chapter 3 for more) and presented their results at a directors' meeting. It was a daunting endeavor, and the team enjoyed a sense of fulfillment.

But the ABC analysis alone could not answer the problems their strategy needed to address and identify concrete action items.

Here Nagao and his team entered the project's next stage. They went back to the starting point: *choosing key products that have strategic importance for the Division to compete and grow.* With the ABC analysis complete, they now had profit-margin data for each product. Over a series of meetings, Nagao and the task force decided to choose key products in order of highest profit growth over the next three years.

"To do that," said Nagao to the task force, "Let's find the average growth rate over the last three years. Based on that, we can anticipate growth, sales and profit for the next three years."

Do you see the flaw in Nagao's logic?

Nagao presumes that products with 30% growth in the last three years will continue to grow 30% in the next three years. This is absurd. If all products grew at a constant rate, the future growth rate would automatically be the same as the past. Everything would simply continue along the same course, and strategy would be useless.

The effects of the previous year's sharp recession were still reverberating through the economy. The business had been hit hard, its growth rate falling from positive to negative territory. How could he ignore that and simply extrapolate the historical growth rate into the future?

Nagao had reverted to his pre-ABC behavior. Again, he jumped to a conclusion without any real basis for doing so. Now that groundless conclusion was driving his actions.

## No Patience Left

The task force headed to the CEO's office in high spirits, confident their weeks of hard work would be met with the same praise their ABC analysis garnered.

Instead, he rebuked them sharply. "You haven't changed, have you!?"

He didn't hide his disappointment. This was the fourth time. Until now, he had been patient, allowing the team to try different approaches, and waited to see some progress. But now his patience had worn thin.

"Nagao," he said. "Look over this table, top to bottom. Where is there information that helps me determine whether we beat the competition?"

Reforms based on flawed logic will generate strategies that are fated to miss the mark. And if the first strategy implemented is unsuccessful or a waste of effort, people will mistrust anything labelled *strategy*. He knew the first wave of reform strategy needed to be *guaranteed* to succeed.

"Realize that strategy is about *winning* or *losing*," he told them.

Saegusa felt that now was the time to step in and sever ties with old mindsets. Not with brute force, but with logic.

He explained. "Why does a product have low growth? Is it because its market has matured? Or is the product in a market that is still in a very early stage? Or has the product lost to the competition? Look at this table and pick any product. Can you tell whether it is slowing down or about to take off?"

"Take any of our high-growth products. If our competitor is growing even faster, we are losing. We are trying to make a call to arms. How does this table help us purge products that appear to be successful, but are actually losing?"

"This tool could cut the wrong way," he continued. "It might lead us to select the wrong strategic product. In that case, we would be better off without it."

### Riddle-solving for Business Leaders (20): What is Strategy?
Strategy is to:

Monitor (1) **the *battlefield* and your *enemies*** by taking (2) **a *bird's eye view*,** and based on the understanding of (3) **your *strengths and weaknesses*.** you find the (4) ***key factor for success*,** and you discern your (5) ***alternatives*,** and gauge the (6) ***balance of risks*,** while by (7) ***narrowing down and concentrating*,** you allow yourself to secure victory within the prescribed (8) ***time frame*** by having all these (9) ***logic*.**

You then make clear (10) ***the order*** for implementing your strategy, as (11) ***a long-term scenario*,** which you (12) ***present to the people in the organization*.**

Strategies that have been written down but are yet to be implemented are merely *hypotheses*. The key to separating the good strategy from bad one before it is implemented is the *concreteness of the logic*.

"This is not an academic exercise," he went on. "Your proposal will be used as the basis for top management to take action, assign work to real people, and invest real money in the real battlefield confronting the competition. You can't look back in hindsight and say that you didn't think it through properly, or that you picked the wrong strategy."

"The future of this business depends on the logic you create," he concluded. "Logic. That's what this is about."

Nagao and his team went back to their desks to contemplate their next move.

## Training Leadership Talent

Saegusa was disappointed, but this situation was not unlike his past struggles turning around businesses. Even apparently talented people do not change easily. You need to relentlessly shake their sense of values until you have inculcated the correct way of thinking to instill change at the company.

It was Nagao who held the key. Over the last four months, Saegusa had spotted his weaknesses.

When Nagao understood something well, he could tackle challenges with impressive speed. He exhibited exceptional leadership, worked with efficiency and agility and set his own deadlines. He had a strong personality with a hint of a wild streak. This unique combination of attributes made him a rare talent.

However, like many, he tended to avoid or put off things that weren't clear to him, or didn't suit him, or didn't feel necessary. Ordinarily, rather than trying to learn new things, he stayed within his comfort zone. This is why his work product often fell short of his corporate responsibilities. After the ABC analysis, the team resumed its work. But Nagao was navigating without a compass. Once again, he was leading his team toward a massive undertaking, all for naught.

Could Nagao and his team be molded into business leaders? They were all hard workers, with strong individual personalities, who were motivated to advance through the ranks. But to succeed they needed to understand their shortfalls. They had to dig themselves out of the hole they were stuck in.

Some say it is fruitless to try to train management leadership because those who have such potential develop on their own and those who don't won't, no matter how you try. But Saegusa believes that executive leadership can develop by learning and experience and he chose to take an *active hand* in training his cadre of future leaders.

**Key Turning Points: Riddle-solving and Decision-making as a Business Leader**
- Leaving Nagao's business strategies under-developed would set a low bar for other strategies, and for leadership talent across the company.
- The business strategies developed here had to be sophisticated from a global perspective. If its business strategies were third-rate by international standards, Misumi could only be a third-rate company.
- So Saegusa decided to develop a system where he could convey *firsthand* his experience in strategies and workplace improvements to potential business leaders. First, he introduced business plans, a methodology he had used in past turnaround situations. This equipped leaders with a tool for application of strategic theory to their own businesses. Second, he championed the role of *missionary of strategy* at Misumi. He began Misumi Strategy School, where he acted as sole lecturer. It was a lot of work to develop teaching materials, but there were enough stories of success or failure in the company for discussion. It was the most effective way to suffuse a strategic mindset across the organization.

## Back to the Starting Blocks

It was already July, four months since the project had launched in March. Saegusa couldn't leave Nagao's task force to their own devices anymore. He decided to push Nagao to overcome his weakness: a lack of drive to seek out what he couldn't see.

"Nagao, remember I taught you about PPM at last year's executive strategy training?" Saegusa asked. "Many think it's outmoded, but what I shared at the seminar came from my own unique experience and can't be found in a textbook. It's a practical tool I've used in real-life situations. How about going back and reading up on it, then starting over from there?"

Nagao re-read one of Saegusa's books, *Professional Strategist*, and his notes from the strategy training seminar.

At the training seminar, he'd been tasked with the challenge of making his business bigger than the competition's. Back then, Nagao felt it was like someone else's fight. But now the problem was staring him in the face.

He remembered how Saegusa had told them it was more important "to be the dominant top player in a narrowly defined, unique market segment," than "be a minor player in a huge market," even if that meant only securing modest sales.

Nagao remembered the chief executive's chart, Stage-based Product Strategy (PPM Model), which had been included in the training session notes (See Saegusa's Management Note 3).

Nagao was shocked to find written right there were all the strategic elements Saegusa was pressing him for now. He'd attended the training session but had probably forgotten it the same day.

"This is it," he decided. "Let's go back and draw up a PPM chart."

And so, the team spent the last week of July on the PPM chart. They had all the basic data they needed from their previous work.

## Management Literacy Fuels Groundbreaking Change

On July 30, Nagao's team finally completed the FA Division's first PPM chart. When they brought it to Saegusa, the tone of the conversation felt dramatically different.

"I see," Saegusa said. "The FA Division is growing, but many products are still in the zone of *Defeat*."

"Yes," Nagao replied, "for the products on the left side, we enjoy the number one position in the market. But there are very few products here." He spoke as if he had known it all along, but he actually only realized it after completing the PPM chart.

"Yes, that's right," Saegusa said. "We can lower the bar for victory and accept those products with a number-two position. But many products are even weaker than that. We certainly can't call the FA business as a whole a success."

When GE's Jack Welch implemented major reforms, he decided that market-number-one or -two businesses were acceptable. Before heading GE, Welch led its plastics division. That was the 1970s when GE was dedicated to PPM.

"Yes," Nagao replied, "and there are several products in the *Defeat* section in the bottom right. In theory, we should withdraw from the products in this quadrant."

"Well," Saegusa cautioned, "theoretically we should. But it's best to proceed carefully. PPM doesn't show the synergy between businesses. That's its shortcoming. There are other elements to competition, so it's best not to decide based solely on PPM. For one, products in this corner aren't necessarily losing money.

We can look to the ABC data you've put together for the real picture on profitability."

Nagao concluded, "We've established that even though the FA business as a whole is growing, many products are seeing only lackluster growth. There must be a reason why we hadn't noticed this before. We can probably point the business toward victory if we solve each issue correctly." His choice of words had changed dramatically, eliciting a smile from Saegusa.

"But the PPM chart shows," Saegusa noted, "the overall picture is not bad. There are many promising products in the top right *Creation* box."

"Those products have a low share, but high growth, so their share will increase automatically. If we focus on them as key products, we can speed up the growth of the business as a whole," said Nagao.

"Yes, but you need to investigate the prospects of products in the Creation box carefully," Saegusa cautioned. "The key products you want to bet on in the market for the time being are those further left, on the winning side."

The conversation felt more balanced. Nagao and his team were beginning to speak and think more intelligently about their business.

"So, this is what he expected from us," thought Nagao. "Strategy is about having these conversations. Management literacy is what generates such changes."

Last time it had been ABC. This time it was PPM. Without those frameworks, you wander about in an endless fog and embark on misguided policies and strategies without ever finding the light. Nagao was starting to assimilate these two distinct frameworks.

## Riddle-solving for Business Leaders (21): Mastering a Key Theory

Business leaders are not scholars, and therefore cannot master all management theories. Nor should they be swayed by trendy theories of the day. Choose one *key theory*, study it extensively, apply it in the workplace and make it your own classic theory. Like a plant, your key theory feeds new frameworks that sprout from there.

If a team equipped with management literacy takes on a team that is not, which will prevail in the market? The answer is clear.

## Something Still Missing

Nagao's team was convinced they should go with the PPM analysis, confident in its utility for selecting key products.

But they had been through this before. They thought the fog had cleared as they reached the top of the climb. But their optimism vanished as another tough ascent appeared before them. Within minutes, another fog bank had rolled in and obscured the peak. As with climbers attempting to summit a mountain, business leaders will at some point confront seemingly insurmountable obstacles. Nevertheless, successful leaders will continue to push on toward the summit, gathering experience along the way.

Saegusa asked Nagao, "What is the strength that drives the success of our winning products? Why do customers buy from us? Or, why do they buy from our competitors?"

These were fundamental questions relevant to any business or service. But Nagao hadn't given it enough thought.

Despite this, the FA business had grown. Until then, in his own way, he had developed the right answer to this question and provided a valued service to the customer. That was why customer orders continued to grow. But had he *consciously* understood what made all that possible? Nagao understood Saegusa's questions hinted at a new starting point for devising a business strategy that was particularly important for the FA business.

Putting aside cost and delivery times, nearly any subcontractor with a certain level of metal-machining expertise could make most of the same precision components. The so-called commodity products they sold were also commonly distributed components that you could pick up anywhere.

Why would a customer choose one supplier over another? It had to be because the favored supplier offered some kind of *value* to the customer. Nagao felt he was being guided to identify that value. He had to develop strategies to *consciously* execute what they had already been achieving somehow.

"If we can formulate actions that will enhance the strengths customers recognize in us," he thought, "and minimize our weaknesses, we can leverage those actions to grow product sales."

Nagao and his team understood that such a process was essential for putting together a strategy.

## What Value Does Misumi Offer?

Nagao and his task force set out to analyze the value they offer. They listed all conceivable types of value, including areas where they were losing out to competitors.

Value as perceived by the team did not necessarily translate to actual value for the customer. The key to this process was to uncover these differences. Here are some of the points they identified.

| Misumi model | Value for the customer |
| --- | --- |
| Catalog provides prices and delivery lead time. | Takes less time to put together estimates. |
| The part number from the catalog is all you need to order. | There's no need to make a blueprint for each product. |
| Complaints are handled by the customer center. | Negative: It's a hassle to call the customer center. |

| Conventional distribution model | Value for the customer |
| --- | --- |
| A salesperson from the distributor comes by to take orders. | It's convenient because they can respond to customer needs quickly and accurately. |
| Distributor handles only certain manufacturers. | Negative: It's cumbersome to place and manage orders across hundreds of suppliers. |

They covered the whiteboard with items of value they thought they provided customers. The process clarified the strengths of the Misumi business model and led to a realization.

They noticed this tick-or-cross method with subjective judgement on several items did not show who was the *ultimate* winner: Misumi or a competitor. Nagao wondered if they could *quantify* these value points. The team spent a lot of time inventing an alternative method and finally came up with a quantified analytical tool. The method is still considered proprietary for Misumi today and unfortunately cannot be shared here.

Nagao took the analysis results to Saegusa, who had not been directly involved in the project for about a month, due to overseas business trips and other management duties.

Saegusa was very surprised to hear Nagao's explanation. The task force had made significant progress in the last month and generated a new tool for analyzing the competitive landscape. After patiently waiting for Nagao to develop as a strategic leader, Saegusa felt as if his patience was finally being rewarded beyond expectation.

Saegusa instructed the team to give the concept a unique name. "Try coming up with something inspired!" he said, laughing. They settled for plain vanilla: *Relative Customer Merit*.

And so, a strategy concept unique to Misumi was born. It may not seem like much to you, but the concept Nagao had devised would generate immense value for the company in the years to come.

### Riddle-solving for Business Leaders (22): One Critical Slide

A successful presentation on a reform scenario contains at least one decisive moment—one slide, or even one sentence—that lands with the audience and sparks a change in how they view your leadership.

A successful presenter knows in advance what that one critical slide will be. Those who don't haven't done enough fact-finding, or they haven't given enough thought to rooting out what problems lie at the bottom of things.

Your slide deck may comprise 30, or even 100, slides. But to make your presentation effective, identify which is your one critical slide.

Nagao felt gratified by the unexpected praise, and relieved to have proved himself and avoided spinning his wheels.

## Nearly Complete, but Something is Still Missing

In September, six months after they had started, Nagao and his team were putting the finishing touches on the project.

"Nagao, I'd like you to present your new strategy to the entire company," Saegusa requested. "I'd like you to demonstrate what strategy is and set the stage for a new era at Misumi. It's a crucial step in changing the company culture."

The presentation was to be given on October 13 at the Misumi Management Forum conference, and everyone from the company would be in attendance. The Tokyo International Forum in Yurakucho would be the venue. Steps away from Tokyo Station, the Forum often hosts large-scale trade fairs.

This created a hard deadline for the team. But again, they hit a wall. They had plenty of talking points—PPM, Relative Customer Merit, and so on—but they lacked a unifying theme that tied the presentation together into a clear, cohesive story.

Saegusa sensed that if they could cobble together their work, it would pave the way for great progress here. On past corporate turnaround projects, he had found that when he uncovered something effective, it brought him a feeling of conviction—*This is going to work*. He had a hunch that a similar breakthrough to a new strategy was within reach here, too.

As chief executive, it was his role to find that breakthrough. It would be unfair to put that onus on Nagao's team. As more seasoned leaders, they would eventually acquire the ability to discover a new logic themselves. That would make his job easier, too.

He sequestered himself and distilled the true breakthrough into one critical chart. That chart is proprietary information that cannot be revealed here for competitive reasons. What follows, however, is the concept in broad strokes.

He drew up a strategy map with Nagao and his team that incorporated all the following elements *in one chart*. It was designed to help them make comprehensive decisions about product strategy.
- The PPM relative share (winning or losing) and market growth (growth potential and its risk)
- Profitability by product (potential profit and cost positioning as seen from the company) per ABC analysis
- The Relative Customer Merit of the value customers see in the products and services they receive

Saegusa named his chart the Misumi Product Strategy Map.

It was a practical tool for defining action items and was easy to grasp even for less-experienced staff. The tool represented a milestone in the company's strategic management.

### Riddle-solving for Business Leaders (23): Contradictions among Frameworks
Simply using two different strategic frameworks *side by side* complicates decision making because *contradictions* often emerge. One framework says Go, the other says No. It's best to first organize the frameworks into a *cohesive* tool. The Misumi Product Strategy Map was integrated in that way.

The map would have enough utility if it could confirm they had enough wisdom to *outmaneuver* the competition. Genuinely impressed by the tool and convinced of its utility, Nagao's interest grew. They finished their work on the tool by October 1.

Next, they needed to quickly put together a presentation they could give to everyone at the management forum in just two weeks' time.

Nagao would be giving the presentation, but it was also a decisive moment for Saegusa. They needed to convince the audience and impress them with the originality of the strategy. This was to be the first salvo in a clever display of fireworks needed to instill strategic thinking here.

Following the onset of the recession, FA domestic sales had fallen to about $132 million. The plan was to take it to $410 million in five years. It was an aggressive strategy for a company in post-bubble Japan.

The number was basically the same as the $410 million sales target that Nagao had first presented to the CEO. But there was a world of difference in the work that went into formulating the strategies and action items to achieve it.

## Working Saturday to Draw Up the Presentation

As the task force finally started preparing the presentation, it came up against another roadblock.

A presentation needs a well-organized story. It needs a *clear introduction, development,* a *twist*, and a *conclusion*. They couldn't figure out how to tell their story. They had plenty of analysis charts. But how far into the weeds did the CEO expect them to go?

Saegusa popped into their office, looked over their script briefly and left the room without a word.

At that point, he sensed danger. The window had opened briefly, revealing a dark landscape. At this rate, with just a few days left, they would not come up with the kind of presentation he was looking for. If Nagao's presentation fell short, people would question the meaning of strategy and fail to see the point of making reforms.

Inevitably, a difficult reform will run up against a gamut of challenges. These struggles offer a golden opportunity for developing management talent. Up to this point, Saegusa preferred to let his people think through problems on their own. He tried to keep a bird-eye's view, like a hawk circling high above, checking in on progress from time to time. If his people seemed to hit a wall, he would swoop down and intervene just in time to avoid a complete breakdown. This was his style of training people.

Nagao came to the office that Saturday morning, frazzled. They only had a few days left. They had plenty of graphs and figures. But the presentation had no *storyline*. Unless they could connect the dots somehow, the presentation would not be ready in time.

Early in the afternoon, Saegusa suddenly appeared. It was the first time he had come to their workspace on a Saturday. Worried about that dark landscape he had seen the day before, he decided to make an unannounced appearance. The task force needed to tell a dramatic story in a compelling way.

### Riddle-solving for Business Leaders (24): Reform is Drama

Reforms rely on accurate logic to be a success. But they also need to have a story or a hint of drama that inspires people. There needs to be some element of good vs. evil. As you fight to overcome a tremendous hurdle, you get help from an unexpected quarter, only to meet another setback. To improve your management skills, you need to write your own script. Tell it yourself. Do it yourself. And experience success and failure along the way. The story needs to resonate with people to effect change in the culture or behavior of an organization.

The drama doesn't come from deft presentation skills. Your audience will immediately see through a flashy delivery if it lacks substance. It needs sound logic, corroborating facts and figures, and a clear tie-in to the business. Identify the obstacles that stand in the way, and what will be achieved by overcoming them. Then, explain what you will aim for next. Cover these elements in a clear and logical order, and your presentation becomes a story.

"So how about it? Still working on the presentation?" asked Saegusa.

"Well, we've tried all kinds of things, but nothing seems to work," said Nagao.

The team was in a real fix. Saegusa sat in the corner of the room watching them work for a while. Suddenly, he stood up and fired off a series of bewildering requests.

"I'll help out," he said, "First, I'll need plenty of white cards. Sheets of paper cut in half will do. And a pencil, eraser, tape and scissors. Oh, and a ruler. Lay out your script and all the graphs and charts here on the table." The team followed his instructions, without knowing where he was going with this.

He surveyed the charts and slides that covered the table and selected graphs to be photocopied in a smaller size. The team took turns running copies.

He took his scissors to the copies—*snip, snip*—clipping out the parts he wanted. The rest fell to the floor. Then he taped the cut-outs to the half-sheets of paper.

He spread these sheets out in front of him and reviewed them carefully. Then he jotted notes in the margins. Occasionally he would rethink an idea, erase and re-write it.

Soon, he had one slide ready.

"This is the quickest way to revise the *story* of a presentation created by someone else. Scissors, ruler and tape. A computer just gets in the way. Here, low-tech tools work best," he explained.

"Good writing or eloquent delivery alone does not make a good presentation. It's about a flow of logic that makes the story clear to the listener. Your audience will see through flimsy substance in no time. No matter how impressive your delivery is, it won't leave a lasting impression."

He had made countless revisions and still had only one slide to show for it. Seeing that, the team realized just how much energy must go into each slide.

Finally, he gave the slide a title. It was short and punchy.

## Watching the CEO Create a Story

Saegusa drafted one slide after another.

The floor was covered in scrap paper: the graphs he had cut away, and the manuscript he had discarded in its entirety. Someone brought a wastepaper basket and started to gather up the clippings.

"No, no," Saegusa said brightly, continuing his work. "Leave them as they are for now. If the floor is buried in scraps, that means the work is going well."

Once he had a few pages on a certain topic, he would talk through the slides as if he were narrating.

He went through each slide as if he were addressing an audience. He ran his index finger over each point as he muttered an explanation. He was checking that the narrative and the slide were in alignment.

If something didn't flow well, he would rewrite the heading, change the order of the text, take the scissors and cut one page into two, or change the order of the pages.

He seemed like one of the team, as he cut and taped pieces of paper together. On the one hand, they were impressed. He had made quick work. And the presentation became more compelling. On the other hand, they were ashamed for making their CEO do the work.

Saegusa paid this no mind. Eventually, there were more than twenty completed slides. Each page was stiff from the tape holding together the graphs and charts. Some pages had pieces of paper sticking out over the edge.

He went through his story one last time—*speaking aloud*. The presentation was smooth, flowing from one page to the next without a break in between. "So, this is what he meant by having a story," thought the team.

Finally, he gathered up the pages and wrote a page number in the bottom-right corner of each slide, attached them with a paperclip, and handed the stack to Nagao. "Here you go," he said. "Now it's up to you. You can revise or cut out what you like. This is about thirty minutes' worth. With a little more effort, you can fill the hour you have to present. Okay. My work here is done!"

Then he promptly left. The team was confounded. Saegusa showed them exactly what he expected from them. What's more, he hadn't done everything himself. He had shown them a sample and then left, telling them to take care of the rest themselves.

"So, this is how leaders can effectively intervene in their team's work," Nagao thought. He had never given—or received—guidance like this before. "I had always thought of a chief executive as a distant presence. But when it came to the crunch, this new CEO joined us in the trenches, worked alongside us and carved away a *clear path to the exit*. Back on track, our work for that afternoon suddenly felt much easier," Nagao reflected.

This episode gave Nagao a real sense that the company was in for a big change. It felt like he was starting out at a *new company*.

## The Misumi Management Forum

On October 13, around four months after Saegusa had officially taken over the company, everyone gathered offsite at the Tokyo International Forum for the Misumi Management Forum. With more than 300 attendees, including staff from the regional sales offices and overseas, it was its largest companywide gathering ever. No one there could have imagined that, in 13 years, they would be part of a global workforce of 10,000 people.

Nagao took the podium and explained the first business strategy that would spark this growth. For many, it was their first contact with strategy. Such a strategy would have been unthinkable in the past. Proof positive that the company was about to change tremendously.

Later that evening, Mr. Taguchi and his wife joined them in the main banquet hall, for a special event held to thank their company's founder.

All personnel attended. It was a lavish party, and that in itself was a novel experience for them. By holding a first-rate management meeting and a first-rate party at a first-rate forum, Saegusa hoped to demonstrate that a new era had dawned.

Now, let's summarize the overall workflow of FA's strategy-formulation project. This is the actual chart Nagao used in his presentation.

Nagao's workflow chart resembles the framework chart contained in Saegusa's Management Note 8: The Four Forces Driving a Passionate Organization. To understand those similarities better, you may prefer to skip ahead to that section first (page 183), and then come back to this page.

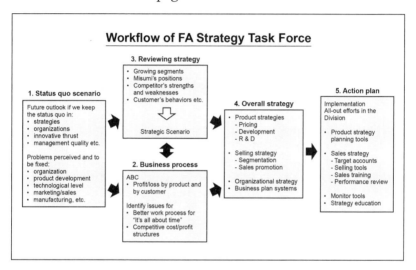

## Growing Domestic Sales More Than Threefold in Five Years

Let's look ahead to the results the FA business strategy eventually delivered. Nagao drew on his own unique strengths to implement his proposed strategy and produce a truly excellent outcome.

The following fiscal year, the FA business overtook the Die Components Business—the company's key business since its founding—on a quarterly basis, and later widened the gap. Nagao's new strategy grew domestic sales from about $132 million pre-reform to about $447 million five years later, easily surpassing the target of $410 million.

The FA business had already done a small amount of exporting pre-reform. Nagao expanded the FA business internationally in line with Saegusa's global strategy. During the same five years, overseas FA sales grew from just $14 million to $117 million.

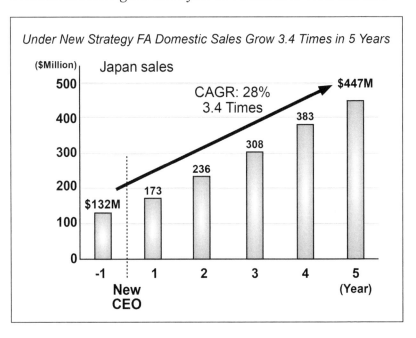

Total FA sales (domestic and overseas) consistently rose by $100 million each year, growing from $147 million pre-reform to $563 million five years later. Sales grew almost four-fold in five years, a compound average growth rate of *31%* per annum. At the time, most Japanese companies were shrinking or eking out only anemic growth in the wake of the bubble economy's collapse. But Nagao's FA business strategy combined with Saegusa's global strategy to achieve impressive growth, making Misumi a stand-out name on the Tokyo Stock Exchange.

The FA business continued to grow in the following years. In the 13th year after implementing Nagao's new strategy, worldwide FA sales exceeded $1.1 billion. The global financial crisis wiped out four years' worth of sales growth. Nevertheless, over the 13-year period, FA sales grew an average 17% per annum including the period of recession.

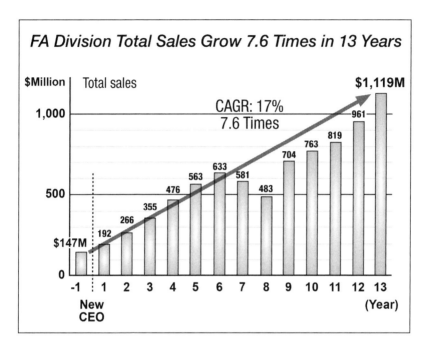

**FA Division Total Sales Grow 7.6 Times in 13 Years**

$Million | Total sales | $1,119M

CAGR: 17%
7.6 Times

961
819
763
704
633
581
563
476
483
355
266
192
$147M

1,000
500
0

-1  1  2  3  4  5  6  7  8  9  10  11  12  13
New CEO                                    (Year)

Before Saegusa's tenure, many associated Misumi with die components. Even within the company, the Die Components Business had received preferential treatment. But Saegusa rejected this view in his second year there. He positioned FA components as the company's new key business and encouraged people in the die-components business to open their eyes. They could no longer afford to rest on their laurels and overlook the threat of new competition in the marketplace.

The decision to select the FA business as his first reform target yielded key strategic value. Operating profit margin gradually expanded from around 10% in Saegusa's first year to around 13% despite increased spending for dramatic expansion of overseas operations.

The FA business had been neither the *main stronghold* nor a peripheral unit. Choosing it as the first target for reform delivered the desired results.

*Testimonial from K. Nagao (At age 42, corporate officer and general manager of the FA Division. Later became executive vice president of the holding company.)*

*The first factor that led to our explosive growth was that top management got involved hands-on in the strategy formulation project. We would never have come up with that strategy by ourselves.*

*Awareness of the importance of strategy improved across the company almost instantly, as if we had been lifted upward by some enormous force. There were twists and turns, but we eventually arrived at a new strategy by drawing on the wisdom of our predecessors and using the correct methods and many frameworks. The things I learned then are applicable to developing any management scenario.*

*On a completely different topic, I got an abrupt phone call from the CEO one Sunday evening around two years after growth in the FA business really took off.*

*"How would you like to see the Grand Canyon?" he asked me. "The FA business has made such great progress thanks to your incredibly hard work. Bring your wife and another key player, too."*

*For a second, I couldn't understand what I was hearing.*

*Mr. Saegusa didn't bring an assistant to handle logistics during the trip. We can't speak English, so he did everything for us. He drove us around in a Lincoln Towncar, fixed any issues with the hotel rooms and even ordered our meals for us. We felt bad for having our CEO work like a tour conductor!*

*The Grand Canyon was amazing, so majestic! You would never see a landscape like that in Japan. An unforgettable experience for me and my wife!*

## SAEGUSA'S MANAGEMENT NOTE 4
# HOW COSTING IS CRITICAL FOR STRATEGY

### The Harmful Effects of Inaccurate Costing

Nagao and his team decided to go back to costing the products before devising their business plan. Before examining that in the next chapter, let's go over the basics of costing in this note.

Costing refers to calculating the *cost of goods* of products the company manufactures or sells. Inaccurate calculations can give rise to misinformed strategy such as investing to expand sales of high-cost products that are therefore not actually making a profit, and instead neglecting products that are making a profit.

Most companies think accounting is a job for specialists. So, most people avoid meddling in the accounting division's methods.

As a result, once costing methods are integrated into a company's system, no one, including executives, scrutinizes them. This is why it is essential for people working in business units to remember to *question* whether the profitability information they refer to is based on the proper costing logic. Saegusa could not rely on an accounting department to innovate its costing because such a department didn't exist under his predecessor's outsourcing policy.

### The Level of Accuracy of Costing

Imagine a manufacturer's factory. Absolutely accurate costing requires that you ascertain exact data piece by piece for each product at every manufacturing process at each moment. Such a number fluctuates, due to factors like operator changes, equipment malfunctions, or small mistakes in manufacturing procedures, and so on.

Accurately measuring these costs from morning to night at every manufacturing process is a colossal task (i.e. information cost become enormous). So, you need to simplify the method by sacrificing detail enough to give yourself a break. Minimize the time spent gathering data and allocate a roughly calculated average cost to each product.

The tradeoff between *accuracy* and *convenience (easy to calculate)* arises most notably in the allocation of so-called indirect expenses. Take a factory's quality control team. To accurately calculate quality control costs by individual product, you would need every quality control staffer to record how much time they spend on each and every product—by the minute from morning to night at every production process. Also, the different salaries of each staffer would need to be reflected.

That's a lot of work. Instead, at the end of the day, each staffer could submit a rough percentage allocation of time spent on each product. Also, use an average salary in place of actual individual salaries. Calculate time spent by broader product categories instead of specific items. These are effective ways to simplify costing that let you slack off a bit.

If you need to cut even more corners, you can allocate the quality control team's monthly total expenses based on monthly product shipments by monetary value. With such a method, the calculation can be made on a monthly basis by the accounting division without involving the shop floor. But if you slack off this much, you are almost completely overlooking the differences in the cost of goods by individual product.

In fact, underperforming companies hardly calculate the cost of goods for each product at all. They go for a kind of *rough estimation* where they throw everything in together.

It is best to balance the simplest method with the greatest possible accuracy. So, where is the ideal compromise? Costing has been a field of academic study at universities for years. The level of costing at a company reveals a lot about that company's management literacy.

## Why Do ABC?

I hope that this explanation has made clear the importance of costing. Now, let's look at ABC. The key point of Activity Based Costing (ABC) is that it is *activity based*. But why use it at a trading company? Why did we have to go that far?

At a trading company, the *accurate cost of goods* of a certain product purchased from an external supplier for $10 per unit will be $10. If we sell it for $15, our gross margin is $5. At first glance, it would seem that the accuracy of cost of goods is not a problem for a trading company.

That works for the gross margin of products. But we do a lot of indirect work between order intake and product shipment. That series of activities involves the same kinds of costing problems that manufacturers face in a factory.

Let's use the above example of a key product with a $5 gross margin. Our salespeople are diligently promoting this product. Assume that we analyze and learn that our salespeople dedicate one-third of their time on average to promoting that one product. We find that the personnel and promotional expenses for that product are $3 per unit, or more than half of the gross margin.

Moreover, we find that the customer centers receive many inquiries and complaints from customers due to technical difficulties with the same product. Summing up the hours operators spend addressing these inquiries and complaints leads to an average cost of $0.60 per unit.

We also find that the warehouses have to make a special package for the product. With delivery included, logistics costs add up to around $3.70 per unit for this product.

So far, these costs total $7.30, completely eroding the gross margin of $5, incurring a loss of $2.30—a shocking discovery for an unsuspecting product manager who has been vigorously promoting the product. The more the sales force sells, the more they lose. What was considered a key product will in fact lead to mounting losses if it continues to be promoted.

I hope this illustrates the significance of costing being activity based. Survey in detail the work done at each step from beginning to end and measure the time spent on each activity. Ultimately, you add all the costs incurred through this chain of activities to the cost of goods for each product. That's ABC.

ABC was originally developed by accounting and management scholar Robert Kaplan in the late 1980s. But more than a decade later, he reflected that many companies that have tried to implement ABC in their organizations have abandoned the attempt due to high costs and employee resistance ("Time-Driven Activity-Based Costing," *Harvard Business Review*, November 2004). This is the same issue as the "cost of information", including the cumbersomeness for managers and staffers who have no interest in using the ABC information for their own work, but have to spend time to provide data for someone else. A reminder of the importance of applying a filter of practical utility to the theories.

Knowing its history, one might think it worthless. But I had found accurate costing information to be *essential* in my corporate turnaround projects. Before the concept was unveiled, I was experimenting with my own simplified costing methods in real-life turnaround situations.

I drew on that experience to introduce ABC at Misumi, where I got involved hands on. Rather than pursuing excessive detail, I sought to strike a balance where we slacked off just enough that it could be run cheaply and still deliver strategic value.

As a result, we successfully averted the common pitfalls of adopting ABC. It has been in place as a standard methodology across the company for over 12 years now. Misumi business managers use it to make decisions on strategy.

This was one innovation generated by the combination of strategic orientation and practical management literacy. I believe we succeeded in incorporating a system that is rare not only for Japan, but globally.

I can't reveal all the intellectual expertise that we have built on ABC developed over the 12 years, but I can describe how ABC was introduced and its outcomes in the next chapter. If you take care to avoid its pitfalls, the method can generate enormous strategic value.

# Chapter 3

# Correcting a Costing System that Misguides Strategy

Inaccurate costing calculations can lead to serious strategic errors.

Misumi built an activity-based costing system into a strategic tool for broad everyday use, something many companies around the world have tried and failed to do.

## Innovating the Business Model With a Chain of Reforms
(Competing Against the International Megatrend)

Growth Acceleration

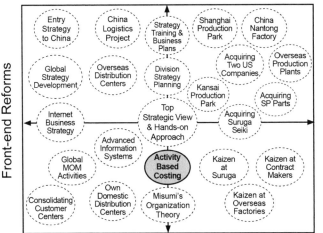

Front-end Reforms

Back-end Reforms

Increasing Quality and Efficiency

## The Dawn of Misumi's ABC System

Recall when, shortly after launching his reform project, Nagao, FA business general manager, brought in a chart to Saegusa, only to have it rejected out of hand. Here, we will cover what happened between sections 1 and 2 of the previous chapter. ABC is important enough to merit its own chapter.

Before the dejected Nagao left, he had this conversation with Saegusa.

"About the operating profit margins shown along the horizontal axis," Saegusa asked. "Are these true profit margins? Have you deducted all indirect expenses including sales and logistics costs?"

"We have millions of SKUs. We couldn't possibly calculate different expense ratios for each product," Nagao protested.

This was a classic debate on costing. The method Nagao described resembled the approaches used at many underperforming companies.

"How can you be sure your products with high gross margins are truly most profitable? The reality is often the opposite," Saegusa continued.

Is there any truth to the idea that products with high gross margins make a lot of money and those with low gross margins do not? All too often this misguided concept leads to improper pricing or failure to cut costs appropriately. So, he advised Nagao and his team to implement ABC.

## Project Launch

The ABC project launched on May 14.

Three people were appointed to the ABC task force. With Nagao, it made a team of four.

Amusingly, they started by visiting a bookstore. They bought four books to gain a basic understanding of ABC. Unfortunately, the books only touched on the concepts. Perplexed, the team struggled with where to start.

"Anyway, first we're supposed to create a workflow that captures all the processes that take place from order intake until the product delivers to the customer."

The chart shows each step that Nagao's team took to implement ABC.

**Step 1: Identify the business processes that take place across the company and clearly illustrate how the activities of each department tie into one another.**

First, focus on customer activities and the product.

The customer orders product online or by fax and can call Misumi's customer centers with any questions. If there is some problem with the delivery, the customer calls to file a complaint, and so on.

Fortunately, Nagao could draw on his experience in the company's IT department. He was familiar with internal workflows because he had helped build the IT systems.

With help from the customer center, logistics, IT and other functions, the team was able to identify the work processes involved from order to delivery in just two days.

They showed their chart to Saegusa, who intended to review their work step by step to ensure they didn't delve too deeply into the weeds, as many ABC projects are prone to do. He was impressed by how quickly they had created the workflow.

Their flow chart showed not only the processes from order to delivery, but also covered product development, catalog publishing and contract manufacturers. It provided a bird's eye view of the company's business processes.

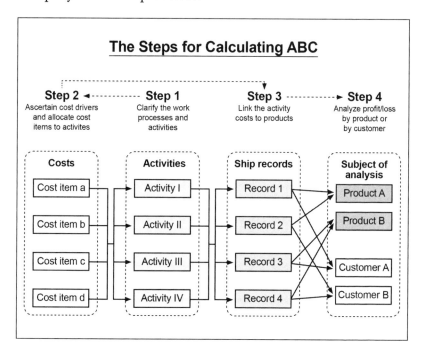

## Step 2: Analyze the relationships between activities and expense-item categories and define cost drivers.

Step 1 focused on customer activities and the product. Step 2 looks at the activities of people in each department.

Start by considering a single employee's work activities and how they tie into multiple workflows identified in Step 1. Moreover, some activities may take place before or after the sale. Consider a product-development staffer. Activities involving preparing a product for commercialization would take place before the sale. If that same staffer helps respond to a complaint, those activities would obviously take place after the sale.

Or consider a situation where multiple people, from sales, customer-care and logistics functions, work together with the product specialist to respond to a complaint. The point is, to understand the companywide costs tied to workflows supporting complaints, you need to capture personnel and other expenses that arise in various areas.

Perform this analysis for all activities conducted across the company and you can connect the flow of costs between organizational units and workflows.

Staff across the company were very cooperative with Nagao's team. Sure, the CEO had ordered this project. But it was also a hallmark of Misumi's culture: People here don't slack off or play spiteful games.

Without such a cooperative culture, the ABC project might have already run aground.

**Step 3: Tie expenses for each activity to product-shipment records**

Nagao was so immersed in the ABC project that, for the first time, he was barely taking time out to eat. As general manager of the division, he had other responsibilities as well. He carved out time for the ABC task force whenever he could afford to delegate regular business to others.

The team went to see Saegusa. They made a practice of seeking his advice whenever they hit a wall or needed direction on the next step. He maintained his hands-on approach to devising the FA business strategy and occasionally visited their work room unprompted.

On June 10, as scheduled, the team finished allocating expenses across activities and went to Saegusa to deliver its fifth report.

"Good work. Even professional consultants couldn't get it done this quickly."

The praise made the team feel rewarded for their hard work and proud of their accomplishment.

They had 20 days left until the two-month deadline they were given at the outset of the ABC project. Time to start work on their ultimate goal—to allocate the total costs of a shipment to each product record included in that order.

## Step 4: Use ABC to analyze profitability

Eventually, the task force completed its analysis, pleased to reach the finish line.

But the data revealed something seriously alarming—*the FA business is losing money on many shipments*. The business was only profitable as a whole because profits from other shipments were offsetting the losses—a shocking discovery.

- Here's one extreme example. One product sold for $0.40, with a gross margin of $0.22. But it incurred $6.21 in expenses, resulting in an operating profit margin of negative 1500%.
- They knew freight cost them a lot, but they identified various other logistics expenses to account for as well. And the cost of collecting receivables was much greater than they expected. IT costs also weighed on profitability when allocated to each product.
- The company had made a practice of packaging and shipping products with lower prices together with products with higher prices to dilute freight costs for lower priced products. But the ABC analysis showed that practice to misguide pricing for many products.
- It wasn't just the products. It was assumed that high-volume customers made a lot of money for Misumi. In fact, there were many customer accounts causing substantial losses.

- Moreover, Nagao had believed until then that new product development was the key to growth, and that sustained development would fuel prolonged topline growth. That assumption, too, crumbled under scrutiny. At first glance, new products appear to have a high gross margin. But if the product requires heavy support or services that increase indirect costs, it was actually adding to the losses with each order. That reality called into question the wisdom of over-emphasizing new product development.
- Some on the sales force were busy as bees promoting products, unaware that those products were losing money. Moreover, the additional sales expenses were making matters worse by widening the loss.

The team finally understood the purpose of the ABC analysis it had been tasked with.

On June 26, the team went to Saegusa to report its conclusions.

He looked at the graph showing profitability by product and nodded. "I knew there was a skunk somewhere."

It wasn't the first time he had said that. But until then, no one understood what he meant. Now, the team got it. All along, he had suspected the company was losing money on many products.

Nagao recalled a conversation he had at a New Year's dinner party earlier that year, when Saegusa was still an outside director. "We have some seemingly minor products that sell for just pennies per piece," Nagao boasted. "And we make tons of money on them." Nagao proclaimed that, with a 60% gross margin, the products were cash cows.

In hindsight, Nagao felt embarrassed by his misplaced confidence. The ABC analysis showed those products were losing ridiculous amounts of money.

## The Numbers Don't Lie

On July 1, Nagao's team reported its ABC analysis results to the company's senior management meeting. Slide after slide of thought-provoking analysis, rooted in data, was displayed on the screen.

"The FA business is making many shipments at a loss."

"This product has a gross margin of 40%, so we thought we were making money. Instead, its operating margin is negative 72%!"

"Products we thought of as cash cows are losing $1 million a year."

Thunderstruck, the audience was aghast to hear its assumptions turned on their head.

People in the business units had always been sensitive to their own team's profitability. But they had no clue how much operational costs (such as logistics) or indirect expenses (such as corporate overhead) were impacting profitability.

At Misumi, those costs had been ignored at the product level. But the team's presentation laid bare the fallacy of those profitability assumptions.

The entire talk was rooted in rigorous analysis and backed by numbers. The facts landed on the audience with a deafening thud. The ABC analysis upended long-established concepts of profitability and pointed toward a new strategy for the business. It not only brought clarity, shedding light on profit structures by product and customer account, but also pointed toward approaches to winning tactics.

The people on the project team were given many opportunities to stretch their skill sets. Over the past three months, they had gone from a warm bath to being thrown into the deep end of an ice-cold pool. But by the time they completed their ABC work, they had come so far that their peers barely recognized them.

The benefits would spread beyond the project team. It may seem obvious, but the understanding of profitability on a product-by-product basis alone would greatly impact the actions of employees and the business as a whole.

### Testimonial from a sales office general manager

*I was asked to help the ABC project team analyze profitability by customer account.*

*In our sales office, we only tracked total gross profit and total sales by customer. We figured anything more than that would be impossible.*

*Even so, from many years in the business I thought I had developed a sense for which accounts were making money and which weren't. Well, it turned out that my intuition was completely wrong.*

*We learned that one of our top customer accounts by sales was losing us tons of money. The account showered us with orders—one of this, one of that. But they came in so randomly that our logistics center pleaded they couldn't handle any more.*

*The ABC analysis made it painfully clear that this unsustainable way of doing business was leading to more losses. So, we decided to ask the customer to bundle their orders. We showed them the numbers so they could understand our pain points. Their buyers were sympathetic and promised to improve purchasing methods. Soon, we were in the black. The ABC analysis was essential to presenting such a compelling argument.*

### Testimonial from a logistics staffer

*The ABC analysis shined a spotlight on costly tasks and wasteful practices, things we had been doing, completely unaware of the consequences. But the analysis made clear that our gut feelings were far off the mark, that you can't make snap decisions.*

*Now we put serious consideration into the size of containers we use to store products to wring out greater storage efficiency. No more using larger containers that leave buffer space inside.*

*Our efforts opened up more warehouse space, allowing us to put off investing in an expansion. The ABC work highlighted the importance of using data to drive continuous improvement activities.*

*A review of the overall workflow from incoming order to outgoing shipment spans multiple organizational units. So, it requires a top-down decision, and that's what triggered the ABC work.*

## Two Steps toward a Companywide Rollout

Privately, Saegusa feared that the ABC tool would be forgotten once the team finished its project. Many other tools have met the same fate in all kinds of companies. He wanted to make ABC a permanent management tool here.

### Riddle-solving for Business Leaders (25): Barriers to Introducing ABC

Most companies have failed to implement ABC as an evergreen tool, as I mentioned in Saegusa's Management Note 4: How Costing is Critical for Strategy. There are four barriers to introducing it:

1. Introduction involves complex and heavy tasks;
2. ABC's quest for more granularity drives up hidden personnel expenses (such as time reporting);
3. ABC needs to be updated as workflows change to remain fresh; and
4. Unless ABC is incorporated into routine management systems, people fail to appreciate its importance and tend to avoid the heavy lifting associated with it.

So, Saegusa implemented two measures.

First, ABC was positioned as a tool for strategy formulation, making the information it generated an essential part of strategy to be presented to top management.

Second, the ABC system created by the FA business was rolled out to other business units under a system accessible to all employees.

For the costing tool to take root throughout the company, the data needed to be made available for people to use in their businesses. Saegusa launched an ABC Navigator project.

The tool would make it easy for managers to leverage costing information to assess profitability by product or by customer and glean insights for continuous improvement activities and strategic guidelines. The tool would highlight losses and cost issues and inform employee initiatives without the need for management direction, as if the team were navigating the ship itself.

And so, the ABC Navigator was launched as a widely accessible tool, with the aim of tying costing data to continuous improvement activities and enabling teams to launch profitability-improvement efforts autonomously. Empowering teams to determine the sound-ness of their business for themselves and take corrective actions without relying on top-down directives had the added benefit of enhancing management skills.

The Corporate Planning Department, which reports directly to the CEO, was charged with developing the software tool and disseminating it across the company. Having seen ABC fail before at other companies, Saegusa knew that Finance, with its indifference to product-by-product profitability, should not be put in charge. It had to be an organization more closely tied to the activities of the business managers and decisions made across the Create→Produce→Sell cycle.

Many managers joined the team and helped build the ABC Navigator tool. Once complete, all personnel received intensive training on how to use it.

Saegusa got personally involved in efforts to inculcate ABC across the company. He exhibited the same passion as Jack Welch did when he implemented Six Sigma at GE. Inspired by Japan's strength, Welch awarded employees who mastered the improvement methodologies with Black Belts, like those awarded in karate or judo.

Of course, Misumi was a much smaller organization, and ABC and Six Sigma are entirely different methodologies. Nevertheless, Saegusa was committed. A hard-to-master tool like ABC needed to be driven by the top to truly take hold.

## Commitment and a Sense of Urgency

The development of the ABC system started as part of the FA team's strategy-formulation process. The Navigator tool for companywide use took about five years to complete. The resulting tool was quite exceptional, even by global standards. While consultants tried to build ABC into a behemoth with impeccable precision, Misumi focused on balancing granularity with convenience, and cutting corners where possible.

In its heyday, the ABC system was touted to have benefits for industries outside manufacturing, such as insurance, advertising, commodity trading, retail and airlines. Nevertheless, Misumi may be the only company in the world that derives four-in-one benefits from it, namely: companywide, evergreen, as a strategic tool, and for the additional purpose of driving operational improvements.

ABC's global popularity has faded, and most books written about it have long since gone out of print. Yet Saegusa wanted to develop it into a powerful business tool at Misumi. As mentioned before, the same applies to PPM. The out-of-vogue concept is alive and well at Misumi as a fundamental strategic link between product development and salesforce activities.

Instead of chasing trends as if they are fast fashion, it's better to pick what you like and milk it for all you can. And, importantly, layer on your own customizations to facilitate ties between the C-suite and the front lines in your company.

You may find it odd that Saegusa spent so much time on one project for so long. Didn't other work fall by the wayside while they were focused on a single project?

To that, Saegusa's answer is clear.

It would have been ideal to leave the work up to someone else, if possible. But the CEO needs to get involved if there is no one else there who can see it through to completion on important corporatewide projects. It takes an entrepreneur's devotion to the business.

But doesn't that strip employees of autonomy and retard their development?

Quite the contrary. Having a skilled professional stand with them on the front lines, tackling the details together, actually promotes rapid growth.

That said, it is important to get in and get out quickly. Keep an eye on the situation and step in when necessary. Once you have redefined the challenge by breaking it into manageable pieces for your people and feel comfortable they can tackle it, you can leave it up to them.

You can't do everything, so you must prioritize for the sake of maximum returns. You have to accept that some things will fall between the cracks or get delayed.

Misumi's people are single-minded and earnest. They are willing to try something with no guarantee that it will generate the desired results, as long as they are convinced it's the right thing to do. They are coachable and open-minded. The corporate culture encourages people to review their own work carefully and reflect with brutal honesty.

Of course, the culture gets diluted as a company grows. Such is the fate of a large corporation. Without realizing it, employees eventually begin to behave like cogs in a wheel.

What can a company do to head that off and retain its vitality? Talks on spirit or words of encouragement from management will not do it. No, there must be concrete *mechanisms* embedded into the organization and the strategy. Saegusa knew that the only way to escape the trap of red tape in a bloated organization was to persistently drive innovations to internal systems and constantly challenge the actions of its people.

Systems like ABC and PPM are exactly the mechanisms needed. ABC was more than just an accounting tool—it was closely tied to the organization's strategic orientation and entrepreneurial spirit.

## SAEGUSA'S MANAGEMENT NOTE 5
# INTERNATIONAL MEGATREND IN BUSINESS INNOVATIONS

At first glance, this book may seem to recount a random grab bag of unrelated reform efforts. In fact, Misumi's corporate transformation was guided by three reform concepts, each with distinct historical roots.

### Trend 1: The Basic Cycle of Business

The first reform concept introduced to the company (Trend 1) was a framework I acquired while running a business in my 30s.

It was the late 1970s. At the time, I was CEO of a joint venture between companies from the US and Japan. In the Prologue, I mentioned my struggle to turn around the slumping business.

One day, I had a revelation. Decision-making within the company was separated into silos by business division, which delayed decisions on important matters. That is when I generated my framework of Create→Produce→Sell and called it The Basic Cycle of Business.

Sole proprietors who stand on their shop floors selling their wares to customers achieve a rapid cadence in this cycle, which begins with the customer. Nevertheless, the cycle slows as corporations grow larger and organize themselves into discrete functional organizations. More people become desensitized to the customer's needs. A company can beat the competition if it can achieve a fast cadence in its Create→Produce→Sell cycle. But it will lose if that cadence slows down. By then, it's too late for excuses.

Obvious, right? Yet nearly every failing company suffers from this syndrome, unbeknownst to almost all of its employees.

Create→Produce→Sell. It sounds simple enough. But don't under-estimate the power behind the words. When I came up with the framework, the idea was to emphasize the importance of "time" in business.

About ten years later, the concept of "time-based strategy" and "reengineering" emerged in the US, which in essence focused on the same internal cycle of Create→Produce→Sell.

At the time, I was not well versed in the true nature of the Toy-ota Production System (TPS). But the mechanism at play when work-in-progress piles up between processes in an inefficient plant is the same as that which allows important business matters to accumulate between organizational boundaries. I made this connection when I came across TPS during an earlier turnaround project. (For more on Create→Produce→Sell, see Chapter 3 of *A Crisis in Japanese Corporate Management*.)

Before long, I began to employ this framework as a business manager. It became an even more powerful weapon for me as a turnaround specialist, because the Japanese companies that retained me suffered the same ailments.

I touched upon Create→Produce→Sell during my presentation on Misumi's Eight Weaknesses (Chapter 1) just before the news that I would become CEO was made public. Without that framework, I would not have been able to diagnose Misumi so quickly, and the reform story that followed might have been off the mark. Therein lies the power of a framework.

## Trend 2: Time-based Strategy Imported from Japan

I did not create this second reform concept (Trend 2) myself. It first gained hold in the US in the late 1980s, and eventually crossed the Pacific to Japan, where it has challenged Japan's competitive edge over the past 30 years.

Its roots, however, can actually be found in Japan, with TPS. The Japanese failed to develop the innovative idea into a strategic management concept, though, and the Americans beat us to the punch. That was the late 1980s, when companies across the US had their backs to the wall, forced to restructure to meet the competitive threat from Japan.

Seeking to emulate Japan's success, many American companies tried to introduce TPS to their plants. The method has been extended to not only manufacturing, but also to non-manufacturing sectors such as air cargo operations, trucking, construction, parcel & mailing delivery, and so on. I was surprised to hear that TPS was also applied to patient treatment at hospitals, and I confirmed it by visiting several hospitals on the East and West Coasts of the US.

Intrigued, Boston Consulting Group's founder, Bruce Henderson, decided to look into how Japanese continuous-improvement techniques make companies stronger. How does something as simple as reducing inventory strengthen a company?

Henderson sent two BCG consultants, George Stalk and Thomas Hout, to Japan to look into the mystery of TPS. (I worked with both of them before I left BCG 15 years earlier.) Leveraging their deep familiarity with Japanese management styles, they spent two years on a deep dive into the true nature of TPS.

Their conclusion surprised Americans. "TPS is not just a technique for reducing inventories. Japanese companies are actually using it to pursue the *value of time*. The pursuit of this new strategic element—*time*—can lead to the development of new competitive advantages."

It revealed the importance of time as a weapon in a company's competitive arsenal. The book containing their findings, *Competing Against Time*, came out in 1990, and was a bestseller in the US.

As a business leader, I had been keenly aware of the importance of time as an element of management since the 1970s. But I was impressed to see that these two BCG consultants derived the concept of *time-based strategy* from TPS in the late 1980s.

## The Evolution of Trend 2—Megatrend in Business Innovations

In 1993, MIT professor Michael Hammer and James Champy published *Reengineering the Corporation*, which sparked a fervor in the US. Professor Hammer delved deeper into BCG's time-based strategy and advocated reform techniques that dramatically increased the cadence (i.e., shrank the time) of the overall process from development to production to sales to customer.

I was surprised. A concept that was similar to the Create→ Produce→Sell cycle—a framework I discovered myself ten years earlier—had emerged in the US under the name of *time-based strategy* and *reengineering* in a more theoretical and literate fashion.

As a turnaround specialist, I felt I should study Professor Hammer's theories in depth. I went to Boston to attend one of his seminars. It was held in a large assembly hall seating more than 1,000 people. Despite the exorbitantly high lecture fee by Japanese standards, the hall was filled with kaizen leaders from across the US. While attending the all-day seminar, I came to a sudden realization: the enthusiastic atmosphere of the hall resembled the heated conferences of Quality Control held in Japan in the 1970s.

It felt as if we had been beaten to the punch. Kaizen activities in Japan had already lost steam, but that passion was being rekindled here in the US.

The passion I witnessed there spoke volumes about how the US was beginning to stir after three decades of decline. And by a strange coincidence, the timing overlapped with the collapse of Japan's bubble economy, which resulted in nearly three decades of stagnation in Japan. An uptrend of industrial vitality in the US intersected with the downtrend in Japan. On the airplane back to Japan, I reflected on the enthusiasm of the more than 1,000 Americans who attended the seminar. It felt as if the US might have finally found a path toward regaining its industrial might.

The flow of innovations touched off by reengineering is what I refer to as the *megatrend in business innovations*. Three major breakthroughs flowed out of that.

The first was a significant change in how leaders considered and approached corporate reform. Grudging restructuring implemented only when deteriorating performance made it unavoidable would not save a company in the long run. It often would only lead to another round of restructuring further down the road. To avoid that fate, reform needed to be sweeping enough to effect a dramatic transformation. This realization led to more decisive reforms at US companies.

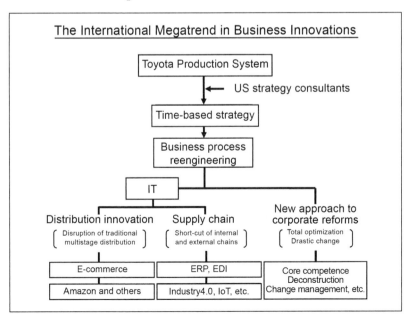

The second was even more impressive. New concepts derived from *time-based strategy* and *reengineering* were merged with Information Technologies. SAP, Oracle and others developed Enterprise Resource Planning software, leading to a wave of supply chain reforms.

This trend also triggered the transformation of accounting firms from mere auditors into enormous consulting firms with staffs of thousands helping to guide clients' operational reforms and systems development. Later, this trend would give rise to cross-industry innovation techniques embodied in Europe's Industry 4.0.

The third innovation was the success of e-commerce businesses built on maximizing the benefits of IT. The 1990s gave birth to countless e-commerce ventures. I myself funded a venture in Japan launching an online grocery store. Despite tenuous starts, ventures in the US vacuumed up risk money from venture capital, emerging from intense competition for survival with stronger business models.

This megatrend in business innovations breathed new life into the American corporate sector and led the way out of a three-decade decline dating back to the 1960s.

What about Japan? The slump following the end of the bubble economy has dragged on for nearly three decades now, but we have yet to develop the sorts of innovations that can extricate us from it.

The reason is clear. Although the megatrend originated in Japan, no one here exhibited the vision to harness its power as a new business weapon. Instead, the Americans did. In the intellectual (management literacy) battle to theorize and amplify inherent strengths, Japan only trails the US.

The Japanese business tendency to fall in line with others, and the reflexive reluctance to make quick decisions that entail risk, are not conducive to leading innovation. Japanese companies need to establish their own unique management theories and frameworks by taking advantage of their people's unique characteristics and organizational strengths. They need to generate management concepts to innovate and develop a pool of creative management leaders.

## Trend 3: Misumi's Short-time Delivery Model

So far, we have looked at my Create→Produce→Sell framework and the megatrend that was sparked in the US. This third trend sprang from different historical roots. What tremendous foresight Misumi's founder had to launch its short-time delivery model in late 1970s, more than two decades before the US!

Short delivery time is a time-based strategy. Moreover, Mr. Taguchi created an organizational structure divided into small teams to achieve a fast cadence in business strategy. It is a time-based strategy for organizational theory, according to my frameworks. (More on this in Chapter 8.)

After I took over as CEO, these three trends converged within the company. Internally, we refer to this strategic concept as, *It's all about TIME*. We have enshrined it as the company motto in our annual reports.

*It's all about TIME* gave birth to a variety of reforms. In the beginning, the reform themes appeared to be only loosely inter-related. However, as the years passed, the reforms began to feed off one another, eventually developing into strengths not only for the divisions that implemented them, but also integrating into strengths of the business model for the entire company. That would lead to sweeping change at Misumi inherent in the term *corporate transformation*.

The people who spearheaded the reform efforts would develop into the next generation of leadership talent to take the helm after my retirement. They are the ones who ensured Misumi would not wither or drown in the wake of the global megatrend.

Please consider the rest of this book in light of the strategic implications of the megatrend outlined above.

# Chapter 4

# Launching a Global Strategy

Lacking a headquarters organization charged with driving an international business, Misumi expressed little interest or strategy toward deploying a business overseas. In only 13 years, the company would grow to employ 7,000 people outside of Japan and derive 50% of its sales from overseas markets. This chapter looks at how Misumi built and executed its global strategy.

## Innovating the Business Model With a Chain of Reforms
### (Competing Against the International Megatrend)

Growth Acceleration

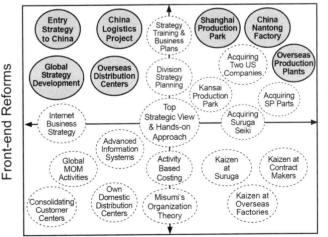

Increasing Quality and Efficiency

## Section 1:
# Breaking Spells to Unleash New Strategic Directions

Any company is going to have its "spells"—old ways of doing things, received wisdom, habits that don't die out—that regulate the thoughts and actions of employees. The more time you spend there, the more desensitized you become to these spells. Even the corporate officers were in thrall to the spells at work at Misumi.

## Existing Overseas Business

Saegusa considered developing a global strategy to be the greatest challenge to transforming Misumi.

With much of Japan in the economic doldrums, Saegusa sought to cap off his career by molding Misumi into a global competitor. It was that ambition that led him to accept the CEO role. And ambitious indeed was his aspiration to build a solid business overseas. Much needed to be done.

Until then, the company had engaged foreign markets only episodically. The Tokyo headquarters was filled with people, from top to bottom, focused solely on sales in Japan. Expanding overseas did not fit the mold here.

Proposals to develop business outside of Japan were typically met with a shrug and a "why not?" But there was no central support and no global strategy.

Despite a dearth of support, in the preceding decade, several individuals showed personal interest in setting up local subsidiaries in eight locations abroad—Taiwan, the US, Singapore, Thailand, South Korea, Hong Kong, the UK and China. Most of these offices had less than 20 local staffers and operated with virtually no local inventory on hand. Nearly all sales were fulfilled by air from Japan as orders came in.

When Saegusa took over as CEO, there was no central headquarters organization charged with overseeing or supporting overseas activities. And there was no one capable of developing a global strategy. Just a few temporary staffers processed paperwork for export to the foreign subsidiaries. At the executive level, there was an officer responsible for overseas markets, but he also held domestic responsibilities. To him, the overseas business was a side job.

Given that reality, the company's overseas business grew little over the decade before Saegusa's appointment. Sales from all overseas subsidiaries combined barely reached $50 million, a mere 8.6% of total sales.

In the 13 years following Saegusa's arrival as CEO, overseas sales would grow 17-fold to about $750 million organically (excluding acquisitions), accounting for 36% of total sales, and eventually to about 50% today. What strategy made this kind of growth possible?

## Visiting the US

Saegusa chose the US as his first overseas trip. The aim was to uncover problems and potential solutions involving the global strategy, just as he had uncovered Misumi's Eight Weaknesses before becoming CEO.

By then, Chicago-based Misumi USA had been in business for 13 years, with meager sales of about $12 million. If that was all they could muster in more than a decade, perhaps the company's business model would not work overseas.

He visited the local subsidiary in Chicago, and within two days of his arrival, alarm bells started to ring in his head.

Misumi USA was being run by H. Asakawa, a long-time company man. He came across as a lighthearted, straightforward character. He explained the company's business performance to Saegusa, showing a slide tracking the gradual growth in US sales.

"Here, we hit a period of growth, and then things really surged," Asakawa explained.

Saegusa stared at the screen intently. The line graph rose modestly across the page. There was no surge anywhere. What's more, after 10 years, sales had reached only about $12 million. Such a flat "curve" left no room to speak of growth, maturity or other lifecycle concepts.

Asakawa had volunteered for the US job as had all other people working overseas at Misumi. In his mind, he had done all he could, and had done it well. Meanwhile, Saegusa realized that he would have to set things straight. To redirect the trajectory of this company, he would have to make a clean break.

Saegusa explained, "Asakawa, this graph doesn't show a period of growth. Sorry to say it, but this business is nothing more than a fly on an elephant's back."

The unexpected criticism hurt Asakawa's pride. But someone had to break it to him. Saegusa was seeking a global strategy. Peoples' blinders needed to be removed so they could change their perceptions about business scale and global opportunities.

As the conversation continued, Saegusa began to sympathize with him. For years, headquarters had constrained investments in new business ventures to miniscule amounts—part of the reason the company's ventures, including overseas offices, looked like random bets at a penny-ante poker table. Asakawa had come to the US in high spirits, only to receive minimal support from headquarters. Constrained by a stingy expense budget, he was unable to execute any bold strategies. Left to fend for himself, he had convinced himself that he was fighting the good fight.

## Drafting "Sheet 1"

Saegusa visited the US to identify problems with the company's global strategy. His three-day trip to Chicago had given him clarity on the answer. Once again, it was the power of his frameworks that helped him shorten what might otherwise be a long process.

He had arrived in the US armed with the Misumi QCT Model (Chapter 1)—a framework he had generated while observing Misumi's headquarters and other domestic sites. The model enabled him to highlight the factors that had stunted growth in its US business.

The catalog distributed to US customers was paper-thin, its product lineup scant. The US pioneered the catalog culture. How did they expect to make inroads into a market like that with such a meager catalog?

Moreover, the company did not own a warehouse in the US; it outsourced shipping to third parties. Experience in Japan had shown that this approach increases shipment errors. The local customer center—which serves as the customer contact point— was under-resourced and inefficient. The problems here appeared to be even more complex than in Japan, where 13 small centers were dispersed across the country.

To make a long story short, the US business was scoreless on the front end of the Misumi QCT Model.

On the back end (product sourcing), the business relied almost exclusively on imports from Japan. Customer orders were forwarded to Japan, and the product was sent to the US by air freight. Clearly, that means a long delivery time. The three-day shipments that were standard in Japan were out of the question here.

Years before, contract manufacturer Suruga had built a plant in the Chicago area at Misumi's request. That provided a foothold for local production in the US, but the plant was losing money left and right. Saegusa visited the plant and observed a half-baked short-time delivery regime, with capability in only a limited range of production items.

Clearly, on the front and back ends, the US business was a poor imitation of Japan's Misumi QCT Model.

Visits to local subsidiaries in other countries revealed similar situations. His first visit to the US was enough to answer the question of why the company had failed to achieve significant growth overseas. The fact that the strengths of the company's business model had not been properly transplanted overseas kept the local businesses in suspended animation.

## Upending the Penny Poker Table

After returning to Tokyo, Saegusa sketched The Concept for Misumi's Global Expansion. It would serve as "Sheet 2" of the reform scenario for the overseas businesses.

He explained to the management team, "As part of our global strategy, we need to faithfully replicate the Misumi QCT Model in every market we enter. Otherwise, we'll lose to the competition wherever we go."

The diagram, though unremarkable, would effect a drastic change in management's thinking and free the overseas businesses from the spells cast on them.

He went further. "Forays overseas are *strategic investments*. The aim is to grow the business. To that end, we will permit local subsidiaries to sacrifice profitability, possibly even book losses. The business in Japan is profitable enough to cover it."

Talk of permitting losses was revolutionary at Misumi and proved enough to break the spell.

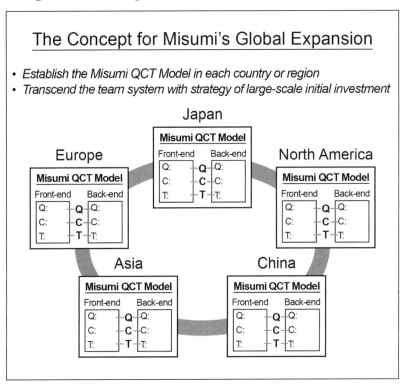

## The Concept for Misumi's Global Expansion

- *Establish the Misumi QCT Model in each country or region*
- *Transcend the team system with strategy of large-scale initial investment*

Until then, the company had almost no internal controls. Once a business plan was approved, it might go unsupervised for a year, no matter how far it veered off track. To compensate for the weak controls, the general manager of accounting set a safety valve, capping a team's annual losses at about $1 million, regardless of the size and the growth stage of business in each location. That fostered a culture of penny-ante poker.

To encourage more ambitious business aspirations, Saegusa removed the safety valve. Of course, he was aware of the risk. What might happen if he encouraged investment without strengthening headquarters controls over it? Leaders of subsidiaries overseas might go on a shopping spree.

So, he decided to focus priority on only two overseas markets—the US and China. He clearly instructed that other subsidiaries would have to sit tight until they got the green light.

He decided to start with a narrow focus because a framework he had put in his mind's freezer 30 years ago was setting off alarm bells. While running a business in his 30s, he had allowed the battle lines to expand too quickly. The ensuing struggle to bring things back under control remained with him as a bitter memory and a management framework.

## Launching in China

Why choose China as a priority strategic market? At the time, the company had a subsidiary set up in Shanghai's bonded zone. But it carried no inventory. Incoming orders were forwarded to Japan. Sales were only about $1 million.

However, historical context guided his approach. That framework would drive the company's China strategy over the following decade.

Let's look at the history he contemplated. After its defeat in World War II, Japan rose from the ashes to overwhelm American industries over a 30-year span from the 1960s through the 1980s. From the late 1960s, Saegusa's time at BCG and Stanford Business School had given him a front-row view of the battle between an ascendant Japan and a faltering US.

One after another, Japan's industries grew in strength and over-whelmed their American rivals. First, it was textiles. Then, major household appliances, followed by televisions, steel, automobiles, and finally, semiconductors.

A similar battle was brewing between China and Japan.

Only this time, it was China, not Japan, that would be the aggressor, and Japan, not the US, that would falter. First, China made inroads into Japan with textiles, produce and foodstuffs, then high-tech wares as Chinese industry grew more sophisticated.

"We're getting into China 10 years late," Saegusa realized. "Unless we act now, we may never establish a meaningful presence there. As Chinese companies grow in strength, they don't stay there; they come to Japan. Once that happens, we could lose our home market. To keep that from happening, we need to bring the fight to them. It's now or never."

Along with customer center reforms (Chapter 7), he positioned the project to launch in China one of two risky undertakings for the company.

The risk of expanding battle lines emerged immediately. Once the China project was up and running, it consumed enormous amounts of his energy. Thank goodness he had the foresight to instruct leaders of local subsidiaries outside of the US and China to stand down. Along with his involvement in other reforms at headquarters, Saegusa was stretched too thin across multiple battle fronts. Both he and Misumi were on the brink.

But no one else in management could see the looming crisis. It was Saegusa's battle to wage, and no one else's.

## Forming the China Business Team

In the February before Saegusa became CEO, one young staffer volunteered to oversee the launch of the China business.

K. Kagami was 30 years old. He had volunteered at the Vision Presentations and was thus selected as a leader.

As a college student, he had spent a year studying abroad in the UK. While there, he encountered racial discrimination against

Asians, which solidified his own Asian identity. His first job out of school was at a trading company. In his fourth year there, the company collapsed in a sensational bankruptcy widely covered by the media. After a brief stint in an unsatisfying job, he came to Misumi to develop his professional abilities.

After two years here, Kagami volunteered for the post in China. He was exceptionally young for the position, even in a youthful company like Misumi. He could not have known at the time the travails he would endure preparing the launch.

Saegusa called Kagami into his office immediately. Surprised at his youth, he sized up this young man who would be leading the vanguard of his global strategy.

"So, you are the one headed to China? What does your initial organization look like?"

"Well, I've selected three other young guys to work with me," answered Kagami.

Saegusa was at a loss for words. Kagami planned to break into the Chinese market with three twenty-somethings? Not one of them had worked overseas, spoke Chinese or knew the local market. They hadn't even been with the company long enough to establish a track record.

Actually, a team of four would be the largest the company had ever dispatched to open a new market overseas. Until then, no one would have thought to wish for more—the work of that penny-poker spell again.

Saegusa asked, "What do you plan to do with such a small team? Merely reconnaissance?"

Now it was Kagami who was at a loss for words. This was a conversation he would remember.

China would be the first and largest testing ground for Misumi's global strategy. The company needed to send its best. Saegusa felt uneasy entrusting the fate of the entire project to Kagami.

So, for the first time as CEO, Saegusa made two personnel changes.

First, he nominated *M. Aragaki* as the officer responsible for the China Launch Project. The youthful Kagami would report to Aragaki.

Aragaki was a veteran salesperson, instrumental in growing the company alongside Mr. Taguchi, the company's founder. You may remember Aragaki from the sushi dinner where Saegusa sketched out the company's business model on the back of that chopsticks envelope (Chapter 1). Saegusa liked his earthy manner, developed over the course of his career in sales.

Second, he replaced the three young staffers Kagami selected with two more-experienced people, per Aragaki's request.

Under the existing rules for team-based organizations at Misumi, team leaders had the authority to choose who would report to them and decide personnel matters and compensation. Even before taking over as CEO, Saegusa had his doubts about this system (more on this in Chapter 8). With this move, he over-ruled it to form the best team for the important China business.

Angered by the unforeseen decision that stripped him of his team, Kagami considered resigning. Some of his peers criticized Saegusa's intervention as too heavy-handed.

Their criticisms were understandable given the systems and management direction of his predecessor. But they were prioritizing existing personnel systems over the strategy to be pursued. To accommodate a new CEO and a new strategy, the organization and systems would have to change.

So, Saegusa felt comfortable brushing aside the criticism. There was no compromising. In the end, no one benefitted more from the decision than Kagami. Efforts to take on an unknown market like China could easily fall apart. If Kagami attempted that with the team he selected, he might have ended up trapped in a *Death Valley*.

As the story unfolds, you will see it wasn't long before Kagami encountered exactly the kinds of difficulties Saegusa had anticipated.

## Projecting Capital Requirements

Sometime later, Saegusa asked Kagami, "How much money do you think you'll need to launch the China business?"

Kagami had never given it thought. A business leader may not require experience in accounting, but surely does need to understand the mechanisms that make money flow.

"A business leader needs to have an idea of how much money is needed to do the job. You can't just charge in blindly," Saegusa warned.

Until then, the company had outsourced financing functions; unfortunately, there was no one at the company who could help Kagami. So, Saegusa showed Kagami how to build a budget.

Kagami drew up a tentative business plan. With some difficulty, he projected funding needs. Doing so helped him understand the mechanisms behind cash flows. In that sense, he was already improving his management skills. The problem lay in the numbers his projection produced.

He projected capital injections into Misumi China peaking in the fifth year, at about $20 million. After that, the business would begin to turn a profit, at which point the capital injections would taper off.

Kagami couldn't believe his own calculations. Formerly, the company had capped annual losses at $1 million—part of the old penny poker spell that choked new business ventures. Yet Kagami's numbers foresaw a $20 million outlay. At the old Misumi, that would have gotten him laughed out of the room.

For Kagami, the sheer scale of what he was taking on was beginning to sink in.

With trepidation, Kagami brought his numbers to Saegusa.

## The CEO's Resolve

Saegusa closely examined the calculations behind Kagami's numbers. The silence seemed to confirm Kagami's fears that the China project might be shelved. The reality was quite the opposite.

Saegusa thought, "He'll need to double that at least."

China was growing by leaps and bounds, and Misumi was a latecomer. If $20 million was all they needed to play catch up and grab a significant market share, who wouldn't be happy?

Still silent, he continued his train of thought. "Set aside the capital discussion for now. There's a bigger problem. This kid is quaking in his boots about $20 million. Not only is he still in the grips of the penny-poker spell, he doesn't have enough management experience."

He wondered, "Can he really be trusted to launch the China business from scratch? Does he know how hard it will be? He put himself forward for this assignment without a second thought, but will he surrender once the real battle begins?"

"Maybe Kagami expects that he can simply replicate Misumi USA there," he mused. "That would be another sign that he hasn't broken the spell. It took Misumi USA 13 years to reach $12 million in sales. That anemic performance is no template for a China strategy."

"In China, we need to be targeting sales of $100 million, $200 million, or even more," Saegusa thought. (Indeed, by the time this book went to press, the business Kagami launched was approaching sales of $500 million, and total Misumi headcount in China had grown past 2,000.)

The spell needed to be broken. Kagami's role would be to achieve a breakthrough for the company's overseas business. It would mean a new strategy, a new culture and a new challenge.

During the long silence, Kagami had no idea what Saegusa might be thinking.

Finally, Saegusa broke the silence, speaking nonchalantly. "This business concept should be fine for now. You don't need to do more in Tokyo. Go to China and get a real feel for the landscape," he said.

Saegusa had taken the helm at Misumi as one last challenge to close out his career. And here he was about to entrust a 30-year-old with such an important link in the chain. Neither Kagami nor anyone else in management here would understand the anxiety and sense of isolation he was feeling. Nevertheless, he had given the green light, making a strategically risky personnel decision.

### Riddle-solving for Business Leaders (26): Bold Personnel Decisions

Bold personnel decisions give people with potential and drive the opportunity to grow beyond their current abilities. There is a good chance of success if the size of the opportunity is a good fit for the individual to overcome their limits. But miscalculate the individual's limits and you risk inviting failure. Bold promotions are an essential shortcut to developing management talent, but they also invite jealousy from peers. Their success relies on the manager's willingness to protect the individual.

Such a decision to change the team's makeup could only have been made by a CEO committed to cultivating management talent, as Saegusa had proclaimed when he took the job. Just as Saegusa had feared, within a few months of arriving in Shanghai, Kagami would face such difficulties that he would consider giving up entirely and quitting the company.

## Spellbound in a Foreign Land

In high spirits, Kagami and his team left for Shanghai in July, shortly after Saegusa's appointment to CEO was approved by shareholders. Aragaki fell ill, so his relocation was delayed until September.

Kagami and his team began by setting up an office in Shanghai. Further, they would need to set up a customer center, a warehouse and a distribution center. They would have to find buildings to house the operations and hire and train operators. Their most challenging task would be to find local contract manufacturers and build out a sourcing network in China that would meet Misumi's high standards for quality and delivery times. They would also need to build IT systems for processing customer orders. Another daunting task was to create Chinese-language catalogs providing information in the local currency with local delivery times. At first, they didn't even know where to find a printer to produce them.

It would take an inordinate amount of time to set up personnel and accounting functions, and interview and hire local staff. How would they assess the capabilities of Chinese job candidates?

Kagami and his team found themselves lost in a dense fog.

They learned that accomplishing anything in China took three, even four, times as much time as it would in Japan. They needed to bring interpreters with them to visit potential customers and contract manufacturers. Shanghai's snarled traffic bogged them down as well.

They spent a third of their day interviewing job applicants. After meeting 32 candidates, they finally made their first hire.

Kagami worked every day of his first four months there, staying at the office until at least midnight. The long hours clouded his ability to make decisions.

Already, he had made a number of serious errors in judgment.

First, it proved impossible for a Japanese team of three to launch the business alone, given the sheer volume of work involved. When Saegusa asked if they planned to go there to do only reconnaissance, he was implying it would be difficult to achieve much more with limited resources.

By now, you may be wondering, "What did headquarters do to support them? Couldn't they send reinforcements to help out?"

Tokyo did nothing of the sort. At the time, company rules treated overseas businesses as independent entities, even if they handled the same products as existing business units in Japan. So, the apathetic headquarters was uninterested in supporting Kagami's business in China. In return, Kagami didn't report to headquarters, either. The people at Misumi thought nothing of it; they were still under the influence of old spells.

- For example, not a single corporate officer took issue with fact that the US subsidiary had achieved only $12 million in sales after 13 years.
- People returning from stints overseas after many years often

struggled to find the right fit at headquarters. Frustrated, many left the company. Saegusa was unaware of this talent outflow until he witnessed it firsthand.
- A young leader like Kagami, relocating to a place like Shanghai, became exhausted fighting a solitary battle with no backup from headquarters. This fact points to an organizational problem. Saegusa discovered this during his first visit to Shanghai.

One of the spells in effect dictated that details from the front lines would not be reported to the CEO. It was a legacy of Mr. Taguchi's management style. He did not get involved in how the team ran its business. If he had something to say, he would do so at the annual Vision Presentations conference. People across the organization had a bias toward omission; they thought they weren't obliged to, or shouldn't, report to the CEO.

Saegusa was able to replace the people Kagami had selected for his team because they were still in Tokyo and the CEO had learned of Kagami's initial choices early on. Once you realize a spell is inhibiting strategy, break it without hesitation. As long as the spell goes unnoticed, the organization will remain paralyzed.

In reality, it took nearly three months for Saegusa to catch wind of the struggles Kagami and his team were having in Shanghai. Given proper reporting, assistance could have been provided earlier. But the communication gap was wide, leading to numerous miscues.

## Struggling to Nail Down the Basics

Aside from the spells at work here, there were other problems that exacerbated Kagami's struggles.

Aragaki, the officer overseeing the China project, instructed Kagami to issue catalogs in China by November. That was only four months after Kagami and his team had arrived in Shanghai. And Aragaki was still in Tokyo.

The directive put tremendous pressure on Kagami. When the three of them arrived in Shanghai, they knew nothing about the local situation. To put out a catalog, you first need to have a distribution center in place. And a customer center for taking orders, and then there's the IT systems…and so on.

Impossible. The catalog deadline was smothering them.

Moreover, Kagami had personal issues that added to his distress. His wife joined him in Shanghai one month after he arrived. It was her first time living overseas and her first time in China. She didn't speak the language or have any friends there. Her husband came home late at night exhausted and left early in the morning. Home alone all day, she began to feel depressed.

Even now, it pains Saegusa to recall their struggles. A company accustomed to doing business overseas typically provides temporary housing for a while, like a hotel near the office. That gives them time to learn the ropes before family joins them. Saegusa had not walked Kagami through that during the preparation phase, and Kagami's wife bore the brunt of it.

Meanwhile, the deadline to publish the catalog was fast approaching.

Kagami had completely underestimated the amount of work that goes into launching a business. Nothing was ready. No way it could have been. He had volunteered for the post in China, but now he was at the end of his rope, both physically and mentally.

But these struggles didn't arise from fending off the competition or facing the customer. It was something far more fundamental. It may sound harsh, but Kagami was crossing a *Death Valley* entirely of his own making. He had miscalculated the complexity of the job and the feasibility of the plan.

Later, Saegusa would learn that they had decided to push back the catalog release from November to the end of December. But what good would one month do?

Kagami later reflected on his struggles, "I thought I would make the catalog release my legacy there. That would be enough for me. Once the catalog was complete, I was ready to leave the company."

He seriously considered quitting. Only four months in, he had been pushed to the point where all he wanted to do was throw it all away and take it easy for a while.

Despite his youth, he was responsible and earnest—a hard worker. Nevertheless, if something truly can't be done, a responsible leader needs to say so. That is the best way out of a bind.

Historically, the company was a very top-down organization, requiring that orders be obeyed, consequences be damned. But he didn't realize that he was now in a place where he needed to exercise leadership over his bosses.

In that sense, Kagami was failing to exercise the prerogative of his position. In effect he was shrinking his own position, or in other words, demoting himself. He had volunteered for the post, but he had no experience in a position as important as spearheading a major company's operations in China.

## Riddle-solving for Business Leaders (27): Shrinking a Position

After rapid promotions or bold personnel moves, the people installed in the new positions often drag along the thoughts and actions of their previous posts, even though their responsibilities have increased. I call that shrinking a position, and it erodes an organization over time. The spread of salarymen in Japanese companies is what happens when this shrinking process occurs repeatedly over a long period of time.

No one at the company knew at the time what a tough nut to crack the China launch would be. To date, the company had undertaken only safe, cautious bets overseas, so it couldn't have known what potential troubles might be lurking there. Its former small-team organizational structure did not encourage the company to throw its entire weight behind high-risk strategies. This was yet another spell cast on Misumi's organization.

If Kagami were to fail, it wouldn't just be his personal problem. It might doom the company's global strategy into the depths of *Death Valley*, and it threatened to wreak havoc on this closing chapter of Saegusa's career.

The company's outdated structure produced an invisible spell that forcefully restrained its people. If young staffers who hadn't truly been challenged before were entrusted with important responsibilities, they might falter like Kagami. Such was the reality on the ground.

Let's look next at how Saegusa dealt with this situation, and how Kagami put himself in a position to enhance his managerial capabilities.

## Section 2:
# Raising the Bar

### Saegusa Visits Shanghai

Saegusa flew to Shanghai in October, three months after Kagami and his team had set up an office there. It was his second trip overseas as CEO of Misumi, following his trip to the US the previous month. Finally, he had made it to the main battlefield for the company's global strategy.

He was met at the airport by Kagami and Aragaki, who had recovered his health by then. Kagami's facial expression revealed pure exhaustion. But there was no way of knowing at the time that his distress was so severe that he was considering quitting.

Aragaki had booked Saegusa a room at a top-class hotel in Shanghai's Pudong New Area. After check-in, he was shown to a luxurious suite offering a sweeping view of the Bund, Shanghai's historical international settlement area. But the hotel was located far from the company's office, making travel through the gridlock very time-consuming.

Formerly, Misumi made a big deal out of the founder's annual trips overseas. When Aragaki came to pick up Saegusa at the hotel the next morning, Saegusa laid down some rules. No suites. No need for a room with a view or proximity to tourist sites. To avoid traffic congestion, pick an ordinary hotel close to the company's office.

Another spell had been broken.

At the office, Kagami briefed Saegusa on the status of the operation.

It was the first time Kagami and Aragaki had held a formal meeting with him. The former CEO's visits were more like courtesy calls. It was probably the first time in the company's history that the CEO had flown overseas to discuss a local business project in detail.

The meeting marked a key turning point. For the first time, Saegusa learned the details of the plan they had developed to launch the China business. The catalog Kagami had been putting together per Aragaki's order was a flimsy 140 pages. More like a measly pamphlet compared to the 1,200-page catalogs distributed in Japan.

Moreover, the report revealed that their sales force was not in order. The status of 13 action plans—order intake, shipments, supplier selection, price negotiation, quality inspection, IT systems and the like—all key to the launch's success—read "TBD," "under discussion," or, "problem needs resolution." And there was only a month to go before the scheduled catalog release.

Nothing was ready. Kagami should have recognized that. Instead, he confidently declared, "we still face many challenges, but we hope to resolve them while we race ahead following the catalog release." Despite the fact that Aragaki's order to begin operations in only four months after Kagami's arrival in Shanghai was virtually impossible to accomplish, Kagami considered it his duty to make it happen. That kind of top-down mentality had always been the norm at Misumi.

To Saegusa, the report was deeply unsettling. This launch was nowhere near complete. There was an enormous gap between the plan Kagami wanted to execute and what was ready to go. With only a month left, it seemed that they had already run out of time.

If Saegusa didn't give them his unvarnished opinion, his trip to Shanghai would have been a complete waste of time. Before taking issue with the catalog deadline, he first questioned its substance in harsh, cutting terms.

"This catalog is unacceptable. You really think you can win in China with this?"

Kagami was dumbfounded. In Japan, the company sometimes published thin catalogs like this as supplements to the thick standard catalogs. Saegusa had only recently become CEO. What did he know about catalogs? What's more, the launch plan was the culmination of four months of grueling work. How could a newcomer to the catalog business call our work unacceptable?

## Why the Catalog Was Unacceptable

Saegusa wasn't just blowing off steam. He had the following three things in mind.

First was The Concept for Misumi's Global Expansion, a guideline Saegusa had shared with the entire company after returning from the US. It was a revolutionary guideline that called for the Misumi QCT Model to be recreated faithfully in every overseas market the company has entered. The catalog is the most important *detonator* for the business model.

Aragaki and Kagami should have been aware of the guideline. So why were they in such a rush to put out a flimsy catalog after only four months in China? Saegusa recalled the performance "curve" he was shown in Chicago the month before. Only $12 million in sales after 13 years in the US. And they called it a surge in growth. Boy, had they set their sights low.

Their problem was the enemy within. They needed to aim higher. And they needed a strategic mindset to make dynamic inroads into new markets.

Another reason Saegusa called the catalog unacceptable lay in the stark contrast with the situation in Japan.

In Japan, where the company already occupies a major market position, the small supplemental catalogs made sense. But can you apply that rationale to the first catalog you release in a foreign market?

If the first catalog is shoddy, people in that country will conclude that your company is nothing special. Most likely, the catalog would be tossed straight into the trash and a potential customer would be lost. You never get a second chance to make a first impression.

But let's be generous. Assume someone actually places an order. The customer center isn't ready yet. The customer calls in, but the local hires are unaccustomed to handling inquiries. The warehouse and distribution center are not operational. With nothing more than a shell of a business, the system would no doubt struggle to fulfill the delivery deadlines that the company motto promises. Moreover, there would likely be many shipping errors. Why take on all that risk this early in the game?

If the customer has a negative experience, they will not come back. As other customers have similar experiences, word gets around.

Saegusa calls this *slash-and-burn* business. When a business like this sets fire to the field (market), the dry grass burns in an impressive burst of flames (booming sales). But grass only burns once. After the fire has spread across the entire field, the flames die out. By then, all that is left is some smoke and scorched earth. Sales growth halts. That's how *slash-and-burn* businesses fail.

Here is another important point. Even a poor catalog, once distributed, would spark reactions from potential competitors. This could prove fatal.

Potential competitors and copycats who knew of the company's strength in Japan would learn of our entry into the local market and take counteraction immediately.

We won't know what the competition is doing to counter us until their business or products hit the market. In the meantime, if we engage the market with only penny antes, we risk showing our hand to the competition.

### Riddle-solving for Business Leaders (28): Slowing the Competition's Response

If a weak player or latecomer releases a new product or technology over a half-baked business structure, it risks giving the competition ideas and triggering a faster response. In the end, it gets outmaneuvered and bounced out. It's important to thoroughly prepare behind the scenes so that when the time is ripe, you can make a rapid push into the market. If you need to test the market first, find an inconspicuous corner of the market, keep the scale small and do it quietly.

Such were the thoughts racing through Saegusa's mind during the first few minutes of his meeting with Aragaki and Kagami.

### "Are You Trying to Put Misumi Out of Business?!"

As the meeting progressed, Saegusa grew more concerned. Let's summarize the logic of his thoughts on strategy.

- To the extent possible, delay triggering a competitive response, which you will not be able to monitor.
- Once you've played your hand, push forward rapidly to make it a one-point match.
- Lay down in advance all the infrastructure you need to compete. Be fully prepared when you start the battle and seize the advantage in the opening stages to capture a meaningful market position.

Kagami's plan ran counter to all of this logic. To Saegusa, releasing this catalog was comparable to an act of suicide for the operation.

"Are you trying to put Misumi out of business?!" Saegusa delivered another harsh blow.

He was fully aware of how unforgiving that might sound, but he felt he should shake Kagami to the core to break the spells that held him in their thrall.

Such a rushed foray into the Chinese market would quickly end in failure, as so many other Japanese attempts had. History dictates what would come next—the Chinese competitive threat would make its way to Japan. Already, many Japanese companies were seeing their prospects fade with the gathering threat from China.

Kagami couldn't believe what he was hearing. He had worked his tail off for four months. He wasn't doing anything wrong. " 'Put us out of business'? What an awful thing to say!"

Once he had time to settle down, however, Kagami began to see the situation more clearly. He wanted to think that he had done nothing wrong, but in reality, nothing was ready to open for business. He had been working to the point of burnout trying to make progress. But with only one month to go, he was clearly running out of time.

Saegusa's words stung, but the dressing down helped Kagami change his state of mind.

"When Saegusa told us to halt the catalog release, I was thrown for a loop," Kagami later recalled. "But deep down inside, I was also relieved. What I really wanted was for someone to put a stop to it."

Kagami realized Misumi's strength in Japan was the result of decades of work—work that had been done long before he joined the company. He naively thought it would be easy to replicate that in China.

As if under the influence of another spell, Kagami had not expended the intellectual effort to develop his own approach to launching the new business.

"I figured if we just put out a catalog, we would enjoy the same success we had in Japan. It would all just work out," Kagami thought. Yet look at how much energy it took just to make one local hire.

He was spellbound, blindly trying to follow orders and issue a catalog in only four months. In fact, it was an impossible task, and Kagami was finally coming to grips with the real-life difficulty of doing business overseas.

For his part, Aragaki realized how little thought he had put into his instructions. Sure, supplemental brochures were commonly issued in Japan, but this was an entirely different game. And he had overlooked the sheer scale of the task of building out infrastructure, something he had taken for granted in Japan. His strength in sales had led him to order a frontal attack, severely underestimating the amount of arduous groundwork needed to pave the way for this sort of entry into a new market.

## Release from Constraints

The meeting on day one of Saegusa's Shanghai visit had laid bare all of these problems.

He spoke harshly to urge his people to "think things through." For, "even with the best of intentions, you may be damaging the company's strategy. Think over the strategy carefully."

The meeting had tremendous significance—it helped avert failure.

So where would they go from here? He showed them the simplest way out.

"Postpone the catalog release," he said. "First, focus on building out the organization, the sales force and the product-sourcing network. The real battle begins once that work is complete."

Together, they decided to shelve the catalog until the following September, nearly a year later.

They arrived at the decision so quickly because Saegusa, with the authority vested in him as CEO, got personally involved in the discussions. An illustrative example of a release from constraints.

### Riddle-solving for Business Leaders (29): Release from Existing Constraints

Assumptions, habits, beliefs and established practices can serve as constraints that bind your people' thoughts and actions. Removing them frees your people to think and act in entirely new ways. Someone with the authority to remove the constraints needs to get personally involved to revive a stagnant situation. If the release is too small, its benefit will be limited. Too bold, and the cost will be too great. Striking the right balance requires intimate knowledge of your people' state of mind. Releasing constraints is one of the hard calls that makes management an art. It's also one of its most rewarding acts.

Kagami abandoned his plans to leave the company.

If he had quit as he intended, his legacy would have been one flimsy catalog—a far cry from the mark he wanted to make on Shanghai. He would have been replaced by as many resources as necessary to recover the situation, and his peers would have soldiered on under committed leadership. Before long, his presence would have been completely forgotten.

And given his earnest disposition, he probably would have been haunted by regrets for the rest of his life for leaving the fight.

## Riddle-solving for Business Leaders (30): Rescue from Chaos

Whether at a corporate or on a personal level, the quickest escape from chaos is to buy time. Extend the deadline. That gives your people the mental space to sort out the problem and the energy to execute countermeasures.

In just four months, Kagami had gone through several years' worth of personal growth.

It wasn't the last time Kagami would be admonished by Saegusa. But Saegusa remembered the many setbacks he himself had suffered in his 30s, recognized that Kagami was alone with little support from Tokyo, and resolved to continue his commitment to Kagami's development.

Kagami's wife eventually became accustomed to life in Shanghai and began to feel like her old self again.

Kagami—in terms of his thoughts, his actions, even his look—would evolve into a nimble business leader. Returning to Japan four years later, still young at 34, he would become the company's youngest deputy general manager of a business division.

## Local Contract Manufacturers

While in Shanghai, Saegusa toured the plants of several Chinese manufacturers that were candidates to supply Misumi. This would trigger the next major episode.

At the time, the most pressing issue for Aragaki and Kagami was building out a local product sourcing infrastructure. They wanted to create a network of contract manufacturers similar to what the company had in Japan. But it was no simple task.

In Japan, the company received high marks for its quality (the Q in QCT). The Chinese-made products paled in comparison.

Kagami and his team hustled to survey potential suppliers. By expanding their search to include new suppliers in Taiwan and Hong Kong, they were eventually able to come up with a list of 20 candidates.

During Saegusa's visit to one supplier, Aragaki told him that it was fairly advanced, compared to its local peers.

Saegusa asked, "Who gives direction on quality improvements?"

Aragaki answered, "We use the same approach as in Japan. We communicate customer complaints to the manufacturer and request improvement. At first, they weren't too responsive, but they have gotten better over time with some guidance."

Aragaki did not pick up on the change in Saegusa's facial expression.

"Do you sign exclusivity agreements with these suppliers?"

"That would be impossible. The suppliers have long been selling to other customers, so we can't constrain them in that way."

"If that's the case, the benefits of quality improvements led by Misumi can be reflected in products sold to other customers as well, right?"

"Well...yes."

Saegusa's expression turned grave.

"So, as these suppliers grow along with the Chinese economy to a scale where they can expand overseas, they'll be free to sell to our customers, right? At a bargain price. What are we supposed to do then?"

Aragaki had no answer. He hadn't thought that far ahead.

As far as Saegusa was concerned, it is management's job to think that far ahead, and to put things in a historical context.

From the 1950s into the 1960s, many Japanese companies sought technological assistance from their American counterparts. The Americans generously handed over many of their secrets. Perhaps their openness to cooperation arose from an avuncular desire to help Japan recover from the ravages of WWII. The Japanese applied these new technologies with passion and creativity that surpassed anything the Americans had done. As a result, Japanese companies rapidly emerged as competitive threats to the US. One after another, American industries were overcome by the Japanese and pushed to the brink. The US economy began a decline that lasted three decades—a very long time.

Now, history was set to repeat itself. Japanese companies had wholeheartedly responded to Chinese requests for technologies. During the war, Japan had inflicted enormous damage on China, so perhaps Japanese people harbored a desire to help China grow, to atone for past sins. Toyoko Yamasaki's novel, *Daichi no Ko* (Child of the Earth) provides an account of how Nippon Steel helped develop China's steel industry.

Saegusa realized that Chinese plants lagged behind Japan at the time, but they nevertheless had enormous potential. Someday, he thought, China will do to Japan what Japan had done to the US.

### Key Turning Points—Riddle-solving and Decision-making as a Business Leader

- If unable to find appropriate local suppliers, the China business would be forced to rely on imports from Japan and thus be unable to fully replicate the Misumi QCT Model.
- Forging a network of local suppliers overseas was not enough. Long-term risks and rewards also needed consideration. If Misumi were to openly share its business model and quality standards with local suppliers without an exclusivity agreement in place, it would be helping to build its own future competitors.
- The problem clearly needed to be addressed quickly. Failing to do so would spell defeat for the company's business model further down the road.

In future forays into foreign markets, Misumi would meet the same challenges in each country. Saegusa mulled over a solution during the flight back to Japan.

## A Startling New Direction

Saegusa made two key moves after returning to Tokyo.

One was to establish a Global Strategy Committee, comprising a China Subcommittee. The new body was made up of key management personnel from headquarters.

In the past, Misumi executives would not involve themselves in businesses other than their own. That was how the company worked—like a collection of independently run fiefdoms. Even Saegusa was held at arm's length by the China business until his trip to Shanghai.

Saegusa set out to break that spell as well. Aragaki and Kagami flew in from Shanghai to attend the first committee meeting, joining other officers and key management personnel.

"Business teams do their own thing. Management across the company is disjointed. That ends today," Saegusa declared. "From this point forward, we will place utmost importance on *strategic directions and priorities set at the corporate level.*"

"The organization must change. Executives in Tokyo will no longer ignore the struggles of overseas businesses. The China business is the company's riskiest project. From now on, all headquarters divisions must support it."

Almost overnight, the company shifted its attention overseas. The change was historic. General managers of business units and other key management personnel began to make frequent trips to Shanghai, gaining on-the-ground exposure to the company's global strategy. Chaired by Saegusa, the subcommittee held monthly meetings in Tokyo or Shanghai.

The other major move was announced during the next China Subcommittee's meeting held in December.

It was one of the measures Saegusa had been mulling over since his return to Japan—and it caught the committee off guard.

"For many years, we have worked closely with our contract manufacturers in Japan," he began. "The team in Shanghai has sought to build out a network of local suppliers there, but the outlook for getting the operation started in time is gloomy. So, we're pulling the plug on that."

The audience was taken aback by the sudden pronouncement. If it didn't work with local suppliers, how would it source products in China?

"Instead," he continued, "we will ask our Japanese contract manufacturers to follow us to China."

Astounded, the audience considered the possibilities. If it worked, it would resolve both the sourcing and quality issues.

He added, "Let's build a Shanghai Misumi Village to house our Japanese contract manufacturers."

The attendees tried to wrap their heads around the idea. Secure an industrial park in the outskirts of Shanghai for our partners to build their plants while Misumi sets up a distribution center and customer center. That would consolidate all the functions right there in Shanghai. It was a completely new concept, a break from the traditional way of thinking at Misumi.

He continued, "We can provide financial support to companies that lack the capacity to set up shop in China." It would be an unprecedented degree of involvement for Misumi, because over nearly 40 years Mr. Taguchi had always tried to keep some distance in the company's relationship with its suppliers. No money-lending was allowed even if a supplier asked to borrow money to get through a bind.

Many doubted the idea would actually come to fruition. It seemed far-fetched, even for a chief executive who was a proponent of free thinking and considering all possibilities.

That day, he released the company from a series of spells and indicated his commitment to the global business.

Moving forward, Misumi would encourage its Japanese suppliers to think globally. If they could go to China and become cost-competitive, it would take Japan's unmatched manufacturing prowess a step higher. The village to be built there would serve as a foothold for Misumi to pursue further global expansion.

Privately, Saegusa was mulling over another idea. Modeled on the Shanghai Misumi Village, build a similar village in every other market the company was fully committed to. Together, Misumi and its contract manufacturers would accelerate their global expansion.

It wasn't a new concept; the idea resembled the practices of Japanese automotive makers. They brought their parts suppliers with them overseas. It was just new to Misumi.

Looking ahead, the Shanghai Misumi Village would quickly become a reality.

## Building the Shanghai Misumi Village

Change began to occur with lightning speed following Saegusa's three-day trip to Shanghai. Already, he had broken numerous spells that had gripped the company.

To support the team in Shanghai, Tokyo's business units implemented Saegusa's orders to recruit Japanese contract manufacturers to join the Misumi village in China.

The contract manufacturers were all small companies. They hadn't given much thought to global expansion or the Chinse market. After Misumi's business units introduced the idea to each candidate supplier, Saegusa would follow up with a personal visit to secure top management's buy-in.

Traveling across Japan, he offered to lend out Misumi staffers to assist the contract manufacturers in launching overseas. Misumi would act as a local agent, selecting plots in the industrial park, and submitting all the required paperwork to the Chinese authorities on the manufacturers' behalf. The company also offered to help hire local employees and extend assistance in the form of capital or equipment as necessary.

Some rejected the idea flat out. Even today, Saegusa can recall each disappointing encounter.

Meanwhile, Kagami and his team personally surveyed 20 industrial parks, eventually selecting one located south of Shanghai. In January, the company led a tour of the site for interested suppliers.

Fortunately, five of them, including one from Taiwan, agreed to join Misumi in China. The following year, four others involved in the FA business joined in, bringing the total to nine suppliers.

The developments overwhelmed Kagami. Saegusa's outside-of-the-box thinking made him feel that the scale of the China business was now expanding beyond what he could have imagined.

### Comments from Saegusa

*I understand how he felt, but I don't think that Kagami was in over his head. True, he needed to start thinking in an entirely different dimension. But true reformers need to go through the process of breaking the spells that bind them to move forward. Theoretically, Kagami could have come up with the Misumi village idea himself.*

*Alibaba, Apple and Dell Technologies were all founded by people who were about the same age as Kagami at the time.*

*For me to truly cultivate tomorrow's leadership talent, I need more people with backbone to step up to the plate. These people need to know how to execute leadership and manage their bosses.*

## A Rapid Launch Overseas

The first group of five Japanese suppliers launched in China quickly, with Misumi providing an unprecedented level of support.

Among the key Misumi staffers supporting the suppliers' launch was someone who had only recently joined the company. She was an experienced hire from a major automotive-parts maker, intimately familiar with the launch and management of overseas plants.

Ordinarily, it would take at least two years to go from planning and site selection to finally making the plant operational. But Misumi Village launched in record time.

Kagami had relocated to Shanghai in July, soon after Saegusa was officially named CEO. Saegusa first visited him there in October and proposed the Misumi Village idea in Tokyo in December. By February, the suppliers had signed on. Production operations began in October, only 8 months later. It was an unbelievable pace for launching plants in a foreign country.

It wasn't just the production facilities. Inside the village, the team leased a rental factory. It was an empty building, with exposed-concrete walls and not much else. They repurposed it into a distribution center.

Additionally, the company built its first logistics center outside of Japan, handling everything from the building design and operational-flow layout to the delivery-vendor selection and local staff hiring and training.

The customer center was housed within the logistics center building. Saegusa named it the Misumi QCT Center. It would serve as a template for future expansion into other markets.

Building out the IT systems proved to be enormously difficult. China was the first overseas market where the company had built a comprehensive IT system covering the entire cycle of Create→Produce→Sell. Language barriers and tax and regulatory issues presented significant challenges, the most vexing of which was complying with China's unique value-added tax system.

## The Business Goes Live

Launch preparations advanced with tremendous speed. Saegusa visited Shanghai once or twice a month to monitor progress.

Recall that the initial, flimsy catalog was to be issued in October. Then it was postponed by nearly a year to the following September. Only three months out from that new deadline, it became clear that preparations would not be ready in time.

He sent an email to all company executives instructing the entire management team to work together to support the launch in China. Here are some of the salient points.

1. We are launching an Emergency China Support Project at headquarters. If you receive a request for support, please place top priority on providing it, even if that interferes with your other responsibilities.
2. On Monday, July 14, the China Subcommittee will meet in Shanghai. All interested executives from Tokyo should plan to attend.
3. If concerns with launch preparations arise, the September catalog release will be postponed again. At the July 14 meeting, we will determine the *Point of No Return*, the point at which the catalog release can no longer be postponed.

At the July 14 China Subcommittee meeting in Shanghai, Saegusa checked the status of each department's preparations.

The results weren't entirely reassuring. He had a nagging feeling that something they hadn't thought of could go wrong at any time. In particular, there were stress points in the distribution center and the IT systems. Nevertheless, there was one more month before they reached the Point of No Return. So, the final decision about whether to go forward with the catalog release could wait until then.

One month later, on Sunday, August 10, the final decision was made.

The day before, Saegusa had returned to Tokyo from Shanghai and sent an email to all executives stating, "We will postpone our first order intake until October 6, following China's National Day vacation. Use the one-month delay to finalize all preparations."

After a year and a half of preparations, the China business was set to go live.

Beginning in late September, catalogs were distributed to potential customers, based on the planned commencement of order intake on October 6.

The day before China's business launch was a Sunday. Saegusa was at home, unable to relax. He kept it to himself, but deep down he was worried that the business might not truly take off.

It had been over a year since Kagami and his team had first arrived in Shanghai. Over the past 15 months, they had endured dramatic twists and turns as they proceeded by trial and error. They pushed preparations forward at breakneck speed and eventually launched the China business. The operation involved a lot more than just acting as a distributor of imported goods from Japan.

The catalogs were in the local language, priced in the local currency, and the expansive product lineup compared favorably with that offered in Japan. Another distribution center was built in Guangzhou to complement the one in Shanghai. Misumi had never built a distribution center overseas. Now, it had two. And despite the headwinds they faced in recruiting suppliers to follow them to China, the Misumi Village was off to a good start.

## Growth in the China Business

The China business launched. So far, we've only covered the history leading up to that event. Later, other Misumi businesses would launch in China and in other countries as well. Each would entail its own drama.

Again, over the following 12 years, the China business would grow to sales of about $400 million. Headcount at the Chinese local subsidiaries would approach 1,000. Including the two plants run by the production arm, Suruga, Misumi would employ a total of over 2,000 in China.

All of this was begun by a team of three led by Kagami, who was only 30 years old.

By comparison, after 13 years, the US business had reached only $12 million in sales. This stark contrast is proof of the monumental change in ambitions and strategic awareness among the people at Misumi. It's fair to say it had become an entirely different company.

**Testimonial from K. Kagami (Four years later, he would return to Japan and, after a series of promotions, eventually rise to business company president.)**

*Without a doubt, my four years in China were a turning point in my career. I was naïve when I first volunteered for the position, underestimating what it would entail. While in China I nearly quit three times. But I'm glad I stuck it out. I was constantly walking a fine line between chaos and success. You don't get many opportunities like that in your early 30s.*

*To my surprise, I received a major promotion after returning to Japan. I was appointed deputy general manager of the largest division at the youngest age in history at Misumi. Mr. Saegusa had dressed me down so many times, I didn't expect him to reward me in such a way.*

*The year after I returned to Japan, we rented out a hotel banquet hall for the business division's year-end celebration.*

*There was a quiz with prizes, and I was one of the presenters. My question read, "In Shanghai, Mr. Saegusa berated me many times. One of these five lines is something he did NOT actually say. Which one is it?"*

*The crowd erupted in laughter. By then we had all had a few drinks.*

*Mr. Saegusa had said he wouldn't be able to make it to the party. Well, wouldn't you know it? This was the very moment I saw him enter the banquet room! People in the crowd were stealing glances at Mr. Saegusa, trying to read his reaction to the question on the screen.*

*One of the lines read, "Kagami, are you trying to put Misumi out of business?!"*

*The crowd laughed hysterically. Mr. Saegusa was laughing along with them, clapping his hands. Each time someone guessed the wrong answer, I would speak up, "Actually, he did say that." Then I would share my memories of that time, throwing salt on my own wounds, which was met with more uproarious laughter. I never imagined I'd have to relive all of that in front of him.*

## Subsequent International Expansion

When Saegusa became CEO, the company had issued only two catalogs overseas—one in the US and one in South Korea.

Four years later, we had 21 catalogs. That means we launched 21 new businesses in various countries, a rapid pace of expansion considering all the requisite infrastructure that needs to be put in place to support sales activities.

Today, paper catalogs are becoming obsolete. Over 13 years, the business was rapidly migrated online. The investment required was enormous, but today you can search instantly for detailed information on individual products from among a lineup of 24 million items as of the publication of this English edition.

Nearly 80% of orders in Japan are made online now. Even though the humble fax machine still plays an important role in this industry, the company has pursued digitalization with extraordinary speed. Overseas, more than 50% of ordering is done online, still leaving plenty of room to grow.

The Shanghai QCT Center was the first of 11 that the company would build over a 10-year period. Recently, the company added a logistics center in Indonesia. As for sales offices, the company now has 53, including some in China's regional cities.

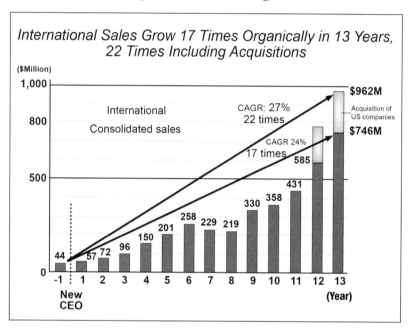

So, how much sales growth did this expansion strategy deliver?

When Saegusa became CEO, overseas sales totaled about $44 million, or less than 9% of companywide sales. Just a drop in the bucket. In 13 years, that grew 17-fold to about $750 million.

That was organic growth in existing businesses. In year 10 of Saegusa's tenure, Misumi acquired two US makers, and adding their performance to the calculation yields 22-fold growth in overseas sales to about $950 million in the same 13 years.

As a percentage of the total, overseas sales went from 9% at Saegusa's appointment to 36%, beating his initial target of 30%. With the North American acquisitions, the number rose to 46%, bringing overseas sales to approximate parity with domestic sales. By 2016, overseas sales exceeded $1 billion.

One of the management indexes that grew the most was the number of employees. The overseas business now employs more than 7,000, including local hires, and many are run by young talent who, like Kagami, started out not knowing left from right, but gained valuable experience in a tough business environment and upped their management skill set along the way. They are the company's next generation of management talent.

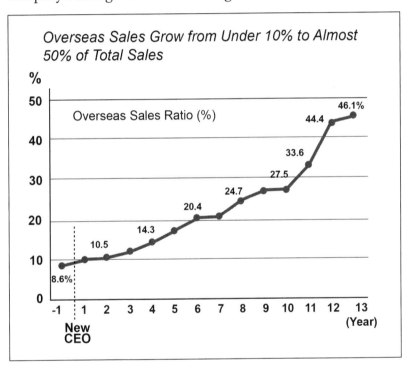

Overseas Sales Grow from Under 10% to Almost 50% of Total Sales

## SAEGUSA'S MANAGEMENT NOTE 6
# MISUMI'S BUSINESS PLAN SYSTEM

### The Role of the Business Plan System

I introduced a Business Plan System to all divisions and business teams at Misumi as a core reform program. The aim was not only the business plans per se but to revamp the corporate culture that had pervaded the company under its founder over 40 years.

From my 16 years as a turnaround specialist, I knew the business plan is the most effective trigger to get people to deeply rethink almost all factors involving strategy. You have already read about Nagao's efforts to develop his business plan for the FA Division. It was not an easy process for him and his task force, but it fueled significant change across the company.

His plan led to years of explosive growth in the business. Moreover, the story of new strategies influenced the state of mind and attitudes of people across the company.

Nagao and his task force astounded the Management Forum audience with the amazing change in the team's demeanor. The team exuded confidence with their logical story-telling and sounded intelligent explaining management theories based on hard-earned lessons from the previous few months. Above all, Nagao's humility in admitting his past shortcomings in managing the division and explaining what he would change moved and impressed the audience.

To achieve a reform successfully, it is important to present new strategies first in sharp but persuasive language, to reset people's thoughts and frame of mind about their business and new leadership. Also, there must be direction on how to redesign the organization best for the new strategies and the people involved. To effect true reform, these changes must all be announced in connection with each other as one cohesive suite of reforms.

While working as a turnaround specialist, I eventually came up with a practical way to nurture management talent. It involved business plans, which doubled as a conduit between strategic issues and organizational issues and a tool to facilitate strategic planning efforts. Without it, people will not sharpen their ability to carry out strategy under the most appropriate organizational structure. Igor Ansoff's "Strategy follows structure" vs. Alfred Chandler's "structure follows strategy" may still be a valid academic argument, but in the reform cases I pursued as a turnaround specialist or as CEO of Misumi, we examined and changed the strategies first, then contemplated organizational changes as necessary.

At Misumi, business plans are not a mere training tool; they are integrated into the real business. The person responsible for the business establishes a real-life direction for the business and sees it through to execution. The team learns real-life lessons along the way that they would not have acquired in a classroom.

Business plans were part of my arsenal in turning around businesses.

## The 40% Review, 70% Review and 100% Review

At Misumi, business plans are formulated at each organizational level, from the business team up to the business division and business company. (The business company is a new organizational layer I added on top of divisions as the company grew. More on this in Chapter 8.) Here, I refer to the business plans formulated at the business-team level. The director of a business team is solely responsible for developing the business plan. Team members may help the director from time to time, but otherwise have little involvement in drafting the business plan.

First, for whom is the director writing the business plan? This critical question is the starting point for the annual business plan development process. The graph shown here is an actual slide I used when briefing directors and executives before they started their work on business plans.

A business plan covers four years. Numbers for Year 1 get reflected in that year's budget. Numbers for Year 2 represent a commitment. Numbers for Years 3 and 4 entail a higher degree of uncertainty but represent a best estimate.

---

## Who Are You Writing a Business Plan For?

1. **For yourself**
   - **Think things through and evaluate the risks**

2. **To motivate people**
   - **Share the feeling that you are in the same boat, including your superior and CEO**

3. **To check the boundaries**
   - **Clarify the scope of autonomy granted**

---

Business-plan formulation season runs from December through March. The first two months in particular take a lot of time.

Strategy is not easy to formulate. As Step 1, your work starts with a sheet of paper twice the size of a letter-sized sheet (A3 size). Place a blank sheet of paper on your desk.

Your instructions are simple. Write what you want to do next year and the following three years.

What you write and present to your boss must have a story. It is called a Solid Main Story. As a business leader, you have to think what *solid* means, what *main* means, and finally what *story* means.

---

## Solid Main Story

Successful management approaches must:

- Align with the 3-Sheet Set
  (Sheet 1→Sheet 2→Sheet 3)

- And become crystallized in a *Solid Main Story*

Once you obtain a solid main story, it becomes a creed:
- **for the leader** taking the helm
- **for the organization** to coalesce around
- **for the people** to guide their actions
- **for everyone** to be reminded of the purpose
  and direction in times of doubt

---

After you finish writing your idea on this paper, you have the first review with your boss one-on-one. It is called the 40% Review and is eventually followed by the 70% Review and 100% Review as the business plan season progresses.

Each review is a gateway for approving or denying the business plan. The review is a one-on-one chess match between you and your boss, who may be division president or even the CEO, depending on whom you report to.

It requires significant thought and energy for both the director and the boss. If, as director, you get ahead of yourself, only to have your boss reject your plan, that creates a lot of re-work, so you want to avoid that. If the substance is thin, better to rethink it sooner, rather than later.

Once the boss gives the Solid Main Story the thumbs-up, the business plan is deemed 40% complete.

Next, the director creates a PowerPoint presentation of a detailed strategic story based on the Solid Main Story. The slide deck explains the business story following the logic of the 3-sheet Set (Sheet 1→Sheet 2→Sheet 3). (See Riddle-solving for Business Leaders (13): "Sheet 1→Sheet 2→Sheet 3".)

All directors, division presidents and corporate executives contribute significant mental energy and time to it. The business plan is also a tool for motivating the team. It's important to cover key strategic elements, but the story must also be simple enough to inspire enthusiasm.

By the day of their 70% Review, directors must prepare a plan they believe to be 100% complete and present it to a review committee, which comprises their boss as chairperson, other senior division personnel, some corporate executives, and occasionally the CEO. Personnel from other divisions may observe with the meeting chair's permission.

After the presentation, the director is excused from the conference room. The committee grades the plan on a ten-point scale and provides feedback on missing strategic factors and other areas that need work.

It is rare for a business plan to obtain final approval at the 70% Review. Unless rejected, most go to the 100% Review, which is typically held a couple of weeks later. Directors continue to work hard thinking and agonizing over how to reflect the suggestions from the previous review.

## Plans are Devised by Those Who Will Execute Them

The final review is known as the 100% Review.

Formulating a business plan is not like doing homework for school. It is a real-world endeavor that mobilizes money and people. What do you need to take into account before you can say that you have thought the strategy through? Directors are asked that question again and again. It hones their skill in strategic orientation.

Some companies have corporate-planning staff formulate the company's business plans. Misumi eschews the involvement of corporate-planning staff in business plan formulation. This represents a fundamentally different approach. Here, the people who run the business make their own plan. It's an absolute must at Misumi. Creating a winning story is closely tied to changing the organization and developing executive talent. The people who run the business are responsible for everything. If a crude strategy is the best they can do, they have only themselves to blame when things don't pan out.

Note that the numbers are not the primary focus of the business plan. The key is the *strategic story*. Who are your competitors? What decides victory or defeat? How do your strengths and weaknesses align with those elements? After answering those questions, what does the business strategy mean to the business leader?

Some want a less burdensome process for business plan formulation. Recently, a lot of the heavy lifting has been simplified. But too much simplification can become a problem. Make it too easy to put something out there that sounds like it makes sense, and they start to think they've actually come up with a strategy. It lightens the load at first, but if the business leader's thoughts remain narrow and shallow, nothing dynamic will come out of the business.

A business plan would not be exceptional if anyone could devise it. At Misumi, our people act like business executives, think strategically, survey the problems broadly, make adjustments themselves and finally execute the plan. Sometimes it works out, sometimes it doesn't, but even when it fails, there is plenty for the business leader to learn.

The business plan system is covered in more detail in Chapter 8 (Organizational Theory).

# Chapter 5

# Acquiring Manufacturing Capabilities

For 40 years, Misumi specialized in trading. However, that chapter of its history would close with
its acquisition of manufacturing capabilities. The
move immediately addressed the weak point of its
trading-company model, but what was the view of
history and the motivation that guided the strategy?

### Innovating the Business Model With a Chain of Reforms
#### (Competing Against the International Megatrend)

Growth Acceleration

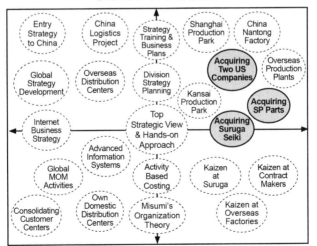

Increasing Quality and Efficiency

## A Stunning Announcement

Amid the whirlwind of developing business reforms and executing strategy, Saegusa came to a realization: Misumi would need
internal production capabilities to continue to grow.

He mulled over the possibilities. Building in-house production
capabilities from scratch would not be feasible: There were no
production engineering capabilities and no personnel familiar
with production.

M&A was the only option. But what would be a suitable target?
Would the target object to the proposal?

Only two years and four months after Saegusa became CEO, he
called a special board of directors meeting. There, the acquisition
of Suruga Seiki (hereafter Suruga) was approved.

Misumi had been a sales company since its inception 40 years
before, but the acquisition in effect closed that chapter of
its history and dramatically changed its business to include
manufacturing.

A holding company named Misumi Group Inc. was established,
and pre-merger Misumi (the sales arm) and Suruga (the manufacturing arm) became subsidiaries in parallel under the holding
company. (Hereafter, Misumi refers to the holding company.)

Suruga was the largest of the nearly 20 contract manufacturers
that made Misumi's short delivery business model possible. At
the time of the merger, Misumi had annual sales of about $815
million (up 17% year-on-year), Suruga about $140 million (up
7% year-on-year). Already, Misumi had begun its rapid ascent.

Moreover, Suruga derived 60% of its sales from supplying product
to Misumi. So, the merger would only add about $50 million to

consolidated sales. Obviously, the companies did not merge to acquire scale.

Talks began under strict secrecy just 17 months after Saegusa started as CEO. The parties rapidly advanced discussions and due diligence. Only 11 months after those talks started, they announced their plans to merge.

Let's start by looking at the strategic rationale behind the acquisition and what management frameworks governed Saegusa's approach.

## Lessons Learned in China

The foray into China had taught Saegusa much during his first 18 months at Misumi.

He had hit upon the idea of creating the Misumi Village in Shanghai as a production park to house the company's Japan-based suppliers. However, recruitment efforts were met with a lukewarm response. Clearly, production functions would be the greatest limiting factor on the company's global strategy. The cycle of Create→Produce→Sell was a pivotal element of its organizational concept, but it lacked the ability to produce itself.

Eventually, nine suppliers agreed to join Misumi in China. But watching the suppliers prepare for the move caused him anxiety and exposed the limits of this approach.

Moreover, the contract manufacturers did little to add international talent to their rosters. That led to an important conclusion: China is as far abroad as our contract manufacturers can go. It would be too much to expect them to follow us to other parts of the globe, such as Europe, the US and the rest of Asia.

That insight forced the realization that The Misumi Village Global Development Plan set forth in the previous chapter would be no more than a pipedream. To execute a global strategy beyond China, the company would have to be bolder and acquire its own manufacturing capabilities.

## Mutual Animosity, Mutual Dependence

There was another reason Saegusa considered acquiring production capabilities.

The contract manufacturers that formed the company's supplier network were small companies. Each was fiercely independent and intensely proud of its own technological prowess. In other words, these weren't the easiest people to deal with.

In developing the Misumi QCT Model, the company had provided various forms of guidance to the contract manufacturers over the course of many years. Misumi set stringent standards for improvement, whether to address problems like delivery delays or quality complaints, or to achieve cost reductions aimed at sales growth. Such demands, paired with workplace improvements and management efforts at the contract manufacturers, gradually enhanced the competitiveness of the Misumi QCT Model. Throughout this process, Misumi and the contract manufacturers added scale together.

Relations with the contract manufacturers had always been tense. That said, if relationships had been too forgiving, the Misumi QCT Model would never have attained its present strength. The friendly rivalry that the tension created was essential.

In times of conflict, words of frustration and anger were hurled back and forth on a daily basis.

With few exceptions, the owners and employees of the contract manufacturers complained about Misumi. "They sit in their cushy offices, pick up the phone and boss us around. They don't see that we're the ones getting our hands dirty. We're the ones with the technology. Without us, they're nothing."

To be sure, Saegusa quickly realized that most people at Misumi possessed little knowledge or experience in production. He found it curious they could keep the contract manufacturers in check despite their ignorance of production.

Misumi's strength vis-a-vis its contract manufacturers was its customer base. It's easy to imagine how Misumi's people might wield that strength as a cudgel and feel entitled to act arrogantly toward the contract manufacturers. At the same time, perhaps their lack of familiarity with the production floor may have caused them to relay unrealistic demands from customers, without any thought to how that might impact production.

Misumi's people had their own bones to pick with the contract manufacturers. "They don't lift a finger to do their own sales or marketing. They forget how lucky they are to be able to just sit around and wait for the orders to come in. They miss delivery deadlines and make defective parts without the slightest concern for our customers. They don't have any idea how much time and effort it takes to grow sales."

Saegusa did not empathize with Misumi's side in this conflict. He knew a bit about how tough things are on the manufacturing floor and thus tried to stay impartial. It was not unlike a sibling rivalry.

"We are completely dependent on each other," he thought. "Familiarity breeds contempt, so of course there will be conflicts of interest and emotional clashes. Nevertheless, our fates are intertwined."

So, conflict was unavoidable. From Misumi's point of view, any production issue had to be *negotiated* with the contract manufacturer. Sometimes they flat out refused to do anything.

And when it came to reform, all of the contract manufacturers would have to move together, or it wouldn't work. Furthermore, coordination took time because there were so many companies to deal with.

Saegusa wanted in-house production functions—even of limited scale—that would move at the pace Misumi required. That would have the salutary effect of quickly boosting its own technology and manufacturing capabilities.

## A New Wave in Global Business Innovation

There was another rationale for setting up manufacturing functions in-house.

Consider the international megatrend in business innovations discussed in Saegusa's Management Note 5. Saegusa feared that the company's inability to implement a production strategy as it saw fit might become a fatal flaw in its global strategy.

Additionally, he worked to strengthen other functions, including customer centers and logistics. The reform themes were named 5C to represent the fact that the reforms involved more than just optimizing isolated parts of the business.

### Riddle-solving for Business Leaders (31): The Five Chains (5C)

To energize a business, you must fundamentally reform the five chains that link the Create→Produce→Sell cycle. The five chains are: time, value, information, strategy and mindset. You can't expect that simply tweaking each of these links independently will deliver impressive results. You also have to address the complexity inherent in an organizational structure divided by function. (From Saegusa's previous work, *Turnaround Task Force*, Chapter 3, Key Point 13.)

The people at Misumi worked frantically, day and night. Sales were growing rapidly. Overseas businesses were expanding dramatically. It would be cruel to expect more of such an overburdened workforce. Nevertheless, there was one piece of the puzzle that just could not wait. That was the Produce in Create→ Produce→Sell. This is the rationale for securing in-house production capabilities.

- The tense, fraught relationships with its contract manufacturers stymied possibilities for rapid expansion.
- People needed to become more familiar with the production side to be motivated to pursue business-process reforms and production strategies.
- The international megatrend in business innovations looked at the business in its totality (Create→Produce→Sell). A lack of control over production would likely become a major liability.

**Key Turning Points: Riddle-solving and Decision-making as a Business Leader**
- It was important to understand that any acquisition of a manufacturer would not eliminate the need for the existing group of contract manufacturers. Misumi could not possibly manufacture in-house all of the products it sells.
- Then what is the purpose of the acquisition? Misumi needed a training ground to hone its production-engineering capabilities. That would also give it the ability to tinker with production itself, without involving any contract manufacturers. The result would be a strong total-reform model encompassing the Create→Produce→Sell cycle.
- The improvement techniques developed internally could be shared with contract manufacturers, who were essentially strategic alliance partners. Instead of chasing after them, Misumi could lead by example.
- The acquisition would deliver significant in-house training and education benefits.

Recall that at the press conference announcing his appointment to CEO, he described Misumi as a test lab for cultivating future management talent. Acquiring a test bed to experiment with production models would position the company to join the leading edge of global competition.

Without it, Misumi could not become a Tier 1 player. It would remain second-rate in terms of future global expansion, business model strategy, and as a magnet for attracting talent.

## Proposing an Acquisition

The lead acquisition target was Suruga. The company had done business with Misumi for nearly 30 years, and fully understood how to run the Misumi QCT Model.

Something else made Suruga attractive. Of all the contract manufacturers, it was the only one to have established its own presence overseas. Suruga owned a plant in Vietnam for manufacturing blanks and small finishing plants in Shanghai and Chicago. It was as if they had anticipated Misumi's global strategy.

An acquisition offer requires a counterpart that is willing to accept it. Instead of mulling it over, Saegusa decided to try a direct approach. He reached out to Akio Hamakawa, Suruga's CEO.

On November 11, Saegusa met with Hamakawa at Asada, a restaurant in Tokyo that Saegusa frequented.

It was their first time socializing one-on-one, so in the beginning the conversation was a bit awkward. Surely, Hamakawa did not suspect there was anything more on the agenda than getting-to-know-you. Once the initial small talk was out of the way, Saegusa broached the idea of a merger between the two companies to pursue a strategy of global expansion.

Hamakawa's eyebrows were thick and dark, and his expression difficult to read.

Saegusa talked openly and frankly about why Misumi needed its own production functions, and disclosed that if Suruga were not interested, he would look elsewhere.

A moment of silence. Then, an unexpected response.

"I understand," Hamakawa said. "It sounds good to me."

Saegusa was surprised. His first choice had responded positively at the first meeting.

Saegusa probed, "Won't there be pushback from your officers?"

"Maybe, but I'll bring them in line," Hamakawa smiled.

That was where they left it for the evening. Saegusa was pleased with the surprisingly positive development.

They met again three weeks later, on December 2. Over dinner, they talked in detail about the post-merger organizational structure. Tremendous progress for a second meeting.

Later talks between the parties went well, but it was too soon for Saegusa to feel optimistic. For one thing, there was a long history of deep rivalry between Misumi and its contract manufacturers. And buying a company was a delicate matter. The deal could blow up at any moment.

As the CEO of Suruga, Hamakawa held the key to the deal's success. Saegusa later found out that, just as he had expected, Suruga's officers unanimously opposed the deal.

Why would Hamakawa push forward with the deal despite such resistance from within? Saegusa felt grateful, but anxious at the same time.

Ultimately, the two companies merged as hoped.

On October 13, only 11 months after the CEOs first met, the boards of directors of both companies approved the merger, and six months later, on April 1, the merger officially took effect.

A holding company, Misumi Group Inc. was established, with Saegusa as its CEO, and Hamakawa as Executive Vice President. Hamakawa also continued to serve as the president of Suruga.

The move came as a shock to people at Misumi. No one anticipated such a dramatic break with its 40-year history as a dedicated trading company. Surely, few understood the strategic aim.

It came as an even greater shock to the people at Suruga. Although it was portrayed as a merger, it was difficult to erase the impression this was actually an acquisition by Misumi.

## Prioritizing International Growth

Separate from the merger with Suruga, Saegusa had also begun work on production reforms. (More on this in the following chapter.) He created a Production Kaizen Department to act as a venue for supporting production improvements at contract manufacturers.

However, Saegusa had instructed the department to target contract manufacturers other than Suruga for the time being. "Stay away from Suruga until I say so."

That's not because Suruga's manufacturing prowess was so advanced that it could wait until later. The reality was quite the opposite.

Pre-merger, Saegusa had visited Suruga plants several times and had thought them mediocre. Poor exhaust ventilation allowed oil mist to linger in the air up to the ceiling. The machines were dirty, the floors covered in oil. One could easily slip and fall. Saegusa felt sorry for the people working there.

Fixtures and tools were not organized. Work in progress was piled haphazardly in several open spaces. Clearly, not even the basics of Kaizen were in practice. If the plant were executing Kaizen, you would see signs displaying relevant KPIs as you walked the aisles. There was no evidence anything like that was in place.

Given the state of the plants, there must be no engineering group pursuing production engineering technologies or production improvements. That much was clear.

But that wasn't an entirely bad thing. He saw enormous potential for profitability upside, as if there were nuggets of gold buried under the plant's dirty floors, just waiting to be discovered. That was his view pre-merger.

Nevertheless, it wouldn't be wise to push through production improvements so soon after the merger. The primary objective of the merger was to have Suruga build plants in other markets to accelerate the global strategy. Suruga had supported Misumi's short delivery times for decades. Even if its plants lacked sophistication, that could wait. The priority was on global development.

## Suruga Gets a New President

Post-merger, Saegusa found every excuse to frequent Suruga's headquarters in Shizuoka, about an hour from Tokyo by bullet train. Even post-merger, he was treated like a visitor at first.

Nevertheless, he donned a company uniform and walked the production floor during every visit, even if he had no specific purpose in mind. It was important to get the people there talking. "Look, he's here again."

Suruga's global expansion ramped up quickly. Under Misumi's global strategy, new finishing plants were set up in several countries. In the fiscal year of the merger, four projects launched—another plant in Vietnam and new plants in Thailand, China (Guangzhou) and the US. There were also plans to build new plants in South Korea and Europe two years down the road.

Ordinarily, it would require a tremendous effort to launch two plants in parallel. But the production-launch team worked frantically to deliver.

Misumi's Japanese contract manufacturers resisted the idea of expanding into countries beyond China. Only Suruga displayed a can-do attitude. Just as Saegusa had hoped it would.

But only a year after the merger, the unexpected happened. Hamakawa submitted his resignation as president of Suruga.

During the year with Misumi, Hamakawa had never revealed a hint of dissatisfaction with how the merged entity was being run or with Saegusa's leadership. He had never complained about how he or Suruga's personnel were treated. After all, it was he who overcame internal opposition to make the merger happen.

Saegusa tried to convince Hamakawa to stay, but to no avail. He insisted, "I have other things I want to do in life."

Saegusa had decided to take over Hayakawa's position as head of Suruga, while continuing to serve as the CEO of the holding company, Misumi Group Inc. He increased the frequency of his trips to Suruga to at least once a week to foster the integration of Suruga into Misumi Group.

No one at either company was aware of how much time and effort Saegusa had expended to foster the post-merger integration. If executives from Misumi were allowed free rein to take over Suruga, many key personnel might have left.

Saegusa felt that initial integration period had gone fairly smoothly, which is often not the case in Japanese acquisitions. The care and attention he had devoted to integration seemed to make the difference in the years to come, as Suruga transformed into one of the most advanced manufacturers of industrial precision components in Japan. Even Toyota executives who visit Suruga in Shizuoka are amazed by the progress Suruga has made over the ten-year period.

## SAEGUSA'S MANAGEMENT NOTE 7
# AN ORGANIZATION'S SENSE OF URGENCY

### Talk Alone Accomplishes Nothing

A company's *crisis* and employees' *sense of urgency* do not necessarily correlate. There's actually more of a negative correlation.

What I mean to say is this: At underperforming companies, where employees should be worried, they're often relaxed. Conversely, it's at growing companies with no reason to panic that the employees are on edge and pushing themselves.

Why is this? Employees at growing companies exposed to market competition respond sensitively to external factors, such as customer preferences, competitor movements or global trends in technology. They hate to fall behind.

In contrast, at an underperforming company, employees are moved by internal factors. They are mostly numb to market competition or the voice of the customer. They are used to losing. Losing doesn't hurt anymore. They just think, "We lost again."

How does a leader instill a sense of urgency? Yelling, "We need more urgency!" won't do it. A leader who seeks to effect change in employees' mindset by simply calling for reform is not exhibiting much management skill.

I learned the futility of that approach managing companies in my 30s. Since then, I've stopped merely speaking of a sense of urgency or the need to reform. Talk alone does nothing.

To effect change, a leader needs to prepare a fully calculated strategic approach and a detailed action plan. With that, the leader needs to stand ready to bear the full brunt of criticism for dismantling the existing organization and value systems.

## It Takes One to Effect Change

One talented leader can artificially manufacture a sense of urgency. No matter the size, when a company on the brink of failure achieves fundamental reform and regains its footing, the transformation can almost always be credited to one powerful leader who effects that change.

Even at corporate behemoths with several hundred-thousand employees, a new CEO can bring about drastic change to the organizational culture. Take GE's Jack Welch or NTT's Hisashi Shinto, for example. They succeeded where several before them failed.

A leader who feels a sense of urgency but takes a calm-and-collected approach to solving problems may be feared but is rarely liked by employees. That's goes with the territory. At some companies in dire need of a turnaround, the CEO is popular. Meanwhile, other officers or employees are widely criticized by the rank and file. That's actually a manifestation of what's wrong.

That is because the CEO needs to take a hands-on approach to instill a sense of urgency within the organization and reform the company. The CEO cannot remain an anodyne and popular presence. I'm sure you recognize that as a common theme in many of the scenes portrayed in this book.

One other thing: The hardships a company endures shape its future leadership talent.

# Chapter 6

# Driving Production Reforms

Production floor resistance against reforms threatened to push all the manufacturing efforts into a
*Death Valley*. How was the effort salvaged? The
result would be a world-class production system
optimized to Misumi's business model, driven by
intellectual efforts involving top management and
hard-won shop floor improvements.

## Innovating the Business Model With a Chain of Reforms
### (Competing Against the International Megatrend)

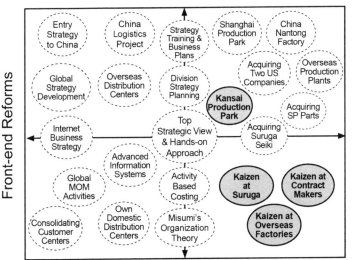

Growth Acceleration

Front-end Reforms · Back-end Reforms

Entry Strategy to China · China Logistics Project · Strategy Training & Business Plans · Shanghai Production Park · China Nantong Factory · Global Strategy Development · Overseas Distribution Centers · Division Strategy Planning · Acquiring Two US Companies · Overseas Production Plants · Kansai Production Park · Acquiring SP Parts · Internet Business Strategy · Top Strategic View & Hands-on Approach · Acquiring Suruga Seiki · Advanced Information Systems · Global MOM Activities · Activity Based Costing · Kaizen at Suruga · Kaizen at Contract Makers · Consolidating Customer Centers · Own Domestic Distribution Centers · Misumi's Organization Theory · Kaizen at Overseas Factories

Increasing Quality and Efficiency

## Section 1:
# Meeting Resistance

### Production Kaizen Initiatives

First, let's step back in time. As Misumi and Suruga were pursuing confidential merger talks, Saegusa was working on a different idea.

Recall the third reason he pursued in-house production capabilities. He was determined that the company would not miss the boat on the international megatrend in business innovations, which comprehensively targeted all business processes, like the Create→Produce→Sell cycle, reengineering and supply-chain reforms.

In pursuing comprehensive innovations to the cycle of Create→Produce→Sell, the company's greatest weakness would be production. No one at Misumi was capable of devising the necessary innovation. No one even recognized the need.

Becoming first-rate in Japan, or in the world for that matter, in the fields of manufacturing, production engineering and production kaizen requires a team to lead the kaizen activities.

Saegusa liked manufacturing. Both operating companies he had led in his 30s were manufacturers. During his 16 years as a turnaround specialist, he came to prefer projects involving manufacturers, and as a result, he had accumulated a wealth of learning and experience in shop-floor kaizen activities.

That said, he wasn't a production kaizen expert. His job was to create the organization and systems that make it possible to pursue kaizen activities and reforms on an ongoing basis.

He searched for a professional instructor to teach production kaizen practices.

There are plenty of instructors out there who teach the Toyota Production System (TPS). Some behave like pitiless drill sergeants—not a good fit for Misumi. But Saegusa eventually found the right person. F. Takagi was 40 years old and took a logical approach to explaining concepts. That would work well for Misumi's people, who knew nothing about production kaizen.

Takagi would spend more than a decade adapting kaizen practices at Suruga and its contract manufacturers.

Misumi's main network of contract manufacturers encompassed about 20 companies. Together, they had more than 40 production lines manufacturing a broad range of products. Clearly, it would be a tremendous challenge to drive the benefits of kaizen activities across all lines. But Saegusa was convinced it needed to be done for the customer to fully realize the benefits.

He asked the contract manufacturers to take in Takagi as an instructor; Misumi would foot the bill. As a first step, they would target just a few of the 20 makers, but most were loath to sign on, just as they had resisted going to China.

Clearly, the manufacturers felt they knew best. They had no interest in hosting a guest instructor. They didn't really know what kaizen was, nor did they care. They were simply being narrow-minded, indifferent to the opportunity to learn kaizen or TPS.

Finally, three of them agreed to give it a try. Some were only luke-warm to the idea, others enthusiastic. But there was a problem: Unless *all of* the contract manufacturers implemented kaizen, there would be no benefit to the customer.

## Riddle-solving for Business Leaders (32): The Benefits of Improving Delivery Times

An important goal of production kaizen is to shorten production lead times—the amount of time it takes to go from start of production to shipment. If the target is the entire supply chain, the aim is to shorten the total time from when the customer places an order until it receives delivery. Consider a scenario where the customer needs all parts to begin its work. If some suppliers have achieved shorter lead times while others have not, there is no overall benefit.

## Impediments to Kaizen

Kaizen activities needed to clear a higher hurdle at Misumi than would have been the case elsewhere. That hurdle is time (T), the most important element of the QCT Model—specifically, short delivery lead times and on-time deliveries, as promised.

There were 2 million product items when Saegusa became CEO. That grew to 24 million items as of the publication of this book in English. Moreover, recall that each product could be made to different dimensions, down to the micron. Count every possible dimensional variation and the number of distinct product variations rose to 80,000,000,000,000,000,000,000, or 80 sextillion ($10^{21}$). An astronomical number.

An order for any one of those variations could come at any time. It might come from Japan, or from Europe. Ready and waiting, Misumi did not know when or where its next order would come from. With no minimum quantities, even orders for one piece were produced and shipped within three days (subsequently shortened to two days).

It would be easy to ship on short lead times if you stocked your product in a warehouse. That works with many consumer products. But imagine the countless number of gargantuan warehouses that would be needed to stock the astronomical number of Misumi products! Most likely, it would not be profitable, as only some of the product lineup would see enough turnover. Instead, it makes more sense to fulfill orders with zero inventory.

Consider a day in the life of a contract manufacturer. Orders that came in from Misumi overnight are made to order down to the micron. Regardless of whether the order is only for one piece, or requires extensive machining, it is made and shipped to Misumi's distribution center that evening.

As you can imagine, the contract manufacturers' order volumes fluctuated greatly from one day to another. That necessitated production-capacity buffers to avoid missing deadlines on busier days. However, too much buffer drives up costs as machines sit idle.

Applying TPS would help balance these variables. Misumi calls its model Make To Order. It's similar to Dell's Build To Order, which emerged two decades later than Misumi.

At Misumi, there is a top-to-bottom commitment to follow through on promised delivery deadlines. That spirit makes it possible to orchestrate the production high-wire act. The company motto is to keep delivery time promises, without fail. Therein lies the customers' trust.

In Japan, Misumi maintains an on-time delivery rate of about 99.96%, excluding deliveries affected by natural disasters. That number captures not only production errors, but also errors in transit from the contract manufacturer to the distribution center, and errors from mishandled orders.

A 0.04% probability of error means that even repeat customers that place several orders a month may experience one shipment delay every few years. Such a low error rate allows the customer centers to notify the customer of each shipment delay.

Delays affecting a customer's production activities are a big problem. The customer may demand that replacement parts be sent immediately. Misumi has its share of stories about the efforts it has taken to keep the customer happy. Once, when Misumi missed the cut-off time for courier services, a customer service staffer rode a two-hour train to deliver the repair parts in person because the customer needed the parts to resume plant operations the next morning. Before the courier industry developed nationwide networks, a staffer once traveled by plane to hand-deliver products worth less than $100.

To keep up the "It's all about TIME" level of service, Misumi and its contract manufacturers had worked together over the past 40 years to refine operations.

Today, due to the advancement of EC businesses such as Amazon, a broad array of consumer products is ready for delivery the next day. In metropolitan areas, same-day delivery, even one-hour delivery, is now commonplace. Keep in mind, however, that none of these services involves *production*, and the products are generally stocked in a local warehouse for easy shipment.

In contrast, Misumi supplies micron-level make-to-order parts. Its business model and extraordinarily wide-ranging product lineup could not be replicated by a competitor overnight. Despite having that competitive edge, Saegusa sought to advance production kaizen efforts. What was he trying to improve?

- Misumi's short delivery times provide tremendous convenience for customers. Saegusa sought to refine the single-piece production method to close the cost gap with mass-produced products.
- Contract manufacturers had yet to introduce even the basics of production kaizen, leaving plenty of room for improvement.

Nuggets of gold were lying there, untapped.
- It was essential that cost competitiveness be enhanced to keep pace with competitors in China and the rest of Asia.
- The short delivery time model of shipping on the third day had not changed for nearly 20 years. A comprehensive review of the Create→Produce→Sell cycle should uncover rich grounds for innovation.

## Cutting Lead Times and Costs

Most importantly, *lead time reductions inherently generate cost savings*. Some find that hard to believe. So, how do they correlate?

Later in this story, you will see how young staffers from Suruga voiced open opposition, claiming, "obviously, single-piece production will lower productivity!" Pretty much anyone with a reflexive opposition to TPS says the same thing. But they are completely wrong.

Try and you will see. You won't know until you try. Whichever way you put it, that's the dilemma you face when implementing kaizen under TPS.

There are plenty of books that explain how to advance kaizen using TPS. But none spells out a theoretical system or formula for how much cost savings can be reaped by implementing those methods.

Each shop floor has its own diverse range of elements. The effect mechanisms (the sequence of effects resulting from a change) are dynamic. Many things interact and fluctuate in a complex fashion. Make a change, thinking it's for the better—if it backfires, change it back. Such is the trial and error that takes place.

"As a business leader, I am driven by logic," says Saegusa. "But I make an exception for TPS. Here, my approach is to first give it a try. The logic is hard to see, so opposition is inevitable. That's why it's impossible to successfully implement this method under weak leadership."

A lot of fundamental know-how is available if you take the time to study it. Stay faithful to the fundamentals and implement the kaizen methodology correctly. There is nothing more to it than that. But once you get through the pain of trial and error, you are rewarded with an epiphany: It's amazing! Once you get there, you will find that many who were dead-set against it are suddenly for it, just like that. And with no logical reason they can articulate.

It's not as if those who joined the *Yes* camp can explain their change of mind. They had no logical grounds for opposing it in the first place, and now they have no logical grounds for favoring it. Chalk it up to tangibility: They were influenced by a physical confirmation of the benefits.

With this logic in mind, Saegusa trained a laser focus on reducing lead times rather than cutting costs.

## Teaching the Contract Manufacturers

The first round of production kaizen activities started with the three contract manufacturers that signed on. Staff from the Production Kaizen Department joined Takagi on site to assist with the instruction.

But they made little progress.

Why? Many people think that kaizen is bottom-up in nature. That is not the case. It's not like QC activities, which emphasize bottom-up proposals. Kaizen is a top-down methodology.

## Riddle-solving for Business Leaders (33): Kaizen is Top-down

Managers who take a hands-off approach to production kaizen activities based on the belief it is a bottom-up methodology will not see significant benefits. The kaizen methodology was imported to the US and applied in many industries, gaining broader adoption than in Japan. That is because it meshed well with the top-down nature of American management structures.

Under a motivated manager, kaizen will generate results. Under an apathetic manager, even would-be quick wins end up as draws. Indifference then spreads through the rank and file, triggering a vicious cycle that worsens with time. The problem always lies at the top. Saegusa had seen it too many times.

As a professional kaizen instructor, Takagi was all too familiar with that brand of resistance. If the leader does not believe in the need for kaizen, that sentiment quickly bubbles to the surface. Ordinarily, Takagi would not waste his time in a place like that. But he pushed through this time, because he bought into Saegusa's dream of innovating the Misumi business model and taking it global.

Nevertheless, the three contract manufacturers were consuming a tremendous amount of time and effort. At this rate it might take a decade to roll out kaizen to all 20 of them. It would be a long slog.

Saegusa began to realize something else needed to be done to prevent the kaizen activities from getting mired in quicksand.

Then, late one night, he was enjoying a drink when he had an epiphany. The idea would shrink the gap between Misumi and its contract manufacturers overnight.

## Key Turning Points: Riddle-solving and Decision-making as a Business Leader

- Giving up on reforms would cause Misumi to lag behind the international megatrend in business innovations. Inevitably, that would isolate the business model, delivering a fatal blow to its contract manufacturers as well.
- Sales doubled to more than $1 billion four years after Saegusa took over. Its contract manufacturers were bumping up against the limits of their production capacity and considering plant expansions. That prompted the idea of an industrial park in Japan modeled after the Misumi Village in Shanghai. The contract manufacturers were spread across different parts of Eastern Japan. Housing their additional capacities all at one site in Western Japan will not only make sense strategically to shorten delivery time to the customers in the area, but also would make it easier for Misumi to guide the Kaizen activities among the contract manufacturers as a group. Misumi would ask Takagi to coordinate all Kaizen activities among the manufacturers at the site.
- Learnings gained inside the industrial park would be brought home to the mother plants, spreading the benefits of kaizen across all contract manufacturers.

It was an outlandish idea, but Saegusa was convinced that it was the right one. Unlike the village in China, this time Misumi would provide the land and building. Contract manufacturers could launch a new plant with nothing more than an investment in their own production equipment. An attractive offer.

Misumi estimated it would need to spend about $40 million on the land and building, not including the contract manufacturers' capital investments. It was an unprecedented investment for Misumi, and a departure from Mr. Taguchi's asset-light model. Meanwhile, the acquisition of Suruga was moving forward on a parallel track. Misumi was set to spend a tidy sum for its size.

Avoiding investment and eschewing the accumulation of capital assets would narrow the company's opportunities for growth. So, he shed outsourcing and the asset-light model, and drove the acquisition of production functions, investments in production innovations, forays overseas and reforms to business processes. He believed these steps essential to ensure the company wouldn't miss the international megatrend in business innovations.

The decision came at a critical juncture, setting the path forward for the next 10 to 20 years. So, Saegusa stuck to his guns. Instead of appeasing shareholders, he went with his entrepreneurial instincts and braced himself to answer to investors.

Eventually, his direction would reward shareholders. And, fortunately, the company was flush with cash. It could pay the $40 million easily with cash on hand.

## Kansai Production Park

Saegusa dubbed the new Misumi village the Kansai Production Park. Just over five years into his tenure, the 16,500-square-meter plant was completed on a plot of land near an existing distribution center.

Once the contract manufacturers had installed their equipment and started production, Takagi began hosting monthly kaizen seminars.

Initially, the contract manufacturers were reluctant to have their own production space openly visible to competitors. But as they shared success stories at the monthly seminars, the village residents grew more comfortable with each other. They worked together to advance kaizen activities, engaging in a friendly rivalry. From time to time, Saegusa would join the seminars to show his commitment as commander in chief.

However, the learnings from the Kansai Production Park were slow to be replicated in their mother plants. There were a few more screws to be turned to stimulate that activity.

## Production Kaizen at Suruga

Meanwhile, kaizen efforts at Suruga had not yet begun. Saegusa had instructed the Production Kaizen Department to steer clear of Suruga, at least for a while after the merger.

However, things eventually got started after Hamakawa resigned and Saegusa took over as president of Suruga.

Saegusa transferred two kaizen staffers to Suruga's plant in Shizuoka.

*Testimonial from A. Asai (Then age 36, a leader in die and mold component production at Suruga. He later became president of the die & mold manufacturing company.)*

*About a year after the merger, a wave of kaizen activities came rolling in. The initiatives were driven by two Misumi staffers from Tokyo who were reassigned to our plant in Shizuoka.*

*Looking back on it now, I see that the plant has risen to an entirely different level. But before kaizen started, our plant was a pitiful place, with mountains of work-in-progress piled up between processes. Machines were placed with no consideration for the flow of production. Defect rates were not posted. And productivity numbers were updated only once a month. There was no concept of lead time. The word didn't even exist here.*

*Nevertheless, we made it a hard-and-fast rule to meet Misumi's shipment deadlines every day. Production worked desperately to get products out on time by that evening. Satisfied just to accomplish that one thing, we thought we were doing top-notch work.*

*The kaizen activities began with the beginner's basic program of 5S. During round one, which took place over 10 weeks, we discarded 12 truckloads of unneeded worktables and racks.*

*Testimonial from S. Ota (Then age 26, part of the Suruga production kaizen team)*
    *I had worked at a plant overseas for a while. Returning to Japan, I was assigned to the kaizen team. That's when I first met Mr. Saegusa. I was told the team would target shorter lead times. I didn't think we needed such a thing.*
    *My job in the team was to change our manufacturing process. But the old way of doing things was ingrained in me. It might not be best, but at least it was better than this kaizen stuff, I thought. I did not like one bit the idea of someone coming from the outside and telling us to change things around.*
    *That reaction was my first resistance, and, in hindsight, it was a mistake.*

The testimonials above were shared by people reflecting back on kaizen activities a number of years after the benefits had started to materialize. They provide an honest account of their mindset at the time.

Saegusa had seen it before. Wherever you go, people who oppose kaizen or reforms pretty much all say the same thing. The consistency is almost comical.

Yet it is no laughing matter. This brand of resistance could push the reform effort into *Death Valley*. The reformer who under-estimates the resistance could be consumed by it. As I noted in Riddle-solving for Business Leaders (2): Battlefield Chaos, people often oppose reform out of prejudice, rather than a logical argument against its merits.

For example, the animosity directed at outsiders is the modern equivalent of Japan's old village mentality. Locals keep to themselves, never realizing how narrow their perspective is.

These modern-day villagers have no qualms about obstructing progress. They might even be officers or upper level managers with a weak sense of responsibility. Unaware of the damage done by their provincial narrow-mindedness or irresponsible remarks, they keep up their childish act until something wakes them up.

### Riddle-solving for Business Leaders (34): The Confident Resistance (Type C1)

The confident resistance (Type C1) has the ability to take action and actively spreads criticisms throughout the company. They do not recognize their actions are pressing leaders into a corner and causing harm by delaying reforms. Instead, they think of themselves as victims, having reform forced upon them. The extreme resistance (Type C2) presents even fiercer opposition and consciously seeks to break things. (For more on this, see Saegusa's previous work *Turnaround Task Force*, "Saegusa's Management Note 2: Behavior Patterns of Those Promoting and Those Resisting Reform.")

The resistance's greatest strength is similar to that of an opposition party in politics—they can criticize everything under the sun knowing they won't have to take responsibility for anything. They use that advantage to spread poison while at the office, or out for drinks, whenever they are outside of their bosses' line of sight.

But eventually word gets back to the reform leaders. The leaders are desperately trying to navigate a path across *Death Valley* at the same time they must overcome sabotage from the resistance. At Suruga, one staffer said, "If it can be done, why don't you do it yourself?" Right to the manager's face.

This is a reversal of roles. Managers should be telling their staffers what to do. But here, the tables were turned.

The historical roots of the kaizen philosophy trace back to Toyota. Today it has been applied effectively across the world. But the people involved in the exchange described above have no understanding of that, no global perspective, no significant knowledge of kaizen, and no clear reason for opposing it. Yet they refuse to follow orders. What's more, they cast off their own responsibilities and tell their superiors what to do. It's like an upside-down world.

A reform leader can feel humiliated being subjected to insolent comments by a young staffer who doesn't know what it takes to manage others. It's a gut-wrenching experience that saps your sense of conviction and leaves you feeling isolated. Saegusa knew all too well how agonizing it could be.

## Typical Resistance to Reforms

For four years after Saegusa had become CEO, Misumi grew at a rate of 19% per year, one of the highest growth rates among publicly traded companies in Japan.

The organization was getting larger and complex. International activities were expanding. Suruga's acquisition was adding complexity to management.

Saegusa was getting stretched too thin. He continued to recruit new talent and make organizational changes.

One such change was to turn over his responsibility as the president of Suruga to an executive he had hired a couple of years before. That allowed Saegusa to shift his focus to other equally important projects, mainly China and other international projects.

The greatest challenge faced by Suruga's new president was to roll out full-fledged kaizen activities there based on TPS. Once the basic 5S work was done, he brought in a group of consultants to Suruga, while instructor Takagi, who Saegusa hired, was still training the contract manufacturers.

Saegusa considered the move to introduce new instructors to Suruga at this early stage of Kaizen an odd approach to reform.

But he was willing to accept the decision, if that's what the new president thought best.

At that point in time, Suruga's people were still resistant to the kaizen activities.

### Testimonial from S. Ota

*Suruga's new president brought in a group of consultants, but I didn't like them. They seemed carefree. I figured they would leave before seeing things through to the end anyway.*

*I was convinced that these outsiders would not understand our manufacturing operations. And I was certain that migrating to the concept of the Toyota Production System (TPS) would erode productivity.*

### Testimonial from A. Asai

*The external consultants were ex-Toyota people and their goal was to improve production, but what they actually did was a lot of generating documents for meetings.*

*Mr. Saegusa came to Suruga after a one-year absence and attended the second report event held by these consultants. He listened quietly all day. We had no clue what he was thinking. After the consultants had left the meeting, he stood up and spoke for the first time that day.*

*What he said next shocked me.*

*"I listened all day today and gained a clear understanding of the true state of your kaizen activities," he said. "I am not the least bit convinced."*

*Suruga's president was sitting right in front of him. Unperturbed by that, Mr. Saegusa went on, "What in the world have you all been doing this past year?! I don't get it."*

*"Just paperwork and beautiful color slides. No smell of sweat. No smudges from machine oil. Only clean hands and no sign of brains on the production floor."*

*Of course, the consultants were fired. We later executed a redesigned approach under different leadership and dramatically improved results. Looking back on it now, that day's scolding from Mr. Saegusa was justified and was a turning point in our history. His comments made me realize that until that point, we had been spinning our wheels.*

## Riddle-solving for Business Leaders (35): Dealing with Resistance

When pursuing reform, plan on running up against people who resist and slack off. A reform leader needs to be prepared to meet resistance, communicate effectively with staff using proper logic and engage those with opposing mindsets. The leader needs to get fake managers to either rethink things or simply step aside.

Reforms at Suruga were not just bogged down: They were on the brink of *Death Valley*.

If you fall off, what would happen then? Misumi would surely lose an opportunity to strengthen itself. How many Japanese companies have gone down that path? That is one way reforms fail at Japanese companies with weak leadership.

### Resolving a Crisis

Production reform wasn't the only thing to hit a wall in Saegusa's reform programs at Misumi. Other high-risk projects such as the new FA strategy, logistics and IT reforms, as well as the new business launches overseas including China and other counties, each met at least one crisis.

In a crisis, first decide, "Is the current leader capable of fixing this?" If the answer is yes, you work with the leader to resolve the issue. If not, replace the leader with someone stronger. No hesitation. A business leader needs to accept that role.

Saegusa stuck to that approach even when a reform went off track. He avoided acting hastily. Instead, he spent time cultivating talent and cast about looking for a breakthrough.

So, how did he resolve the crisis in the production reform?

## Section 2:
# Resolve + Wisdom + Hard Work = Results

## A New Leader for Production Reforms

The reforms Saegusa implemented were not random shots from the hip. They were grounded in solid rationale, aimed at achieving comprehensive innovations to the Create→Produce→Sell cycle that would drive the company into a new era.

Failure in any one of the reform efforts would become a bottleneck, gumming up the whole operation. So, Saegusa was determined to achieve success, no matter how much time it took. He was pursuing a chain of diverse reforms that would culminate in nothing less than a wholesale transformation.

Saegusa's Management Note at the end of the previous chapter described the need for a capable leader to re-energize a reform effort and achieve a breakthrough. Who would that leader be? Who would emerge to steer the production reforms?

### Riddle-solving for Business Leaders (36): Build your Team from Top to Bottom

To create a dynamic business organization, appoint your strongest person at the top of the organization first, and then move downward from there. Here, sequence is key. It sounds natural, but in reality, it is often done the other way around. Managers who fill the lower tiers first will end up appointing a leader based on the level of the people who would be reporting to that leader. Instead, pick a desirable leader and let that leader propose an organizational design based on their own criteria.

Recall Y. Nishi. You first met him in Section 2 of Chapter 1. At age 37, he was the youngest corporate officer when Misumi decided to withdraw from its new business ventures. Saegusa had told him, "Life is short. Snooze now and you'll be dead before you know it."

The decision to withdraw from seven ventures left Nishi's business in place for the time being. Over the following two and a half years, Nishi was given latitude to pursue the business, but eventually it ran into further hardship.

The time has come, Saegusa decided then. Misumi had few promising management leaders, and Nishi was a rare talent. So Saegusa decided to bring him back to the core business of mechanical industrial components, which had begun to take off, creating a pressing need for someone of Nishi's abilities.

But it was a delicate issue. If Saegusa pushed too hard, Nishi might prefer to resign rather than desert his team to accept a post for himself in a more profitable unit.

But Nishi understood his situation. He attributed any management talent he had to the time and capital the company had invested in him. He felt deeply indebted to the company, as if his mission in his next post would be to recoup the losses generated by his business venture.

Nishi dutifully obeyed Saegusa's instruction to return to industrial mechanical components.

That was four years earlier. Since then, Nishi had served as general manager of the electronics division and executive corporate officer in charge of logistics and the e-commerce business. He had also been appointed to the board of directors.

## A Bold Personnel Decision

Saegusa called Nishi to his office. Now 43 years old, Nishi's hair had grayed, giving him a distinguished look.

"It's been four years since you came back to mechanical industrial components." Saegusa said, "Have you thought about your next step?"

Without waiting for an answer, he followed, "You should try Production. Anyway, think about it."

"Think about it? He has already decided for me," Nishi thought to himself. But what he said was, "Production? I have no experience there. It doesn't feel like a fit for my personality, either."

Saegusa replied, "Well, give it some thought. You may not see it now, but it would be an invaluable experience for you."

Misumi does not make personnel decisions unilaterally. Staff can decline reassignments.

Nishi wondered why he was thinking so conservatively when in the past he had boldly tackled new challenges.

Ultimately, he accepted the new position.

Saegusa promoted him to executive director and president of Suruga.

Nishi was shocked. Promotion to executive director in such a large company at the tender age of 43 came as a complete surprise.

Another bold personnel decision. What he would make of it was up to him.

## Casting Light on Problems

Nishi was prepared to be challenged in his new position. But from day one, he felt overwhelmed. Over his 20 years at the company, he had worked exclusively in the business units.

Manufacturing was an entirely different world. He didn't even understand the terminology they used in the factory. He was off to a rough start.

But Saegusa felt confident he would climb the learning curve quickly.

The three companies Saegusa had run in his 30s were all in different industries. Thereafter, as a turnaround specialist he was completely new to many of his clients' industries. Nevertheless, after about three months of feeling his way through the dark, he would eventually get to the point where he could give directions to the employees.

The same could be said about the events described in Chapter 1. From his first day at Misumi until he presented Misumi's Eight Weaknesses, some three months had elapsed. He made quick work of pinpointing what was troubling the company. Catch a whiff of something that stinks and sniff it out. Repeat.

Nishi was getting the same sort of experience.

### Riddle-solving for Business Leaders (37): Broadening Management Skills

Exposing management talent to fields where they have no experience gives them the opportunity to diversify their management skills. That broadens the applicability of those skills. Eventually, they resemble professional athletes who can make a contribution to any team from day one.

Nishi was quick to grasp new things and exhibited strong leadership, so he rapidly acclimated to his new environment. But the situation was serious. Suruga's production-kaizen efforts were on the cusp of *Death Valley*. Kaizen programs at contract manufacturers also stagnated due to a lack of enthusiasm among owners about Misumi's intervention in their manufacturing process. In

short, Nishi's predecessor had left nothing positive behind for
him to work with. Nishi was alone and wondering where to begin
with to fix the tangled situation.

From his bird's eye viewpoint, it appeared to Saegusa as if Nishi
was stuck in a maze. Time to swoop in and provide support.

Saegusa's decision about two years ago to take the position of
Suruga's president had turned out to be one of the wisest decisions he ever made. Although the situation was complex and
challenging, he just needed to figure out what precisely went
wrong in the last 12 months since he had moved on to other
responsibilities.

To help Nishi, Saegusa first visited the sites where kaizen activities were underway. It must be the most effective way to do
reconnaissance.

Adopting a hands-on approach, he quickly visited three
factories—Suruga and two contract manufacturers. He summarized
his observations and findings into a dense, nine-page report. What
an unprecedented phenomenon: the CEO of a public company
"reporting" to his subordinate.

The report was more guidance than it was findings. It was both
specific and practical, based on his observations of the shop floor.
Here are excerpts from the report.

A visit to a manufacturer's shop floor revealed that the KPIs the
Production Kaizen Department posts every month do not reflect
the reality on the ground, giving top management false peace of
mind. It's infuriating.

- The activities of the Production Kaizen Department have been
  spread too thin across too many contract manufacturers, with
  no tangible results to show for it anywhere.

- Worse, the production kaizen staff are too involved. The leaders and their teams from the contract manufacturers need to take the driver's seat.
- The computer systems approved to facilitate kaizen at Suruga are more of a hindrance than an asset. It's better to validate a new idea with pen and paper first. (See Chapter 7 for more.) Eliminate any software that inhibits improvement. Write off the premature investment as a sunk cost.
- Most importantly, no one has envisioned a *finish line* for the production kaizen activities. So, no one knows what steps will get us there. A reform without a goal will not endure.
- The Production Kaizen Department has neglected to address these issues. The team is brain dead and lacks planning acumen.

This is a true story. He actually said, "brain dead." Given the serious state of affairs, what measures did he think would effect a breakthrough?

> **Key Turning Points: Riddle-solving and Decision-making as a Business Leader**
> - The lack of controls was worse than expected. As CEO, he regretted being too hands-off. Left unaddressed, the reforms would surely die.
> - It's important to visualize the *finish line* of reforms. One of the plants should be developed into a *model plant* so that its success story can be shared with the others.
> - Pull in the entire staff, which is currently dispersed across multiple locations of Suruga and contract manufacturers, and have them concentrate on one or two plants. Have the staff reside full-time at that plant and work on getting to the finish line.

The report included solutions and was shared only with Nishi and a limited number of executives. It would function as "Sheet 1" (a Brutally Honest Reflection) to escape *Death Valley*.

Nishi then shared it with his team. It helped clarify the situation they were in. It was also reassuring, in that the report freed them of many constraints. (See Riddle-solving for Business Leaders 29.) They felt free to act without being constrained by legacy decisions.

## The Real Reform Begins

Nishi was joined by two new lieutenants as replacements for the two who had left. One was O. Hoshikawa, who had experience in kaizen activities at an automotive parts maker. The other was Yoji Natsui, who had previously worked at an electronics manufacturer.

*Testimonial from O. Hoshikawa (Then age 40. Later became representative corporate officer for the production platform.)*
*The shop floor was in poor shape when I arrived. I despaired, "Where in the world have they sent me?"*

*Moreover, most of the manufacturing methods were different from those at my previous employer, where we used mass production. Suruga produced a wide variety of products in small quantities. And production volumes changed every day. Shortening production lead times and improving productivity (cutting costs) seem to conflict with each other.*

*I felt like I had been dropped into a fast-flowing river and told to change the current, but the most I could do was keep my head above water.*

*That's about when we got Mr. Saegusa's report. To have my organization called brain dead was a shock, even though the comment was not directed at me personally. After all, I was still new there.*

*At the same time, it was very encouraging to know that he understood the situation on the ground. It was like being rescued from that river.*

*As suggested by the CEO, we decided to focus on the two testing grounds. One was subsidiary, SP Parts. I implanted a production kaizen staffer there.*

*The results confirmed our hypotheses. We found some approaches that work for producing a large variety of products in small quantities as well as in mass-production settings. The successes we had in developing production models boosted our confidence.*

Meanwhile, progress was elusive at the other testing ground, Suruga. There, the resistance continued.

Saegusa knew from past experience that the resistance was not merely a collection of bit players—they were the principal culprits. And they shared just as much blame for delaying reforms as the ineffective leaders.

So, how would things play out at Suruga?

### Testimonial from K. Yamasawa (Then age 41, production kaizen leader)

*I couldn't take Takagi's teachings seriously. I would prepare some things in the days leading up to his visits, but that was it, really. If he reprimanded me, I didn't let it bother me.*

*But then things changed. After Takagi's third study session, we gathered to discuss the experience. In a dead-serious tone of voice, Nishi said, "Let's speak openly. Tell me how you really feel. If you all don't start taking the initiative, this reform effort will go nowhere. Do you realize you are the ones who will decide its fate?"*

*The leaders present were shaken by Nishi's grave expression and tense tone. We finally understood we were the ones who were in the driver's seat.*

*Belatedly, I realized my attitude had been wrong all along.*

*The incident triggered a major change in our approach.*

Do you remember S. Ota? He was the leader in Section 1 of this chapter who was convinced that shorter delivery times were unnecessary and that Suruga's way of doing things was fine; he disliked taking instruction from outsiders. Well, he continued to resist.

That one talk from Nishi was not enough to win him over. So, it would take another episode.

***Testimonial from S. Ota (Age 30. Kaizen leader, three and a half years after his appearance in Section 1 of this chapter)***
*One day, Nishi, Takagi and Hoshikawa invited me to dinner. It was my first dinner with my three bosses. I felt a bit anxious about what was going to happen.*

*At dinner, Nishi told me he knew I had not been fully in favor of kaizen. He encouraged me to speak up. So, I told them the kaizen methodologies made no sense and that our legacy methods worked well enough. Nishi's talk at the previous meeting had made me a little more positive about things, but deep down I was still unconvinced.*

*It made for a tense dinner. To make the story short, after a while, Nishi spoke bluntly.*

*"For nearly three years, you have not given these new methods a fair shake. If you had given them a real try and seen it through to the end by now, we would already know whether the methods are good or bad.*

*"Mr. Saegusa appointed you, hoping you would work out. The company bet on you. But a long time has passed, and we are still only arguing. Without your fully committed effort, we can't tell whether these methods could be effective or not. You're the one standing in the way."*

*It hit me like a powerful blow.*

*I realized I was the problem. I bowed my head in shame.*

*A few more words from Nishi made me realize that I derive personal satisfaction from criticizing others and the company, but I was the one who deserved criticism.*

*It became clear to me that I was not leading anything but holding back the reform effort of the entire company.*

## A Leader's Ability to Sever Ties

If anyone else would have joined that dinner talk, it would have been the CEO. That's how serious the problem had become.

Saegusa felt that the real problem was a matter of innovative spirit at Suruga. No one up to that point had been able to sever ties with the salaryman attitude of not taking responsibility on their own but blaming others, especially management.

Notice that Ota did not change his attitude until the top executive got close enough for him to feel the heat. Over just one dinner, he suddenly changed. He had a "revelation" and "reflected" on his behavior.

That can only mean one thing: Not enough had been done by management to explain the effects of his conduct. No one applied the needed pressure to get him to think more deeply about it. Weak leadership. It is sad to admit, but even senior managers may have been infected by the salaryman syndrome, more interested in reducing personal risks. Until Nishi came onto the scene.

What if Nishi's last attempt to bring Ota around failed, and Ota refused to change? What would have happened then?

Imagine how this situation sounds to American readers. Surely, they would be astounded by the kid-gloves treatment that pervades Japanese companies.

In the US, resistance leaders like Asai or Ota would have been fired long ago. The reform program would have moved forward without a single look back. That's the natural speed for decisive American managers.

In a sense, that dinner talk was the final crossroads. Had the outcome been different, Saegusa and Nishi might have pursued the other path—remove the cancer.

At this point, Saegusa and Nishi were on the same page about the next step.

Before we go on, let's consider what might have happened if the resisters were fired on the spot. In their wake, another 20 or more key people might have left, too. Such a departure en masse would have eroded the stability of the Suruga business model, based on shipping all orders by 5 pm on the day of order receipt. Since Suruga was Misumi's largest contract manufacturer, the business model of Misumi as a whole might collapse. Damage in the marketplace would be enormous.

But what if the risks were not so high? Do you think the two individuals resisting reforms should have been dismissed right away?

No, according to both Saegusa and Nishi.

How many times had Saegusa seen or heard of post-merger integration efforts in the US that failed due to hasty action? Often, they fail to retain capable talent, but more critically, their replacements are worse and eventually get fired.

Delays like this would have been impermissible if Saegusa was still working as a turnaround specialist today. Nissan Motors changed in two years. K. Kuroiwa in Saegusa's book *Turnaround Task Force* transformed Komatsu's industrial machinery business in two years. K. Inamori, the legendary founder of the ceramics and electronics maker Kyocera, took two years to turn around Japan Airlines after taking the helm at the bankrupt airliner. Put another way, if you don't go at it with the intention of wrapping it up in two years, you won't be able to change anything in ten.

However, recall that when Saegusa came to Misumi, he declared that he intentionally took a long-term perspective, a departure from the short, decisive battles he had fought as a turnaround specialist.

So, what did Saegusa do with members of the resistance like Asai and Ota?

Nothing beyond the support he provided Nishi when he swooped in to survey the situation at Suruga. He appointed Nishi president of Suruga. Nishi in turn hired two new experienced kaizen managers from outside. Takagi was brought in to be Suruga's sole kaizen instructor. Saegusa toured three factories under kaizen programs and issued a diagnosis and ideas about how to redirect the kaizen activities. The message was, "Withdraw all the forces from the field and have them focus on building two success stories. Show everyone involved what is the goal."

He gave full authority to Nishi and took his leave.

If possible, he wanted to avoid getting directly involved in the situation at Suruga, even if the efforts there hit a wall. Similarly, as you will see in the following chapter, when reforms to the customer centers ran aground, he picked another leader and awaited the results instead of inserting himself.

A CEO cannot, and should not, be a micromanager. You have to wait and see if the leadership you put in place will live up to your expectations, how they overcome obstacles and whether they will acquire true managerial capabilities. It takes patience to cultivate talent.

Saegusa had his hopes set on Nishi.

And Nishi had grit. He had mastered the basics, engaged others easily and spoke reasonably. He was able to sever ties with the old ways in his own style, and he approached tasks with surprising intensity, earnestness, resolve and passion. Nishi's predecessors were unable to do that; they were inept leaders—mere salarymen.

Nishi said himself that he was new to production, but he got the reforms moving in only three months. Substantial change was afoot.

## Change Paves the Way for Leaps Forward

That was how the production reforms finally got on track.

The organization was beefed up. The work of developing *finish-line* models at the two testing grounds advanced rapidly.

### Testimonial from D. Shibayama (Then age 37 and manager in the Production Kaizen Department.)

*I had volunteered to relocate to the US as a director in the North American Division in Chicago. At 9 pm one day, I received a call from Nishi. To my surprise, he said he would cancel my transfer and he wanted me to be a leader who could achieve a breakthrough on production reforms.*

*I was sad to miss the chance to go to North America, but I had no complaints. It was an honor to be picked by top management for the most difficult task the company faced then. Of the two sites chosen for model development, I was assigned to be a leader at SP Parts. I leased an apartment there and started a routine of being the first to show up at the plant, earlier than any staffers and workers, each morning. Day and night, I practically lived there.*

Nishi issued Shibayama a difficult mission. "Take a back seat. The local plant leaders need to drive this." The instruction reflected the issues experienced at Suruga.

Shibayama kicked things off at SP Parts by soliciting the opinions of local staffers about the kaizen program. Things got off to a rough start.

"Kaizen work will reduce overtime. That means we'll make less money. I'm not for that," the workers in this rural area complained.

Fortunately, however, the production lines were relatively simple. A step-by-step implementation of the kaizen methods quickly produced results.

*Testimonial from Shibayama (continued)*

*Mr. Saegusa, Nishi and Hoshikawa came for their first on-site review about two months after I started at SP Parts.*

*It was no simple tour. Misumi's business is based on a wide variety of products in small volumes, where order volumes swing wildly from day to day. But our promised delivery times must be kept. Top management joined us in concrete discussions aimed at developing new concepts.*

*A helpful reference for me was the metaphor of the tragedy of the chairmaker (see below), which I learned about in a strategy training session at work. It is important that people feel fulfilled by the work they do.*

## Riddle-solving for Business Leaders (38): The Tragedy of the Chairmaker

Artisans who handcraft entire chairs themselves and sell directly to the customer are sensitive to customer satisfaction. So, they strive to hone their skills and designs. Introduce a division of labor, however, and you may end up with one worker who spends the entire day making only chair legs. The legs must fit the other parts properly, so that makes standardization and quality standards important. In that environment, workers must operate like machines. That takes the fun out of building chairs. The workers also become desensitized to customer dissatisfaction. They place more focus on their paychecks. (Based on Moshe F. Rubinstein and Iris R. Firstenberg, *The Minding Organization.*)

*Testimonial from Shibayama (continued)*

*The kaizen meeting took place in a corner of a large cafeteria with high ceilings. But Mr. Saegusa suggested, "the meetings should be held in a smaller room. A tighter space will generate more enthusiasm."*

*We gave it a try. Some of the quieter leaders began to voice their opinion more freely. Sometimes that led to active debate.*

*Leaders from other processes came to see the test line. Positive word of mouth started to spread through the organization.*

Unexpectedly, by focusing on the two sites, the kaizen staff became the conduit for a rivalry between the test lines at SP Parts and Suruga. Fortunately, Ota from Suruga had really changed his outlook and actions. To help confirm the test results of the process kaizen drive, he even took on the role of *whirligig beetle*. That is the person who hustles about the plant delivering parts from one process to another, like a beetle skipping across the surface of a body of water.

It takes time and capital to change equipment layouts. So, first you connect the processes manually to check for gains in lead time or productivity.

Ota's pedometer indicated he was walking more than 10 miles a day. By the end of the day, he could barely stand. He slimmed down, too. The passion he put into his whirligig beetle role inspired other skeptics to cooperate, kick-starting a virtuous spiral throughout the company.

"The tempo of kaizen reforms picked up dramatically. I was surprised that the organization changed so much just because I adjusted my attitude. For three years, I didn't appreciate my own importance," Ota reflected later.

The two production-model testing grounds achieved tremendous progress. In about nine months, they had significantly reduced production lead times and costs.

There was still much to be done, but the production reforms that had stagnated for three years finally got to the point where the *finish line was visible*. Wonderful progress.

The kaizen teams residing in the plants worked together enthusiastically with the local plant staffers. They had delivered on Saegusa's objective in limiting the activities to two sites for the time being. After all, haste makes waste.

## A Compass Guiding Reforms

The Production Kaizen Department that had been called brain dead only nine months ago developed into an organization exhibiting intellect, planning and effective oversight functions, thanks to the coordinated efforts of Hoshikawa and Natsui. The two vice-general managers created work products including Basic Concepts of Kaizen and a Kaizen Manual.

The practical manuals would serve as a guide in the roll-out of the kaizen techniques to other contract manufacturers and defined flexible manufacturing.

But at this point, the real kaizen activities were just beginning.

The next step was to implant the production models across the rest of Suruga and the contract manufacturers. That would impact nearly 40 lines in all—an ambitious undertaking. Later, the production models would be introduced to Suruga's overseas plants and taught to the local staff.

By creating a *finish line* for themselves, the production kaizen staff demonstrated that it had grasped the goals and methods for kaizen, as well as concrete techniques.

Each of the contract manufacturers involved had unique processes and methods, but the principles of kaizen would apply to one and all. It was simply a matter of fine-tuning them to fit the specific workplace.

While Misumi's team was focused on the two testing grounds, Takagi continued to teach at the contract manufacturers, visiting the Kansai Production Park every month.

Now, the time had come to deploy the kaizen production staffers to plants across the country again. Their job would be to help advance kaizen efforts under Takagi's direction.

## Calling an Owners' Meeting

As described in Riddle-solving for Business Leaders (32): The Benefits of Improving Delivery Times, the project to shorten delivery times would not deliver benefits to the customer unless the kaizen initiatives were adopted by all major contract manufacturers. Nevertheless, there were still some skeptics. That problem needed to be addressed. Otherwise, the project would surely hit another wall.

So, Saegusa assembled the owners from the strategic alliance to report the results Misumi had achieved and the path forward. Initially, the meetings would take place on a monthly basis. Misumi and the others would share progress reports on their kaizen activities with all of the owners.

At around the same time, an initiative to distribute a mininewspaper to report on kaizen status reports and other initiatives began.

The purpose of the initiatives was clear to all. Owners experiencing delays would be made aware of that fact and encouraged to make progress. The measures reflected an awareness of the reality that a delay in one place would render the kaizen achievements elsewhere meaningless.

Owners with a strong independent streak would not be enthused about the meetings.

Takagi was making headway with his training at the Kansai Production Park. But the kaizen benefits remained within the park. There was little momentum to carry the initiatives back to the mother plants. This problem needed to be resolved in one fell swoop.

The first owners' meeting was held on June 1 that year. A full eight years had passed since Saegusa became CEO. About six years had elapsed since the Production Kaizen Department was established. Misumi and Suruga had merged more than five years earlier. And Nishi had become president of Suruga 20 months before.

At the meeting, Misumi shared its expertise in production kaizen with the contract manufacturers. Ordinarily, that kind of information would be confidential. The handouts included charts, conceptual diagrams and concrete data to help explain the kaizen methodologies and the benefits seen at the two production-model sites.

The owners in attendance were shown results and statistics with unprecedented clarity. The facts were backed up with logical explanations, leaving no room to argue.

That did not necessarily mean everyone there immediately bought into the idea of production kaizen. Surely, there would be some skeptical holdouts.

After the day's agenda was complete, Saegusa rose to speak.

- Asian competitors have emerged, beating us on price and cost. I want to you to be aware of how tough things are, since you are not directly exposed to the harshness of the marketplace.
- Japan is losing its edge in manufacturing prowess as other parts of the world close the gap.
- Historically, Misumi and our contract manufacturers have acted like quarreling siblings. But since I became CEO, I have worked to forge more harmonious relationships.
- I can share with you now that the true purpose of the Kansai Production Park was not simply to add capacity in Western Japan. It was also intended to spread production kaizen methodologies to all contract manufacturers in the park. That's why we invested $40 million to build it.
- The international megatrend in business innovations is a fight to innovate the entire Create→Produce→Sell cycle. We need

to respond by pursuing a seamless time-based strategy, as represented by our catchphrase, "It's all about TIME."
- Finally, those who fall behind in this project will also fail to keep up with global competition.

Silence fell across the room as the owners averted their gaze. Some looked somber. It was hard to tell if they took his words as encouragement, or as a threat. That was up to them. Just as long as they moved forward.

Even the people from Misumi kept quiet, their eyes fixed on the floor. Something may have struck a chord with them. Some may have intuitively understood that his words were the culmination of a long battle that had unfolded since he was made CEO, marking a historic change in the balance of power between Misumi and its contract manufacturers.

## Gaining the Independence to Pursue a Dynamic Strategy

When Saegusa first became CEO, Misumi relied completely on its contract manufacturers for all production activities. To get anything done, it had to negotiate with each supplier individually. For their part, the contract manufacturers felt they were the ones with expertise in manufacturing and were thus disinclined to follow Misumi's guidance. There was truth to that: Neither the executives nor the staffers at Misumi knew the first thing about manufacturing.

If Misumi were to limit its future strategy to the domestic market, the business model would eventually lose its competitive edge. Unable to achieve growth, the company would start to fade away. It needed to evolve production to better position itself for its next stage of growth. Otherwise, it would not be able to devise a dynamic strategy, nor would it be possible to keep pace with the changes issuing forth from the US.

Don't forget that, for Misumi, the contract manufacturers were, and would continue to be, important strategic partners. However, eight years after bumping up against its limitations during a foray into China, Misumi had finally risen to the level where it could exercise autonomy and independence across the entire cycle of Create→Produce→Sell.

People were undergoing a transformation—from amateurs who devoted little thought to production matters into a group of people who put production front and center in their minds.

*Testimonial from O. Hoshikawa (Age 42. Promoted to general manager of Production Kaizen Department.)*
*Production-model development at the two testing grounds progressed nicely, generating the shorter production lead times we had hoped to see. At the same time, there were productivity improvements and clear cost savings.*
*There were many lessons there for a reform leader, including the following universal points.*
- *Take a hands-on approach as needed, intervening directly and energetically to convey the reform concept to the rank and file.*
- *Clarify where responsibility lies within the organization. Make the organization small enough to be manageable and for the individuals who reside within it to move with agility.*
- *Quickly free people from constraints that inhibit their thoughts and actions.*
- *Ensure that triggers are in place to visualize results. For example, quantify KPI metrics on progress, reward effort, and build in early wins.*

*Testimonial from Y. Nishi (Age 45. Executive director and president of Suruga. Then, after serving as senior executive director, would succeed Saegusa as CEO of Misumi Group Inc.)*
*About two years after I became president of Suruga, we made a sweeping change in our reform program. Instead of adopting the popular Toyota Production System model, we refined a flexible manufacturing*

*system that better fit our business characteristics. It gave us a shot of confidence.*

*Once you get tangible results, it automatically boosts the motivation and satisfaction of everyone involved.*

*I was assigned to lead production, where I had no prior experience. We restarted the languishing production kaizen project that, in two years, started benefiting our strategy significantly. Now, we are actively implementing kaizen activities in our overseas plants, too.*

*The experience reminded me of the sense of fulfillment and enthusiasm I had in the past when we were pursuing new business ventures. I haven't felt like this in 10 years.*

*Plus, I gained confidence in my ability to manage a manufacturing business. Compared to 10 years ago, or even 2 years ago when I first assumed this role, my management abilities have improved a lot.*

## Standard Second-day Shipments: Launching a New Time-based Strategy

Nishi later rolled out the production kaizen methods to plants overseas. Leveraging the benefits, he deployed business-model innovations in rapid succession as new time-based strategies.

That is how the production functions of Misumi's Create→ Produce→Sell cycle went from nearly nothing in Saegusa's early days at the company to an important factor supporting its global network.

Under the business model in Japan, Misumi shipped within *three* days for standard orders. That was shortened to *two* days for standard orders by the time this book was published, thanks to nearly 10 years of production kaizen efforts. Can you imagine how much innovation and hard work went into cutting out that one day? Remember, order just one of the 80,000,000,000,000,000,000,000, or 80 sextillion ($10^{21}$) different micron-level precision components, and it produces and ships within two days. No minimum quantity requirements.

Misumi's ability to drive kaizen reforms continued to improve. The activities have transcended conventional production kaizen efforts, and now target advanced automation and fundamental reforms to the manufacturing methods themselves. The benefits are delivered to customers around the world through the company's global footprint.

Saegusa reflected on the fruits of the production strategy he had pursued. The sense of achievement was on another level entirely from what Kanta Kuroiwa experienced at Komatsu, where he turned around the business in a shorter span of two years, as introduced in Saegusa's book *Turnaround Task Force*. After more than 10 years, Misumi had been transformed, and was positioned for a new stage of growth.

Saegusa reveled in a quiet joy and sense of achievement that could only be felt by a CEO who has spent a decade directing a complete transformation.

## SAEGUSA'S MANAGEMENT NOTE 8
# THE FOUR FORCES DRIVING A PASSIONATE ORGANIZATION

## A Universal Framework

The riddle-solving episodes described in this book are a mostly faithful account of true events. The happenings, the timeframes and the sequence in which problems arose are recounted accurately. In addressing those issues, I relied on a framework for designing passionate organizations that I developed as a turnaround specialist. I also put the framework to use in the turnaround case at Komatsu, the second largest construction machinery company next to Caterpillar, as depicted in *Turnaround Task Force*.

Komatsu was a traditional Japanese company. In contrast, Misumi is a growing company with young, up-and-coming people. But a universal framework was applicable to both companies. The factors that threatened the businesses were startlingly similar.

The protagonist of *Turnaround Task Force*, Kanta Kuroiwa, assembled a task force of talented young staffers and drafted a "Sheet 1" (a Brutally Honest Reflection) so convincing that it left no room for argument. At Misumi, I took action before the reform activities began and drafted my own "Sheet 1". Consider the effect on the audience in both cases. The initial confrontation with the evidence caused them to question their assumptions. As more corroborating facts mounted, their conventional values were shaken to the core. You need to *shake their values* to bring people around to a new direction with conviction.

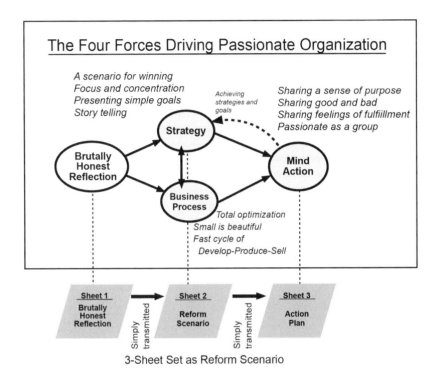

3-Sheet Set as Reform Scenario

At first glance, the framework for designing a passionate organization appears to be a simple chart. All executives at Misumi share the framework for designing a business plan. It explains the six driving forces behind what energizes a business organization. I will describe four of them here.

In a passionate organization, the leader forms a simple strategy and presents it to the team. At the same time, solid business processes have been built. With strong strategy and processes, the organization remains energized as strategy permeates the team's mindset and actions. (See the arrows presented in the chart.)

1. Strategy
   Throughout my career, I have experimented with a variety of methods for communicating a strategic story from top management down to the rank and file.

The key elements of a winning strategy are narrowing focus and concentration, presenting simple goals, and having a narrative. No matter how complex the situation, the Solid Main Story (starting from Brutally Honest Reflection and leading to Strategy in the graph) must be simple to inspire passion. (For more on this, see Saegusa's Management Note 6.) A leader must communicate it enthusiastically and take a hands-on approach to breathe life into the strategy. As that strategy comes to life, it elevates the Mind and Action of all staffers involved.

2. Business Process

Inside the company, there is a flow that connects the functions of Create→Produce→Sell (The Basic Cycle of Business). Products and services follow that flow for delivery to the customer. Additionally, there is a cycle originating from the customer that feeds market demands back to the business. When those demands are reflected in upcoming product developments and service improvements, and the company delivers those solutions to the customer, the customer is happy.

But you can be sure that more demands will follow. So, the cycle continues to turn, as units within the company pass on work, from one to the next. Business processes are workflows, which encompass operational flows, internal ties and internal control systems, among others.

To innovate the Business Process, you also need to start from a Brutally Honest Reflection and then advance to Business Process in the graph. It would also be a part of the Solid Main Story and must be simple (in combination with Strategy) to inspire passion among those involved in the business process. Companies with strong business processes pass off work to each other efficiently. At weak companies, the cycle cadence is slowed by stagnation and disruptions at various points in the cycle. A strong organization:

- optimizes the entire cycle (not just isolated parts of it) in response to customer or competitor actions; and
- speeds up the cycle cadence and enhances competitiveness by

dismantling function-based divisions and re-designing the organization to house all Create→Produce→Sell functions under one roof.

These organizations are smaller than the business units which we commonly find in large corporations, particularly in traditional large Japanese companies today. I like to say, "Small is Beautiful." After reforms, a well-designed organization will have these characteristics:

- The people working there feel closer to the customer than before.
- As in small businesses, people feel a sense of ownership over the business as a whole.
- The sense of ownership increases sensitivity to external competitive forces and the profitability of the business.

Organizational design reforms need to be well-conceived to generate these effects.

3. Mind and Action

Here, Mind and Action refers to the people who, by sharing the Solid Main Story, feel positive about the change and connected with one another through a sense of co-existence that molds them into a cohesive group. They are mindful of the customers and the competition. Based on this mindset, the group is able to take action through teamwork and execute the reforms faster.

An organization designed to have a clear strategic story and quick business processes will show tremendous change as the strategy and processes permeate through the rank and file.

- People share a sense of purpose.
- People experience joys and pains in common.
- People derive a sense of fulfillment from working together to execute the strategy.
- As a result, they become a passionate organization.

As these reforms progress, they generate the dramatic change seen in the Komatsu case described in *Turnaround*

*Task Force.* The team's vitality is enhanced, and the organization achieves a steep increase in competitiveness.

4. Brutally Honest Reflection

   Additionally, the fourth driving force, Brutally Honest Reflection, is shown on the far left of the chart. In fact, it is not a mere addition but a critical step to make a "Sheet 1". In order to clearly build the Solid Main Story, you would always need to go back to a Brutally Honest Reflection.

   That reflection must be rooted in dispassionate logic, as described in Chapter 1, and that logic needs to resonate with people.

   Planning for any reform or strategy begins with a clear "Sheet 1" as shown on the chart. It will decide the success or failure of the overall reform or strategy.

   Once that simplified logic has been drafted into a "Sheet 1", it is carried over to "Sheet 2" and "Sheet 3" (as described in detail in Saegusa's Management Note 2: Riddle-solving Makes or Breaks a Business Leader). Doing so accelerates the execution of solutions in an organization. Companies unable to do that spin their wheels, lack a unified direction and waste time chasing reforms that may elude them in the end.

   Since creating this framework for designing passionate organizations, I call it to mind almost every day. I compare it to the approaches I am considering at the moment, and check for inconsistencies.

   But even veteran executives don't know where *Death Valley* may be hiding or what form it may take when it rears its ugly head. What struggles lay around the corner at Misumi?

# Chapter 7

# Reforming Operations in a Battle Against Time

Misumi reformed its customer centers so that 145 staffers could accomplish the work of 600. This chapter looks at the steps it took to implement reforms in the operational department, and the sweat, tears and perseverance they required.

## Innovating the Business Model With a Chain of Reforms
### (Competing Against the International Megatrend)

Growth Acceleration

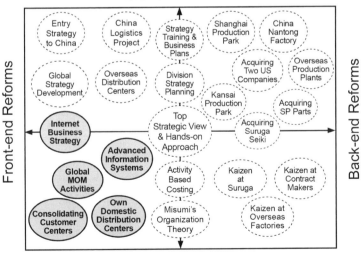

Increasing Quality and Efficiency

## Section 1:
# Choosing the Wrong Concept

### Ailing Operation Chains

Saegusa's list of Misumi's Eight Weaknesses, which he presented before becoming CEO, started with the sales organization and customer centers. Reforming the customer centers was a high priority, as was the launch of the China business (Chapter 4). He called them the "two big, risky projects."

The customer center reforms ran into a series of difficulties. The third time was the charm, however—they finally succeeded after two stumbles. This chapter provides an unflinching account of the reform campaign—both the embarrassing mishaps and the personal growth.

The customer lies at the start and end points of a company's business cycles, and many companies are plagued with problems somewhere along that process. Typically, the chain of operations includes the customer, order intake, internal processing, shipment, delivery, the customer again, and receivables collection.

Consider the low-profile B2B products that Misumi sells. The industrial mechanical components industry typically employs traditional channels encompassing tier-one and tier-two distributors. Long ago, however, Misumi introduced a groundbreaking business model. Not only did it circumvent conventional distributors, it also eliminated the need for a sales force of its own, as all orders from the customer came directly into the customer centers. That was true then, when sales were not more than $500 million, and it remains true today, even as sales exceed $3 billion now. That is why Misumi is seen within the industry as having revolutionized distribution.

The company's customer centers used to receive 80% of orders by facsimile. Today, more than 80% are online. Problems that automated systems cannot resolve are escalated to human operators, who contact the customer by email, phone or fax. The customer centers are the largest customer contact point and are positioned on the front line of sales at Misumi.

Saegusa visited two of these customer centers before he decided to accept the CEO role, and four more thereafter. The visits gave him insight into issues that were imperceptible from his seat at headquarters.

### Riddle-solving for Business Leaders (39): Inconsistencies Surface in Sales

When response to the competition or the customer has broken down, headquarters is often unaware of the incongruities that may lie just underneath the surface at sales contact points. Executive officers must transcend organizational barriers and get out onto the front lines, where the customer contact points are, to uncover the crossed wires and debug the affected business processes.

When Saegusa presented Misumi's Eight Weaknesses, the company was operating 13 customer centers spread across Japan. It seemed to be an outdated concept from the days when long distance calls were expensive and local services on a personal basis were considered important.

Apart from the Tokyo and Osaka centers, they were small in scale. Moreover, outsourcing had delegated the operators' work of customer interaction to part-timers placed there by staffing agencies. There were only one or two Misumi personnel at each center.

*Testimonial from Y. Goto (Then, age 35. Head of Customer Center B. Later, she was appointed by Saegusa to a reform team in Tokyo headquarters.)*

Yes, Mr. Saegusa did visit our customer center while he was still an outside director. I was a bit surprised by the questions he asked. It suggested his familiarity with operations.

"You must have a lot of turnover if you are relying on temporary staffers."

"That's true," I answered. "Half of the operators here today are still in their first year, and half of those have only been on the job for four months."

Mr. Saegusa said, "Wow. So, even if you are fully staffed by budget, they may not necessarily be effective."

"That's right. It takes about a year for a new operator to learn the ropes. The new hires are trained by veterans but often quit soon after they've completed training, meaning all that work goes to waste. I spend a lot of time interviewing candidates throughout the year," I lamented.

Mr. Saegusa also talked to the staffing agency's supervisor on the floor. Then he came back and told me, "That supervisor said the operators learn their work through on-the-job training."

We use the expression often ourselves, so at first, I didn't see what the problem was. Then he said, "Many Japanese companies use 'on-the-job training' as code for doing nothing." It felt as if he had seen right through us.

**Testimonial from H. Yamada (Then age 34. Head of Customer Center C. She would also later move to the reform team in Tokyo.)**

Mr. Saegusa visited our customer center after he became CEO.

Opportunities for women promoted to managerial positions are still limited in other large Japanese companies, and therefore I enjoy this work at Misumi.

At the time, we had seven catalogs, each over 1,000 pages. With 2 million products, no one could remember them all. [Misumi now sells 24 million products as of the publication of this English edition.]

*"If you split the work by product division, the operator only needs to learn one or two catalogs," he said. "Wouldn't that make things easier?"*

*"No, specialization hasn't worked for us," I responded. "We don't have many operators here, and if someone leaves, we lose that person's expertise in a specific area."*

*"So, you mean, each operator covers all products, and interacts with all of our business teams at the Tokyo Headquarters," he said. "In other words, people in each business team in Tokyo potentially interact with all operators in all 13 locations nationwide?"*

*"Yes, that's how it works."*

*"An organization like that doesn't cultivate teamwork," he said. "There must be lots of blame cast both ways where your work intersects."*

Spot on. Our interactions with the business teams were often contentious.

People from the business teams responded quickly for things important to them. Otherwise, they acted as if it was someone else's problem. But we are the ones left to face the customer's fury.

*"You've been doing this for seven years?" Mr. Saegusa asked me, smiling. "No plans to quit?"*

If I quit, that would be the end of it. I complain, but I actually like working here. The constant change driven by growth in the business and the organizations keeps things lively. Getting yelled at by a customer is deflating, but many of them appreciate our hard work. You could call a lot of them fans of Misumi.

## A Double-loss Structure: Costly Outsourcing

Two customer center visits gave Saegusa a feel for the stress points and organizational fatigue. Surely, he thought, all of the centers must suffer from the same ailments.

Kanta Kuroiwa, the protagonist of Saegusa's book, *Turnaround Task Force,* faced similar issues at Komatsu. Disconnects between the business teams and the customer centers severed the cycle of Create→Produce→Sell, which should be the source of the company's competitiveness.

While some viewed outsourcing as progressive, Saegusa realized it was actually causing serious damage. Misumi did not have its own staff positioned on the front lines of sales, the key place to capture the pain points and needs of the customer. That work had been left up to vendors and temporary staffers.

### Riddle-solving for Business Leaders (40): Excessive Outsourcing

Too much reliance on outsourcing might negatively impact internal functions and dull a company's innovative senses. In turn, the company loses the ability to change strategy as it sees fit, leaving its strategies vulnerable to obsolescence, unless the outsourcing partner you have chosen has enough sophistication and resources to deploy advanced technologies.

The purpose of outsourcing is to cut costs, of course. But at Misumi, outsourcing was pushing costs higher. That was Saegusa's important realization.

Misumi products are technologically difficult to produce. Many temporary staffers started to work at Misumi assuming that the products they would handle were like any other simple consumer product. These people would become quickly overwhelmed by the complexity of the job and soon quit. This was the first clue. Simply adding people to cover for high turnover would most certainly drive up costs.

New hires take time to master the work. So, their performance is not commensurate with their pay. In addition, veteran leaders have to spend considerable time teaching new hires and interviewing candidates, so they too are effectively underperforming vis-à-vis their operational work standards. Once these symptoms become the norm over an extended period of time, outsourcing actually becomes more costly and loses its original purpose.

Aware of the importance of condensing complex problems into simple catch phrases, Saegusa mulled it over on his train ride back to Tokyo. Eventually, he landed on *double-loss structure*.

Back at headquarters, he asked management, "How much emphasis have you been placing on improving operations at the customer centers?"

"Operational improvements are locally driven," was the answer.

Gee, *locally driven* sure sounds nice. But, given the complexity of the problems, wasn't that just code for *not our problem*? It seemed the company had neglected reform here. Instead, the strain of that contradiction between policy and reality was pushed onto the customer centers, and on-site staff were left to deal with the consequences on their own.

Structurally, the people working at the local centers were forced to expend an extraordinary amount of effort to compensate for those contradictions. Meanwhile, headquarters treated them as if their status were somehow inferior to the marketing or product development teams at headquarters and seemed to look down on them as "outcasts" toiling away in the local centers, even as they benefited from their work.

And yet, the staffers working in the local centers said they liked the company. How humbling. Saegusa empathized with them and promised to himself that he would improve their status. It wasn't just sympathy: It was a stress point in the business model that, if left unaddressed, could develop into a serious problem that might threaten the business.

**Key Turning Points: Riddle-solving and Decision-making as a Business Leader**

- There were disconnects between headquarters and the front lines of sales. The company could gradually lose its edge without management at headquarters being any the wiser.
- Thirteen customer centers constituted an unusually distributed organization.
- Consolidating the centers would surely be difficult and painful. How to treat operators would constitute the greatest risk. Once the intent to terminate local staffing agreements was communicated, staff departures could disrupt order-intake operations. Mishandle it and operations could come to a grinding halt, crippling the business.
- Nevertheless, the conclusion was clear: These issues could not be left unaddressed. Consolidation of the centers required further study.

Resolving this problem would only become more difficult as the company grew, leaving it saddled with structural inefficiency. Saegusa decided to fix this problem before his tenure ended.

But the reform effort ran up against a series of unexpected risks, encountering two major setbacks along the way.

## The First Major Setback

Soon after Saegusa was appointed CEO, he learned that a department general manager had formed a team to study customer center reform. Saegusa asked him for a status report. His impression was that the leader and team members were both weak and lacked the ability to lead such a critical reform.

So, he threw them a life raft. It would be the easiest method. Hire external consultants.

However, the life raft didn't work.

***Testimonial from K. Yamazaki (Then age 46. Would soon be appointed manager of the reform team.)***

*Under Mr. Saegusa's approval, we hired a consultant group. But it didn't work well. We selected one from a few consultant groups featuring famous names, but after all, the consultants didn't have the experience or capabilities to fully understand our complex problems. We work with micron-level manufacturing and tight delivery times, not simple customer centers handling ready-to-ship consumer goods like stationery or inventory goods. The consultant was soon dismissed by our CEO. That would mean that we were the ones who would need to solve this problem, without relying on outside help.*

*However, at that time, our reform team was not even drawing nearer to any solution, but rather struggling with different, more fundamental, and primitive issues. To be honest, the reform team was terrified of Mr. Saegusa's idea of consolidating all 13 centers into one. Therefore, we worked under strict secrecy, for fear that word would spread, triggering resistance and operator departures at the centers. We had backed ourselves into a corner.*

*Eventually, Mr. Saegusa noticed our predicament. One day he asked, "What are you doing slithered away inside your "octopus creep hole"?*

*I admit octopus hole was the perfect way of putting it, because we operated under the cover of darkness, afraid to come out in the light of day.*

Here, Saegusa saw the limits of Misumi's organizational capabilities—the lack of initiative to resolve problems accumulated over the history of 40 years. Intellectual prowess to seek solutions was weak. The situation resembled the small businesses he had observed in the past.

Saegusa called a cease fire and retreated. It was his ninth month as CEO. The time lost hurt more than the money paid to the consultants.

## The 5C Reform—A Fresh Start

Saegusa did not give up. He formed a new team and called it the "5C" Reform Team. The 5C was a reference to the five chains: time, value, information, strategy and mindset. For more, see Riddle-solving for Business Leaders (31): The Five Chains (5C).

He understood that a lack of leadership caused the previous setback. The complexity of this reform required more than average leadership. The new team needed more people familiar with the details of the job.

So, he appointed K. Yamazaki as manager. Additionally, he made A. Shiga team leader. Among the 13 heads of the customer centers, she was the best fit for the team leader requirements set by the CEO—someone gutsy, having an intimate familiarity with the workplace and practical wisdom to create new workflows at the new center. Then he selected four more people from the call centers, one as a full-time and three as part-time contributors to the reform project.

It would be impossible to develop the plan under complete secrecy. To get anything done, the team would have to emerge from its octopus hole.

There was a dilemma. Once the team began their activities, surely rumors would start spreading. Local staffers and operators would learn sooner or later that the company is preparing to close down their centers. That might spark many of them to look for employment elsewhere.

To complete the reform plan, all operators at a local center needed to be retained through the last hour of the last day of operation. Then, overnight, all customer relations would be switched to the consolidated center in Tokyo. Next morning, the customer services from Tokyo would be activated. This step would be repeated one by one for each local center. There were no better options to migrate operations those days—electronic remote work sharing was still technologically immature, and fax and telephone were the primary means of communication with customers.

Failure would corrupt order-taking operations for weeks or even months because the old centers would have already been closed down. Such a risk could become a fatal blow for Misumi as a company.

It was obvious to Saegusa that coordinated work with key staffers at the local centers would be essential to begin even the planning phase of the project.

Saegusa mulled over the possible solutions. Each alternative had certain risks that might result in the disruption of operations. Finally, he decided to take the most straightforward approach.

He called the reform team together and spoke with conviction, "I have made up my mind about our direction. I will disclose the plan not only to the chiefs of the 13 centers but also all the Misumi supervisors who are managing outsourced or part time operators at the centers."

That made the reform team nervous. Probably, some of them wanted to crawl back into their octopus hole. But some started to express their opinion.

"Tell everyone? That's more than 60 people nationwide. Rumors will spread and people will start leaving."

"No," Saegusa responded in a firm tone. "We will tell them everything. They are a part of our reform team and there can be no secrets among us. Then, there will be no rumors, or at least we can minimize or control it."

Saegusa continued.

"I visited the centers and saw the people there serious and sincere about providing customers with the best service possible. I trust them. They will understand the importance of this project. I will tell them that our 60-plus people will decide the destiny of this company."

The reform team was still worried. Would things really go as the CEO said they would?

## Revealing the Plan

Invitations went out to center chiefs and all Misumi supervisors in the customer centers. During the work week, they were typically too busy, and the only time everyone could gather was over the weekend. They were told to attend one of two meetings, either in Tokyo, mainly for people in Eastern Japan, or in Osaka, mainly for western Japan.

Planning for any reform or strategy begins with a clear "Sheet 1" (a framework of a Brutally Honest Reflection), an important step that decides the success or failure of the overall reform or strategy.

On the day the meeting was held in Osaka, some 30 staffers hailing from western Japan, including Fukuoka and Hiroshima, attended. The CEO's presence suggested a departure from the days when the company was run by its founder.

At the beginning of the meeting, Saegusa stood up, smiling. To this day, he can picture the ray of morning sunlight streaming through the window of the conference room.

He made eye contact with everyone. He could read their facial expressions, as they could his. That was the main reason the meeting was split into two smaller groups in Tokyo and Osaka. It allowed for more intimacy.

"Thank you for coming out over the weekend. I wanted to speak to you directly."

He clicked and showed one slide.

"We looked into the problems you face in your center operations and identified 284 problems."

The problems were split into four categories: (1) intra-center workflows; (2) coordination with business teams at headquarters; (3) IT systems; and (4) problems involving center operators themselves.

Saegusa clicked and provided the following summary.
- From the customer's point of view, we are slow, off-the-mark and inconsiderate.
- From management's point of view, the strategy is stagnant, resources are wasted, and there are opportunity losses.
- Center personnel feel a sense of worthlessness, distrust and helplessness.
- If we don't address these problems, customers will leave us, the competition will beat us, and the business will stumble.

The participants were astonished. They had been complaining about these problems all along, but no one at headquarters was interested in hearing them out. Yet here was their CEO addressing their concerns head-on.

Next, Saegusa revealed something that was not known at the time. With the passage of time, we can swallow our pride and share it with you readers as well.

"In the three years before I became CEO, the total number of operators at all centers grew from 190 to 239, an increase of 49."

Nothing unusual in those numbers.

"But over that same period, 206 operators quit. That means the company had to hire 255 to overcome the turnover."

The audience was shocked by the severity of the attrition. Undoubtedly, the heavy turnover created inconveniences for the customer.

As they tried to digest the numbers on the screen, they all realized they were not the only ones who had struggled. It brought home how much waste there was in their operations, and implicitly posed the question of why the company had done nothing to address it so far.

He concluded that past attempts at reform had failed because:
1. Responsibilities within the Misumi organization had been split by function, geography and product division. Therefore, the organization was not optimized from a companywide perspective.
2. For the same reason, the reform concepts and systems strategies were unclear.
3. The 13 centers were operating independently, which resulted in the development of many local work rules and procedures. Energy for reform was diluted across the 13 centers.
4. To summarize, you have done your best. But, understand that the causes of some of those 284 problems lie within the centers themselves. For that, you bear your share of the responsibility. Nevertheless, overall, this has been a matter of the company's leadership. The fundamental reforms had been too weak.

Saegusa emphasized the fourth point above to convey his commitment moving forward.

He paused a moment to read the room again. Then, he proceeded to the last section of the presentation. It was the CEO's core message of the day—the main point for calling this weekend meeting.

He displayed a slide that foretold consolidation of the 13 centers.

A moment of complete silence covered the entire room. Some in the audience gasped, fearful their jobs would be eliminated.

Truth be told, everyone in the room was exhausted from years of arduous labor. Many of their friends had quit along the way. Surely, many felt fed up and powerless to fix the situation.

In other words, their Desire for Drastic Change had been felt desperately for years, but they couldn't figure out themselves what kind of change it should be, how and when it would occur, and who would initiate and lead the change.

From his experience as a turnaround specialist, Saegusa knew that people's strong Desire for Drastic Change (in other words, strong dissatisfaction with the status quo) was one of the most critical factors for accepting a new reform program. But this time, there was a strong, serious dilemma—the drastic change might mean they lose their own jobs.

The conference room was filled with faces revealing anxiety over the fate of their livelihoods.

The 5C reform team, sitting along the side wall of the room and watching both Saegusa and the participants, wore hardened facial expressions. They thought, "Alas, now that our CEO has broached the topic, we have crossed the Rubicon."

They were worried that many would start considering leaving the company. Headcount would fall. The disruption would threaten to break the company.

Of course, Saegusa was fully aware of what the team was thinking. He again scanned the room, making eye contact with everyone present.

## Easing the Pressure

"Having heard this," he said. "I'm sure you are all worried about what will happen to you."

"Let me be clear," he started to speak again, in a louder voice. "As your CEO, I solidly promise to you. I guarantee you will continue to have a job at Misumi. Even after the call-center operations are moved to Tokyo, there will be plenty of customer service work to be done locally, at the sales offices housed under the same roof. So, please, stay with us."

Both the audience and the reform team were taken aback by the unexpected declaration. Saegusa wanted something more to allay anxiety over their futures at the company. He came up with the idea of guaranteeing their employment the night before and made up his mind over breakfast that morning.

The audience sat quietly, all staring at him. They didn't look suspicious. Rather, they looked moved. Saegusa thought he had won their trust.

But he wasn't done yet.

"I just have one more request," he said.

Surely, their minds had shifted on to the next point of concern. And he needed to make one thing absolutely clear before adjourning this meeting.

The issue was about how to pass this information on to their local subordinates, i.e., the subcontractor operators. Saegusa wanted to ensure the meeting's participants were in full understanding and agreement about how to cope with this issue before they returned to their workplaces.

"Please keep what you heard today to yourselves. This request is absolutely essential to prevent disruptions at centers across the country.

"It's too early to disclose these discussions to the staffing agencies or vendors we use, because we don't have a concrete plan yet," he said. "I am sharing this information with you today because we need your help and participation in shaping that plan."

"I ask all of you to work with the reform team to analyze work processes in each center and determine which are the best practices to adopt in the new center's workflow design. Without that piece, we would be foolish to disrupt our relationships with the staffing agencies and vendors. The disruption would harm them, our customers, and Misumi as a whole. A careless act by anyone in this room might trigger such a disruption, which in turn may spread nationwide."

"Let me be clear. I have no intention of blindsiding our vendors. Once the plan is finalized, we will give them proper advance notice. We'll fulfill all of our contractual obligations. We'll make sure to work with each vendor, acting in good faith until the end," Saegusa stressed. "Again, this is the promise made by your CEO."

The audience was listening carefully and seemed to understand.

After the meeting ended, the participants returned to their workplaces. What happened then about the rumors? To tell you in advance, there were no imprudent rumors or baseless speculation, nor were there any workplace disruptions triggered by information leaks. Everything remained under control, and the reporting line continued to function smoothly, as if the weekend meetings with the CEO never took place.

*Testimonial from K. Yamazaki*

*All it took was a two-hour meeting. The mindset of the whole orga-nization, which had been stagnant for years, changed in just one day.*

*I never imagined that everyone's attitude could change so drastically. What had I been doing back in that octopus hole?*

## Saegusa's Greatest Mistake

The new reform team started to design new workflows and orga-nizations for the new center to be opened.

It was a big challenge. The workflows at each of the 13 centers varied significantly because the centers were opened one by one over a period of 20 years with little effort to drive standardization since.

In the existing organization, the size of one center was 40 operators at largest, only 10 at smallest. The new consolidated center in Tokyo would have a work volume equivalent to nearly 150 operators.

Naturally, the new center must have better productivity, i.e., more work volume processed per person, fewer staffing than 150 operators, and a shortened process time to provide faster customer service.

The reform team tried to benchmark other companies, but no comparable operations were found in Japan. The consultants they hired had proved to be no help. The team realized they needed to invent their own creative model from scratch.

As a first step, they started to work with managers and supervisors of select centers, hiding the real purpose to the operators, to find best practices for each work process to be adopted in the new center.

Saegusa had almost no knowledge about the workflows at cus-tomer centers, but he insisted that the future concept incorporate one thing.

### *Testimonial from A. Shiga (Then age 37. Team leader in the 5C Reform Team)*

*We held a three-day off-site meeting at a seminar house outside of Tokyo. We tried to finalize the work plan for the team. To my surprise, Mr. Saegusa attended all three days. He was mostly listening, but in one session, he spoke up about the concept of workflows to be adopted in the new center.*

*"The key would be to shorten the turnaround time (TAT) for customers."*

*I had not heard the term before. He taught us TAT referred to the total time from the point of a customer placing an order until the point our product or service delivered to the same customer, like a boomerang. He also used the words "elapsed time" or "lead time" in the same meaning.*

*He said, "We must focus on 'TIME'. Then we will gain efficiency and low costs. That is the essence of the Toyota Production System (TPS)."*

Nobody saw at the time it would be a critical success factor for the renewed reform project.

Unbeknownst to them at the time, the seeds of another failure had already been sown, and would grow into the reform effort's second major setback.

Saegusa believed the reform team had fully incorporated the principles he stressed.

As he would later learn, they did not do their homework. They didn't consider his instructions crucial. To them, it was just a lot of jargon that went in one ear and out the other.

Actually, some there advocated an opposing concept, namely what they called *job specialization*. It was the antithesis of what Saegusa explained, i.e., the concept of "single-piece production" from TPS. In more than half a century since its inception, TPS had always countered the traditional beliefs rooted in the job specialization concept. What you just read about the resistance and battle at Suruga (Chapter 6) was typical.

If Saegusa had known there were proponents of job specialization on the team, he would have shut down the belief immediately. But he missed it. The topic had even appeared on the agenda for the off-site meeting he had attended. But he didn't notice, lacking knowledge of internal center operations and unable to keep up with the detailed discussions of work processes.

He did not imagine that immediately following his talk, someone would propose applying a completely opposing concept.

So, the alarm bells did not ring in his mind that day. That was the last time he would be present for a discussion on job specialization.

In the following months, the company poured $10 million into designing IT systems based on that misguided concept.

Saegusa brought in a new general manager from outside the company to bolster reform leadership. The recruit had experience leading the launch of a call center overseas for an American company. Having hired an expert in the field, Saegusa substantially reduced his involvement in the reform effort.

## The Second Major Setback

It took about a year to design and develop the new center's IT systems.

After a lengthy period of preparation, the consolidated center began operations within the Tokyo headquarters building. It was 19 months after the 5C reform team was formed (and two and a half years after the launch of the troubled original reform project). Saegusa named the new center the QCT Center, after the framework of the Misumi QCT Model.

He had allocated more money for its interior design than for the other floors. He wanted to position the QCT Center as an appealing place to work, hoping to boost the pride of the people stationed there.

First, personnel from the nearby Tokyo customer center were relocated to the QCT Center on a trial basis, to prepare for the nationwide consolidation.

Regretfully, Saegusa was still not aware that the center was being built out under a concept that was the polar opposite of the single-piece production model.

"We are still working out some wrinkles as people get used to the new system, but things are going well," reported the veteran general manager he had recruited.

In reality, though, serious problems had begun to surface. Saegusa later learned signs of the problems had already appeared in the trial phase.

There were more hand-offs between work processes in the new center, leading to wasted work and delays. As a result, productivity was lower than at the old Tokyo center. It was as if a factory had reverted to an antiquated system predating TPS.

The same people who did not study even the basics of TPS assumed that the job specification concept would simplify training require-ments for operators down to a month, much faster than the local centers' usual six-month training periods.

Ultimately, reality gave them a rude awakening. New hires failed to achieve the anticipated work efficiency. The new center was forced to increase hires just to keep pace with daily work volumes. The need to make additional hires should have been a red flag alerting them to the holes in their theory.

Recognizing the breakdown exposes the failure for all to see. That's what trials are for. But they failed to capitalize on it.

## The Ability to Sever Ties

After the half-year trial, the time had finally come to begin the migration of work from local centers to new Tokyo center. Once operations were migrated away from a local center, it would be shut down. There was no turning back. Each center would only have one shot at success.

Saegusa received continued assurances from the general manager that preparations were progressing smoothly. Saegusa walked the trial floor, but nothing appeared out of order. No detectable sign that something was amiss. So Saegusa gave the green light to resume the migration.

A full three years had passed since Saegusa had become CEO.

Through repeated and careful advance discussions with local vendors, Misumi had requested that temporary staffers continue to work up through the final day, and incentives had been put in place to encourage that.

Fortunately, nearly the entire staff stayed on to help out until the last day.

*Testimonial from A. Shiga (By now, she had been promoted to director overseeing half of the QCT Center.)*
*In July, we started by migrating the centers in Okayama, Fukushima and Kanazawa into the QCT Center in Tokyo.*
*Those three centers were smaller than the others, but soon I began to sense things were falling apart.*
*The following month, we hit a wall when we tried to migrate the Sendai center. Complaints from customers poured in and productivity took a nosedive. The phones were ringing off the hook, and everyone worked*

*frantically throughout the day. But still we couldn't keep pace with the workload and had to put in many hours of overtime every night.*

*Misumi advertised our commitment to keep promised delivery deadlines. It was our motto. So, we all worked as fast as we could to process incoming orders that same day to ensure that delivery deadlines would be met. But we were in a tough spot. If we allowed orders to carry over to the next day unprocessed, they would only add to that day's workload, and it would snowball from there.*

*We were desperate to keep up. But there were other problems, too. We were spending a lot of time interviewing job candidates and training new hires.*

*It was obvious that if we tried to push forward with the consolidation, QCT Center operations would be overwhelmed, resulting in major sales disruptions.*

The whole business was at risk of collapse. No word from the general manager recruit, as usual. Saegusa caught wind of a rumor that the QCT Center was in trouble. He rushed to the floor.

The management team appeared fatigued, irritable and glum, avoiding eye contact with their CEO. The general manager looked completely exhausted. All he had to say was, "things are bad." No sign that he had a grasp of the causes and potential countermeasures. Saegusa felt a strong sense of distrust toward him.

Walking the floor, one thing immediately became clear. There was a serious, emotional standoff between the planning group, responsible for designing and driving the project, and the operations group, in charge of running the operations. The operations side felt victimized, as if they were being asked to do the impossible. The planning side criticized operations for a failure to execute properly. Both sides felt aggrieved, and they were lashing out at each other.

Saegusa sensed here was an organization being torn apart from the inside, and the person responsible for overseeing it had virtually checked out.

Obviously, the reporting line was dead. Leadership had collapsed. The situation had festered beyond the realm of quick fixes. The problem had deteriorated to the point that Saegusa needed to step in and take corrective action himself.

The course of action was clear. First, any disruptions that would affect the customer had to be held in check. The consolidation plan called for the Fukuoka center to be migrated to Tokyo the following month. Customer notifications would go out in a few days. The addition of the Fukuoka operations to the new center's workload might prove ruinous. There was no other option. The consolidation plan would have to be suspended.

It would prolong the double-loss structure created by the overlap between the old and new. Newly hired operators are in place in Tokyo while the remaining centers will maintain operations. Besides, $10 million had already been sunk into IT systems.

Saegusa felt uneasy having to make an important decision without knowing how much it would cost and how it would impact the company's bottom line. But this was no time for calculations. And he was the only one who could make the decision.

His top priority was to eliminate the risk of inconveniencing customers, whatever the consequences.

Saegusa immediately gathered the management team.

"Suspend the consolidation immediately. Revamp the QCT Center. We'll look at resuming the consolidation later."

Saegusa had exercised his role to sever ties. The team seemed deflated; regret written on their exhausted faces.

Instructions were immediately issued nationwide to put the Fukuoka migration on hold and postpone all further consolidation steps. The order rattled the team. While they felt a sense of relief at the reprieve, it was mixed with remorse for having caused a failure that would saddle the company with major losses.

## The Inescapable Agony of *Death Valley*

It was August, and the reform effort had met its second major setback. Two years and four months had passed since the 5C reform team launched.

The general manager recruit "fell ill" amid the mess and stopped showing up for work. He never returned.

"This is a scene I have witnessed before," felt Saegusa as he recalled the inescapable agony of *Death Valley*. He envied people who could just up and quit in those situations. How many times had he wished that he could do the same? Instead, he sighed and thought, "here we go again."

The struggles continued. This was no time for a CEO to show weakness. Surely, everyone would have liked to escape and leave it all behind. But they chose to stay with Misumi.

By this point, nine local customer centers were operating. In parallel, the QCT Center was largely vacant. It turned out that the double-loss structure would set the company back about $3.6 million a year.

How many months, or years, would it take to finish the consolidation? No one had an answer to that question.

Eventually, they would move on to their third attempt. They would generate a new concept that fit the Misumi business model. The streamlining would result in world-class operations.

And, as management talent, they would learn the valuable lessons and sense of accomplishment unique to those who successfully cross *Death Valley*. It would prove to be a pivotal experience for them.

**Section 2:**
# The Third Try is the Charm

## Arriving at the Scene of the Fire

Y. Takeda (then age 36) was called into the CEO's office. He had joined the company only three months earlier.

Takeda had gone to work for one of Japan's leading trading companies. His employer had financed his pursuit of an MBA. But he had grown tired of his work there and decided he wanted to work for Misumi. Saegusa told him, "Take as long as you need to wrap up your work there. We look forward to welcoming you whenever you are ready."

Six months later, Takeda took the leap. Initially he was installed as executive assistant to the CEO. Saegusa was pleased with his job performance on the assignment over his first three months.

"Takeda, the customer centers are going up in flames and I need you to put out the fire."

Taken aback by the abrupt news, "Mr. Saegusa, I have no experience or knowledge related to that kind of operation."

"I believe in you," Saegusa said. "You would become general manager, overseeing an organization of 300 people. The roots of the problem are deep. It will require your full commitment."

Not only did Takeda have no experience with those operations, he had never led such a large organization.

"If you want to take your career to the next level, this would be a valuable experience," Saegusa added.

Remember? He had said the same thing to Nishi before sending him to salvage the reform efforts at Suruga. Saegusa believed in what he said, though. Taking on the unknown is the gateway to success for talented business leaders.

Takeda assumed the post immediately. Indeed, the place was in flames, as Saegusa had said.

Takeda was in an unusual position then. He had only recently joined the company, and now, at 36, he was its youngest division/department general manager. There he was, alone at the helm of a troubled division. Many of the people he was leading were a generation older.

Takeda was quick to sniff out the internal discord that Saegusa had detected. He soon came up with a way to ease tensions between the planning and operations groups.

Inspired by his leadership, the people who had been doing nothing but fighting had a quick change of heart.

A month after his appointment, Takeda prepared a slide deck entitled "5C Reform Revival Project" and presented it to Saegusa.

Saegusa was impressed with the progress achieved in only one month.

Here are the salient points from his presentation.
- The reality: When the consolidation was postponed, the QCT Center in Tokyo was staffed with 136 people. Before then, local centers handled the same workload with only 88 people. A disastrous 50% jump in personnel expenses.
- Miscalculation of learning speed: Job specialization was expected to simplify tasks and onboard new hires in one month. In reality, it will take at least three months for new hires to get up to speed, and even longer before they're as competent as existing operators. So, of course, there will be staffing shortages.
- Cutting corners in preparation: Saegusa had repeatedly

instructed that work procedures be standardized at the local centers in advance of the consolidation. Instead, the team cut corners. As a result, the new center saw a rise in "exceptions" to standard procedure. This exacerbated the confusion.

- Disregard for KPIs: During the half-year trial period, customer complaint measures were clearly deteriorating. If those indicators had been taken seriously, it should have been possible to predict the breakdown.
- System-design defects: The systems introduced at the new center were supposed to cover 90% of work processes. In reality, there were many deviated procedures brought in from local centers to be covered manually. Requirements for the IT systems were not properly defined.

Saegusa was disappointed with the quality of the work done by the planning team. The leader showed a disdain for the actual workplace. No importance was placed on surveying the workplace to witness first-hand the work being done there.

Duplicative operations at the new and old centers was costing an additional $3.6 million a year, or $300,000 every month.

Saegusa said, "It means we are dumping $10,000 down the drain each day." His words stung the team members deeply.

Takeda shared his executive presentation with the reform-team leaders. That became their Brutally Honest Reflection framework and "Sheet 1", which should serve as a starting point for the new action plan.

## Moving toward a New Start

However, for Takeda, the problem lay in drafting "Sheet 2", to address a new reform scenario.

He proposed to the CEO a new plan to spend the next four to five months to improve current operations at the new QCT

Center, then resume the consolidation of the remaining 9 centers.

Saegusa was skeptical. The workflow designs adopted had been all wrong to begin with. They needed to be redesigned nearly from scratch, and the software must be renewed accordingly. Already, $10 million had been spent, but software changes would cost more.

Can the consolidation be resumed so quickly? Saegusa's misgivings would foreshadow the next predicament. But Takeda was headed in a different direction from what Saegusa had envisioned.

Takeda began to look into possible solutions. He took the time to visit the local centers. He analyzed data and workflows to assess the current situation in each work process at the new QCT center. Based on that, he identified problems and listed them up in a problem-control chart. Then, he gave orders to address each one. He believed repeating that process would eventually iron out the problems and stabilize operations.

As a result, he developed a root-cause correlation chart that identified 18 different problems.

Next, he would plan to form task forces to study solutions to each problem. By this point, two months had already passed.

Meanwhile, the company continued to run the two operations in parallel. There had been no improvement to turnaround time (TAT). Work productivity fell to 50% of pre-consolidation levels. Complaints were up 250%. Customer patience was wearing thin, and organizational fatigue was dangerously high.

At this time, Saegusa's time was spread thin between the China business (Chapter 4) and the Suruga acquisition (Chapter 5), among other things in other divisions. But he was growing concerned because Takeda hadn't recently reported on the 5C reform team's progress.

When Takeda finally came, he showed Saegusa his thick report analyzing 18 basic problems he identified. Saegusa could guess that Takeda didn't come to see him for a couple of months because Takeda was pouring tremendous work hours in this document. Takeda looked confident the report would exceed the CEO's expectations.

Wrapping up, Takeda asked Saegusa, "I am going to hold an off-site meeting with key members to discuss how to address each of these," Takeda said. "Would you please join us?"

The two months spent creating the diagram had given Takeda insight into the problems in the current operation, and he felt ready to make a fresh start.

He was not prepared for what Saegusa would say next.

"Takeda, this doesn't make sense to me."

He continued. "The document summarizes your understanding of past failures. And your idea is to work on each of the 18 problems, one by one? Do you think that will result in true reform?"

Takeda was stunned. He thought he had made a compelling case.

Saegusa said pensively, "This is not what you need now. You won't find a solution in this neat analysis of past issues. You are still relying on the old "job specification" concept. That is where your predecessors erred, despite the direction I provided them based on my own experience to date.

"Takeda, you will fix it? No joke. It was already proven in the trial that 'job specification' was wrong for our operation. You want to stay the course?"

Saegusa continued, "If you ever bring me another telephone book of analysis like this, I'll have it shredded!"

In reality, Saegusa had never torn up a document his staffers had done their best to prepare. He was being intentionally provocative to jolt Takeda. This, too, was a form of severing ties.

## Reflections Guided by Frameworks

Takeda returned to his desk and mulled over what had just transpired.

He had spent the last two months elbow-deep in a detailed analysis of what was going on and directing his team to take corrective actions. But the CEO said that had not brought them any closer to formulating a new reform strategy. They were treating the symptoms without finding a cure.

He continued to reflect.

Takeda realized that he was no longer a salaryman, no longer some cog in the wheel at a giant trading company. If he simply followed a tired old playbook, Misumi's business would fail. Now, he was a business leader. This was a reform effort.

In three months, Takeda managed to find a way out of the tunnel that would elude some salarymen for their entire careers.

Takeda liked two of Saegusa's frameworks—"Small is Beautiful" and "the Create→Produce→Sell cycle". Intuitively, he knew those frameworks held important clues for revisiting the customer center reforms.

Viewing the new QCT Center from the lens of those frameworks inspired an interesting approach to TAT.

Takeda had his team investigate TAT—in this case the time that elapsed at customer center between receiving a customer's order and sending out confirmation back to the customer. He discovered that 77% of total time elapsed was "waiting time"—time spent waiting for the next step to begin, during which Misumi operators performed no work for the order in question. Takeda concluded that cutting waiting time could shorten TAT substantially and improve customer service.

### Riddle-solving for Business Leaders (41): The Benefits of Turnaround Time Reductions

Toyota Production System (TPS) teaches that smoothing out workflows reduces TAT. Not only is time elapsed reduced, but work efficiency (the total amount of time spent to perform that job) is also improved. In other words, TAT reductions improve productivity and costs.

Job specialization is a concept that splits work into simple tasks and has each group focus on its assigned task from morning until night. Each group performs its own task over and over again, so it is supposed to be more efficient.

But Takeda made an interesting discovery.

The work forces in the local centers were smaller, so instead of specializing, experienced staffers performed multiple tasks as needed. Even so, they were able to perform each individual task efficiently.

However, those veterans who relocated to the new center in Tokyo were required under the job-specialization procedures to perform one simple task all day, every day. As it turned out, though, the work efficiency for each task was actually lower now than it was at the local center.

For Takeda, it was an eye-opening discovery. The data could help develop a breakthrough toward a new reform concept.

Not to belabor the point, but Takeda's finding directly refutes the effectiveness of the division of labor, which has dominated capitalism since Adam Smith. It also helps explain the tragedy of the chairmaker discussed in Riddle-solving for Business Leaders (38), the efficiency gains achieved by cell-production methods, and the reasons why many Japanese salarymen have lost their drive as their job responsibilities were divided into smaller roles as their organizations grew.

The findings also gave Takeda visibility into problems involving the staff's hearts and minds and the health of the organization.

When a group focuses its entire day on one kind of task, it loses sight of what is happening in other steps of the process. The most serious flaw of this arrangement is that groups miss opportunities to help each other out, because they no longer see the customer problem in its entirety. Work becomes simplified into tasks and importance is placed on compliance with work standards, similar to the analogy of making chair parts in Riddle-solving for Business Leaders (38) mentioned above.

## Building a New Model Concept

Once Takeda noticed he needed to layer on another framework, he marshalled all of his strengths in service of that goal. He recalled a visit he made to one of the centers shortly after he was tasked with leading them.

*Testimonial from K. Honda (Then age 32. Head of Customer Center E.)*

*Yes, Mr. Takeda visited our center.*
*"This center seems different from the others," he said.*
*"Yes, here we have always had people move around," I told him.*
*"What does that mean?"*
*"We have two small teams here," I explained. "Within each team, the operators' roles change over time. We aren't assigned desks—jobs are. We only sit there while we are performing that job. When our role changes, we get up and move to the next job's desk."*

*"It's like a game of musical chairs," Takeda said.*

*"Our operators are highly skilled because they all have experience in all work processes," I continued. "Everyone knows what comes before and after the work they are doing that day."*

*"Nice," he said.*

As Takeda recalled this episode, he realized the center's practice was completely in line with Toyota Production System (TPS).

Late the next night, Takeda noticed the light was still on in the CEO's office in the next building. He decided to stop by to borrow a book on TPS.

At the time, there was a small room on the executive floor that Saegusa used as his library. He pulled several books off the shelves for Takeda and laid them out on a table.

"It's out of print now, but Professor Shigeo Shingo's work is the best for theory. I recommend this comic book, too. I distributed it to the nursing staff during a reform project at a hospital."

That sparked an impromptu tutoring session.

The next day Takeda immersed himself in the books. The work processes at the QCT Center differ greatly from those of manufacturing plants, but the fundamental principles and methodologies were basically the same. He gleaned many lessons from the books.

## Testing New Operations

It was the beginning of February, five months since Takeda had assumed his post.

Takeda showed his new design concept to Saegusa.

"The concept looks good. Start validating it in trials right away," Saegusa directed.

Takeda was caught off guard by Saegusa's advice. "Don't rush, Takeda. Take your time on the trial. Never mind the deadline. You can delay restarting the consolidation. Don't be hasty. Do it right!"

Takeda stared back at Saegusa, "Got it. I will 'Do it right!' then."

To Saegusa, this was a very *important exercise of management skill*. Takeda was under tremendous pressure to meet a deadline. Saegusa freed him from it.

Takeda moved into the trial phase.

The trial did not go well at first. Productivity fell short of expectations, and there were many operational mistakes. It was a process of trial and error. New work rules were being made up on the fly, putting extra pressure on the operators.

Unable to handle the pressure, one of the operators complained about the burden that the work methods were placing on them. Several temporary staffers of the same mind abruptly stopped showing up for work.

Takeda had optimistic assumptions. He thought that the operators and temporary staffers understood the purpose of the trial—getting the company out of this pinch.

Saegusa thought back to his own experience in his early 30s, when he was let down by someone who worked for him. So, he said to Takeda, "You can talk about your commitment to the business, but don't expect your people to invest the same enthusiasm as you do. Lean too hard on the work ethic of your people and it will eventually come back to bite you."

The project eventually overcame the temporary staffers' walk-out and made progress.

The core trial team comprised a group of women who served as leaders at their respective centers who came to Tokyo to help the trial. They worked very hard.

They were determined to ensure that consolidating operations in Tokyo wouldn't drive up customer complaints. As they developed trial parameters to ensure customer satisfaction, their strong sense of responsibility inspired the other people.

Saegusa was deeply grateful to them for embracing the transfer of operations and agreeing to relocate to Tokyo.

Eventually, interruptions to workflows within the trial center dissipated, portending better times.

*Testimonial from Y. Takeda (Age 36 when he assumed department general manager.)*

*Although we started to see positive signs in the trial run, everyone was exhausted. No one could tell whether their hard work would be rewarded with success, or if we would be stuck forever.*

*They needed to feel confidence in the amazing results we were starting to see. It was time to recognize an "Early Win".*

*I thought it might be useful to present the trial team's early successes to everyone at the QCT Center. I mentioned the idea to Mr. Saegusa, expecting he would say it's too soon. But he surprised me.*

*"That's a good idea," he said. "Why not go bigger?"*

*CEO assembled all key managers of all divisions at headquarters and the senior corporate management team. We rented out a small theater located next to the company's offices and held a two-hour evening event.*

## Riddle-solving for Business Leaders (42): Early Wins

It's difficult to recognize tangible results in the midst of a long, drawn-out program. Employees might lose momentum, confidence and motivation. An exhausted organization is fertile ground for dissent and an emboldened resistance. To avoid that, it is wise to recognize early successes, even small wins, to assure the team it is on the right path. (More on this in Chapter 4 of Saegusa's book, *A Crisis in Japanese Corporate Management*.)

*I turned the stage over to the team and watched from a corner of the theater.*

*The veteran leaders from the local centers, unaccustomed to speaking in front of large crowds, seemed shy and nervous. But there was a sparkle in their eyes.*

*The upbeat account these women provided of their struggles suggested confidence that they were finally headed in the right direction. Seeing my teammates up on stage was so moving that I got a little misty-eyed.*

*It was the first time key personnel from headquarters learned of our work at the QCT Center. Impressed, the audience gave the speakers a rousing round of applause.*

*It convinced me that the worst was behind us.*

## Onboarding the Operators

Around that time, Takeda made another major decision. Historically, most operators had been temporary staffers. He wanted to onboard them as permanent hires. But he hadn't discussed the idea with Saegusa. He thought the CEO might reject the proposal.

One day, Takeda met with him to broach the topic. Once again, Saegusa's reaction surprised him.

He agreed on the spot and told Takeda, "Go for it." The reaction was natural for Saegusa because, when Saegusa had visited the customer centers before accepting the CEO position, he noticed "the double-loss structure". It was clearly caused by excessive dependence on temporary staffers who, consistent with their temporary status, naturally felt little loyalty and commitment to Misumi.

The trials run by Takeda's 5C reform team took five months, two months longer than originally envisioned. At last, they settled on new work processes.

- The trial team's productivity was 75% higher than before the trials.
- Complaint rates were down 27%.
- Order turnaround time was shortened by 52%.
- Operator proficiency index jumped 2.3 times.

The statistics were impressive, but the most dramatic change was in the team's attitude. Specifically, they felt a sense of responsibility toward the customer, freedom at being liberated from robotic tasks in the old operation, the joy of making their own proposals for improvements and a real sense of personal development.

In the eyes of the CEO, Takeda had "done it right." In light of the trial team's success, the new methods were rolled out to all operations across the QCT Center.

At the same time, another major innovation was introduced. The new center's organization was divided to align with the business divisions.

Recall Saegusa's conversation with H. Yamada, one of the local center heads. If you can divide the work at customer center by product lines, you would radically reduce the number of catalogs for each operator to cover, paving the way for big gains in expertise and proficiency. The local centers were too small to make this method work, but the new center in Tokyo had reached the critical mass necessary to move forward with the idea.

## Resuming Consolidation

Now that the critical systems were in place, it was time to resume consolidation of the remaining centers.

In December (15 months after Takeda arrived at his post, and four years and seven months since the original reform project started), consolidation resumed, beginning with the Yokohama and Matsumoto centers.

There were no major problems this time, thanks to the careful preparations made during the trial phase. It was a victory for the strategy that was developed while the operation was put on hold. The success was attributable to an ability to sever ties—an option exercised several times to recover from setbacks.

A month before consolidation resumed, Takeda made one other big move.

He proposed establishing a backup center in Kumamoto, in southern Japan, to assure business continuity if Tokyo were ever crippled by a major earthquake.

The new Kumamoto QCT Center launched in April, a short five months after its approval. Things can move quickly at Misumi.

Of course, all of the methods that proved successful during trials in Tokyo were applied to the Kumamoto center. The remaining local operations would be migrated either to Tokyo or Kumamoto.

## The Remarkable Work of the Center Leaders

In September, Saegusa visited the Kumamoto QCT Center, which by then had been in operation for about five months.

The opening of the new center was covered by the local press. During his visit, Saegusa made a courtesy call to the governor of Kumamoto, who expressed gratitude for the contribution to the local economy.

Upon arriving at the facility, Saegusa went straight up to the second floor, where he found locally hired operators busy at work.

What he saw there surprised him. He had heard that a few key managers and leaders had relocated from Tokyo to Kumamoto to support the backup center launch. But he found out there were not just a few. As he walked the floor, he was greeted by many familiar faces. They were beaming with delight as they welcomed him.

One called out, "Good morning, Mr. Saegusa!"

Saegusa stopped to say hello.

"How are you, Mr. Saegusa?" said another.

"Oh, you relocated, too?"

Soon he was overwhelmed with emotion. Thinking of their commitment and sacrifice moved him profoundly.

They had relocated from local centers to Tokyo before the second setback and had participated in Takeda's trial and seen it through to the end. After stabilizing the Tokyo operations, they moved again, this time to remote Kumamoto.

They were training the local hires in Kumamoto and were committed to remaining there until the operations were running smoothly and the 5C reform effort could be considered a complete success.

Most young people gravitate toward Japan's biggest cities, like Tokyo or Osaka. So, it was heartening to learn that these women felt such a strong commitment to their work that they would willingly transfer to a smaller city more than 1,000 kilometers away from Tokyo. That's equivalent to relocating from New York City to Charlotte, NC, or from London to Belfast.

Long ago, many Japanese companies could rely on a strong employee work ethic. That is less the case today, so Misumi can take pride in its deeply devoted work force.

The consolidation would eventually reach a successful conclusion. The success was attributable to the experienced women who supported the project from beginning to end, toiling at thankless tasks, all the while held in contempt by headquarters.

That night, a dinner party was held in their honor. Saegusa went around the table to pour a drink to each person and bowed to express his gratitude one by one.

After resuming in December, the consolidation took another year to complete. That was two years and four months after Takeda took over, and five years and eight months since the original effort began.

Work with the local vendors concluded smoothly. Nearly all temporary staffers at the local centers worked up through the last day. Not a single conflict arose. Saegusa was grateful for their help. And the operators' performance during the risky transition phase was impressive.

The consolidation was finally complete. Thirteen centers had been rolled into one unified operation.

Saegusa felt a sense of closure as he recalled his pledge to resolve this problem while he was CEO, to allow his eventual successor to focus on other challenges. He rented out a ballroom and invited senior management and staff involved in the reform effort to gather and celebrate their efforts.

As was his practice, Saegusa made his rounds pouring drinks for everyone, stopping for brief conversations. He was happy to oblige requests to pose for souvenir snapshots along the way.

But there was still more reform work to be done.

## The First Signs of Autonomous Progress

Having seen the consolidation through to the end, Takeda's work was complete. His reward was the management experience he had gained, which was what drove him to change companies in the first place.

Saegusa assigned him a new challenge, heading up Misumi's original business—die components. For Takeda—who was still in his 30s—it was a big challenge. Another bold personnel decision.

Meanwhile, the 5C reforms continued. It required more hard work. Takeda was succeeded by K. Yamazaki, whom you may recall from the octopus hole incident. They could laugh about it now that it was behind them. Yamazaki had faced the third try and, in the process, he had grown, both personally and as general manager.

Yamazaki recognized that further productivity improvements would need to leverage frameworks and kaizen tools as a guide. He borrowed from Saegusa and generated something that became known within Misumi as a new framework called "Impact Mechanism Map" for kaizen activities.

The tool mapped out the ripple effects (mechanisms) of specific kaizen actions. The chart's objective was to make Misumi's QCT centers the best in the world in two sub-categories.
- Become the world's top customer center in terms of customer satisfaction.
- Become the world's top customer center in terms of work efficiency (low costs.)

Misumi is in a unique industrial segment. Therefore, read 'the world's top' to mean 'among Misumi's global peers within the industry'.

You have probably already noticed a strong contradiction between the two goals. It's easy to cut costs at the expense of customer satisfaction. And if you ignore costs, you can raise customer satisfaction as much as you like.

Saegusa instructed Yamazaki, "You can't chase one or the other. Aim for improvements that balance the two. Make everyone at Misumi aware of the inherent conflict between them."

So, on the framework chart, Yamazaki connected the dual goals with a line, and wrote "Must be balanced" in between.

Then, he and his team added a tree diagram of specific kaizen measures to achieve the dual goals, including KPIs for the biggest items.

Yamazaki's chart reflected Saegusa's "Strategic Chain" management concept, which emphasized the need to share strategy across all levels of the organization, instead of confining it to the C-suite.

That was the extent of what Saegusa taught Yamazaki. Beyond that, Yamazaki exercised his own judgment and executed as he saw fit. The Impact Mechanism Map was shared across all organizations in the Tokyo and Kumamoto QCT centers, followed and reinforced on a weekly basis.

## Doing the Work of 600 With 145

Six years had passed since Yamazaki succeeded Takeda. The company's sales dipped during the global financial crisis but rebounded thereafter and climbed to $3 billion, and it employed more than 10,000 people globally. Over that six-year span, kaizen activities at the QCT centers progressed at a rapid clip.

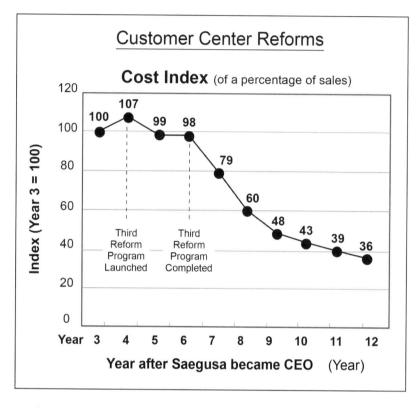

Customer Center Reforms

**Cost Index** (of a percentage of sales)

- Operator productivity more than doubled.
- That made possible a 60% reduction in operator headcount. There were 372 operators upon completion of the consolidation. Now, there were 145, even as sales doubled.
- An index of center expenses as a proportion of sales went from 98 at the time of consolidation down to 36, in six years as shown in the exhibit.
- Customer complaints, as a percentage of total shipments, fell 57 percentage points. The team cut costs while dramatically enhancing the quality of customer service.

Yamazaki and his kaizen activities achieved reforms that would not have been possible if the customer centers had remained dispersed. Saegusa's decision to reform the customer centers during his tenure had paid off.

- If Misumi had continued to operate the original customer centers without change, it would have required 600 operators to support growth. Now, only 145 were needed.
- About one-third of that improvement is attributable to the increase in online orders. The remaining two-thirds is the result of rationalizations driven by Yamazaki.

The operational expertise accumulated over many years of struggle have blossomed into an intellectual-property asset for Misumi that supports its competitive edge.

Yamazaki, the man who had been burrowed inside his octopus hole is now exhibiting business creativity and leadership talent. As your people overcome daunting challenges, the experience accelerates their development into capable management talent.

## Learning from Failures

For all involved, it was a long haul that entailed a great deal of personal growth.

*Testimonial from A. Shiga (Director at QCT Center Tokyo. Then she moved to Kumamoto as its Center Director.)*

*Looking back on the work we did to get the reform operation up and running again, I now realize we followed the framework "Sheet 1→ Sheet 2→ Sheet 3" to the letter. By now, it's second nature for us.*

*At first, we really didn't have a lot of visibility into the future. It was like climbing a mountain. We could see the terrain appearing to level off just ahead, so we would set our sights on getting there, but once we arrived, we could see that there was another climb ahead of us. So, we all worked together to get over the next hump. We made it through that process again and again, and now here we are.*

*After the 5C reforms were on track, I accepted a position transplanting our operational model to overseas subsidiaries. Although each location was different, they had to get over the same hurdles we did. Wherever we went, it was the same journey, different place.*

### Testimonial from K. Yamazaki (General manager)

*I thought my career was going fairly well until Mr. Saegusa came along.*

*When the operational reform project hit its first setback, I realized I had been behaving like a self-entitled employee.*

*As the company started to change rapidly, somehow, I found my footing and started to make more of an effort.*

*Mr. Saegusa exposed me to many management frameworks. Internalizing them helped me regain the self-esteem I lost during the first setback.*

*There were many difficult hurdles to overcome, but I found the challenge invigorating. Even so, as the head of my organization, I still have many other things I want to accomplish.*

### Testimonial from Y. Takeda (Later became president of an internal company and eventually executive vice president)

*With the reform project, it was one failure after another. Each time, we were saved by a new reform concept.*

*We had resilient people who faced the challenges head-on. Of course, some left us. But the great majority stuck it out, even though it sometimes drove them to tears.*

*Collective enthusiasm—that might be one of the strengths of traditional Japanese management, a strength that companies may be losing today.*

- *A business leader must have tools (frameworks) that capture the essence of the problem and provide simplicity and structure to the chaos. Otherwise, the organization grows fatigued and hits its limit.*
- *To develop process reforms, you have to take a step back to see the whole picture and focus on the structure, instead of zooming in on the minutiae. Incremental improvements to individual pieces of the puzzle won't bring about fundamental reform.*
- *Process reforms can't be pursued across all areas of the company at once. You have to apply methods that break up and control the risk.*

## The Misumi Operational Model Goes Global

For more than a decade, Saegusa advanced parallel reforms across all of these support organizations. Each underwent an agonizing trial-and-error process that played out much as it did at the customer centers.

In the end, reforms were advanced across all support organizations to speed up the cadence of the Create→Produce→Sell cycle.

After completing reforms in its facilities in Japan, the company began to migrate the Misumi Operational Model (MOM) globally. MOM teams dispatched from Tokyo headquarters worked closely with local hires at overseas subsidiaries to implement the reforms.

Each reform built on another, so failure in any one of them would hold back the transition to the next one. Failure in any of the links would have weakened the Reform Chain, inhibiting global MOM activities.

It was a long journey, but in the end, our people's achievements helped boost the company's global competitiveness. In business, of course, once you reach the peak of completion, the descent toward obsolescence begins. It is up to the next generation of management to continue to evolve Misumi's Operational Model.

# Chapter 8

# Designing an Energized Organization

In order to build a competitive company, it's essential to establish a Solid Main Story (Saegusa's Management Note 6) to define strategic direction and focus. Then, determine an organizational design that will best fit the strategies taken.

In this chapter, we follow how the CEO developed basic frameworks and philosophies for organizational reforms at Misumi.

## Innovating the Business Model With a Chain of Reforms
### (Competing Against the International Megatrend)

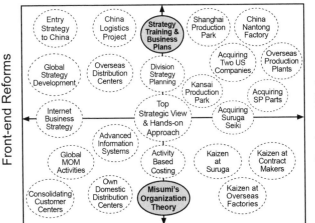

## In Search of New Japanese Corporate Model

Since accepting the CEO position, Saegusa remained committed to transforming Misumi into a new style of Japanese corporate model that would provide a stark contrast to Japan's many debilitated corporate establishments.

In planning corporate reform, the top priority is always to find a strong strategic story. It is not easy, but it always has to be done first. Along those lines, Saegusa made the Misumi QCT Model to confirm the company's business strengths, and "Eight Weaknesses" to identify what needed reform. Through these work products, he came to the conclusion that Misumi held great potential worth spending the last leg of his career on.

But after assuming the CEO position, he felt strongly that, in pursuing his aspiration to lead Misumi to overtake the conventional Japanese management style, he had not yet established a clear framework for the optimal Misumi organization.

He could transform the company into a truly strong international company building on two pillars—the Misumi QCT Model and the Misumi Organizational Model. He intended to make Misumi a testing ground for a new Japanese organizational model.

## What is an Energized Organization?

Saegusa wanted to build an energized organization. But what makes an organization energized, as opposed to a conservative organization?

It was a very basic question that Saegusa had to answer. After giving it considerable thought, mulling over notes on past experiences, study papers and books he referred to as a turnaround specialist, he developed a new framework titled, "A Traditional vs. Innovative Organization".

In the chart, on the left, *traditional organizations* signify old companies. On the right, *innovative organizations* signify companies such as US ventures.

Where on the chart would your company fall—right or left? Here are Saegusa's characterizations of some of the factors included in the chart.

Factor 1: Organizational structure
Traditional organizations typically form hierarchies where authority is centralized. Work process is divided by function. In contrast, an innovative organization is decentralized. It distributes authority across the organization, tends to adopt holistic models and often utilizes flexible project team concepts.

| A Traditional vs. Innovative Organization (Misumi Organization Framework No. 1) | | |
|---|---|---|
| **Factors** | **Traditional Organizations** | **Innovative Organizations** |
| 1. Organizational structure | Hierarchy (centralized) | Decentralized (holistic teams) |
| 2. Work processes | Complex | Simple (full straight) |
| 3. Individual work scope | Narrow (division of labor) | Wide (diverification of skills) |
| 4. Organizational control | Controlling | Empowering |
| 5. Role of supervisors | Managing | Coaching (mentors) |
| 6. How employees see their roles | Employed | As professionals |
| 7. Who employees aim to please | Supervisors | Customers |
| 8. Subjects of evaluation | Effort | Results |
| 9. Form of remuneration | Monthly salary | Performance-based pay |
| 10. Behavior considered clever | Risk aversion | Creating chances (high risk) |
| 11. Behavior that receieves praise | Improvement | Innovative change |
| 12. Corporate management style | Maintain and prolong (farmers) | Pursuit of strategy (hunters/nomads) |

Factor 4: Organizational Control
Traditional organizations emphasize "control" to execute governance. Innovative organizations tend to leverage empowerment.

Factor 5: Role of Supervisors
In a traditional organization, supervisors exert management authority while those of innovative organizations want to function more as mentors and leaders.

Factor 10: Behavior Considered Clever in the Organization
Traditional organizations are mostly risk-averse and value incremental improvements. Innovative organizations value risk-taking
to change and create opportunities.

Factor 12: Corporate Management Style
Traditional organizations tend toward incremental improvements
by correcting manuals, while innovative organizations emphasize
significant jumps and re-writing scenarios.

### Riddle-solving for Business Leaders (43): Farmers vs. Hunter-gatherers

Unlike the US, Japan has seen few ventures grow into
major corporations. While running a venture-capital fund
in his 30s, Saegusa observed that the Japanese agricultural
mentality could not keep up with the hunter-gatherers
in the US seeking instant success in a modern-day gold
rush. Japan has now fallen behind China in speed and
ambition. Even if Japanese business leaders don't morph
into hunter-gatherers, they do need to acquire strategic
skills to help them keep pace. Otherwise, they will fall
behind their global competitors. Professionalism is the
key word.

## Core Factors Causing Misumi's Organizational Weakness

Developing this framework naturally led Saegusa to the next question. How could Misumi's organization be characterized within
this framework?

The founder often put himself forward as a *visionary leader*
when it came to Japanese business models. He said so internally at Misumi, in magazine interviews, and in speeches to
the business community. Based on the founder's statements and
actions, Saegusa felt Mr. Taguchi had truly aimed to design an

innovative organization. What he sought to implement aligned almost entirely with the right-hand side of the framework, "A Traditional vs. Innovative Organization".

Therefore, Saegusa could say the principles underlying Misumi's organizational design were sound. In practice, however, Saegusa observed many disturbing situations as honestly depicted throughout this book. The most serious problems were a lack of strategy in new business ventures, resulting in no synergies between the new businesses and the core business, a low growth rate and poor profitability, high turnover of team staffers, and other serious problems explained in "Misumi's Eight Weaknesses".

As the new CEO, Saegusa had to fix the problems and wanted to build an energetic organization. But where to start the reform? What should he write on "Sheet 1" (a framework of a Brutally Honest Reflection) in accordance with the standard logic (Sheet 1→Sheet 2→Sheet 3)?

Thanks to the framework he developed, one day he tried to use each factor on the list as criteria to analyze the strengths and weaknesses of the Misumi organization.

To make the story short, he identified the two deepest shortcomings of Misumi which had repercussions that rippled out to two other factors.

Basic Problem Set A (dotted line on the framework chart)
Shortcoming A-1: (Factor 6) Weak professionalism among executives and key staffers. The managers at Misumi were nice people, honest and hardworking, but from the viewpoint of professionalism, they were ordinary people. This resulted in the next shortcoming:

Shortcoming A-2: (Factor 5) Weak leadership, mentorship and coaching

Basic Problem Set B (dotted line on the framework chart)
  Shortcoming B-1: (Factor 12) Weak ability to generate strategic scenarios. Focus and goals of the business units were
  not clear. This resulted in allowing the next shortcoming:

  Shortcoming B-2: (Factor 8) Weak follow-up on performance in the business units due to weak focus and goals.
  Management review was conducted only once a year. The
  strong QCT model in the core business (industrial parts)
  generated abundant profit for the entire company. Ironically
  it also allowed loose management of individual units.

Saegusa felt he grasped the basic causes (that he had gotten to
the bottom of things) of Misumi's organizational weaknesses. But
these problems were so fundamental that it didn't look easy for
any professional CEO to cure. By the nature of the problems, no
quick remedy would be available. If you, the reader, were in his
shoes, how would you fix these problems?

## The Founder's Challenge for Organization Reform

Mr. Taguchi, the founder, sought to design a very innovative,
unique organization about a decade ago. It was an unprecedented
concept in Japan, or even in the U.S. or Europe.

As described in Chapter 1, the founder had led the company
toward creating many internal ventures, and introduced a
business "team" concept. Here is an overview of the team
structure at the time.
1. So-called functional organizations, such as human resources,
   sales, purchasing and sales promotion had been dismantled.
   Those roles and responsibilities were all delegated to the small
   business teams which have around ten staffers each.
2. Team leaders were selected by the board of directors based on
   the evaluation of the competitive presentation at the annual
   Vision Presentations for one-year tenures. Anyone could raise

their hand to be a leader (a strong denial of traditional seniority systems in ordinary Japanese companies).

3. For all intents and purposes, the team leader functioned as an employer. Team leaders had the authority to hire personnel from inside or outside the company, decide salaries and allocate bonuses under the profit-sharing scheme.

4. Every year, employees could choose to remain on their current teams or move to another.

5. If a team breaks its annual profit record, a certain percentage of the surplus is paid out as profit-sharing. The team leader has the authority to decide how those profits are divided among the team members. In the event of particularly strong business performance, this distribution might exceed the fixed annual salary.

When Saegusa became CEO, a decade had passed since the founder introduced the team system. As mentioned before, Saegusa observed many disturbing situations.

A big gap existed between the visionary goals originally set and the reality you saw ten years later. Saegusa would have to fix the problems. He needed to look for an additional framework. If he could identify the issues more precisely, he would be able to develop a scenario for organizational reforms as opposed to relying on a random approach.

## The Cycle of Organizational Evolution as a Company Grows

Saegusa again spent considerable time, and eventually he had come up with another framework named "The Cycle of Organizational Evolution as a Company Grows" (Misumi Organization Framework No. 2).

Saegusa believed that a company's vitality would depend on a combination of "energized individuals who enjoy challenges in their business unit" and "strategic focus from a companywide standpoint".

## Stage A

When the founder of Misumi introduced the "team" system (in concept, it was the same as Saegusa's "Small is Beautiful") and started the new business ventures, Misumi had embarked onto Stage A on the chart.

## Stage A→B

A decade later, by the time Saegusa arrived at Misumi, unfortunately the organization had already moved down to Stage B.

Thanks to this framework, Saegusa now understood where Misumi was. The deteriorated organizational state would be a threat to keeping Misumi's growth and profitability even in the core business of industrial parts, which was, in the mind of the CEO, Misumi's last chance for future success.

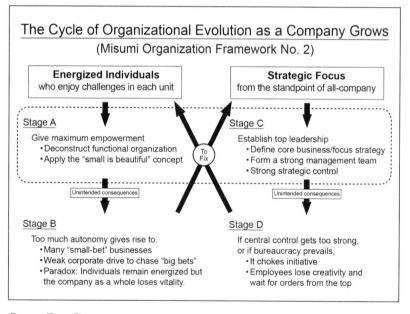

The Cycle of Organizational Evolution as a Company Grows
(Misumi Organization Framework No. 2)

**Energized Individuals**
who enjoy challenges in each unit

**Strategic Focus**
from the standpoint of all-company

**Stage A**
Give maximum empowerment
• Deconstruct functional organization
• Apply the "small is beautiful" concept

To Fix

**Stage C**
Establish top leadership
• Define core business/focus strategy
• Form a strong management team
• Strong strategic control

Unintended consequences

Unintended consequences

**Stage B**
Too much autonomy gives rise to:
• Many "small-bet" businesses
• Weak corporate drive to chase "big bets"
• Paradox: Individuals remain energized but the company as a whole loses vitality.

**Stage D**
If central control gets too strong,
or if bureaucracy prevails,
• It chokes initiative
• Employees lose creativity and wait for orders from the top

## Stage B→C

How should Saegusa remedy the situation? His answer was to go to Stage C. No framework emerged easily—he gave considerable thought before writing down Stage C at the position on the paper.

Once you decide a framework, it would decide a direction for the real business. Saegusa decided to liquidate all the internal ventures and return focus to the core business. If the strategies are successfully implemented and continue to be renewed as necessary, the company will build competitive positions and grow in Stage C.

## Stage C→D

However, if a company fails to stay in Stage C and drops to Stage D, which is defined here as a failure, what would cause such a drop? There can be many reasons, and Saegusa considered organizational aspects in this framework.

Corporate strategies are top-down in nature. If they are enforced too strongly and for too long a period, autocratic style at the top might prevail. The organization below might become compliant and less inclined to take the initiative. As individuals lose their vitality, so does the company.

Alternatively, the company might be successful on strategies in Stage C and grow into a larger company. As is always the case in large organizations, the decision-making process gets more complex, time consuming, and becomes bureaucratic. Again, as individuals lose their vitality, so does the company.

In reality, we see so many companies in Stage D. Saegusa used to work as a turnround specialist for such companies in Japan.

## Stage D→A

To revitalize a company in Stage D, you have to add the elements included in Stage A, as if to move the organization from D toward A. The concepts would be to decentralize authority, or to add the "Small is Beautiful" concept and thereby foster entrepreneurial spirit.

## Sustaining Vitality by Re-organizing with Growth

In this framework, a company would evolve as if it climbs a spiral staircase. As it clears one stage of growth, it is rewarded with a new set of problems to solve. To cure itself, it must re-organize to position itself for further success. It is a fundamental pattern in corporate growth. You might say it's fate.

Combination A+C (An Excellent Organization)
Before your company moves downward from Stage A→B as Misumi did, add the management programs included in Stage C, namely, add strategic focus from a companywide standpoint.

Before your company moves downward from Stage C→D as so many companies commonly do, add the management programs included in Stage A, namely, introduce organizational methods to energize individuals who would enjoy challenges in their organizational unit.

On the chart, Stage A and C are grouped together by a rectangular dotted line. It means the combination of A and C is essential to keep an organization vital.

- A business division is led under strong divisional strategies (Stage C), but its staffers in the middle ranks and below are empowered as much as possible (i.e., add Stage A factors).
- A large company is led by strong companywide strategies (Stage C), but it has organizations below to operate as much smaller units as possible, or offer programs to seed small ventures, or allow so-called bootlegging trials (i.e., add Stage A factors).
- At Misumi, the entire company is divided into internal companies (to be explained) for the executive level, but have many small "teams" for the staffers in the middle ranks and below.

## Riddle-solving for Business Leaders (44): Small is Beautiful

Divide your organization into smaller organizations equipped with the entire set of functions encompassing the cycle of Produce→Develop→Sell. As a small but fully integrated organization, it will be nimbler than the competition. Select a leader with backbone to head the organization and teach that person strategic literacy. Have that leader independently draft a strategy to beat global competition and execute on it.

This framework applies not only to Misumi, but to all companies in general. A top executive who leaves the same organizational design in place for too long might put the company's long-term competitiveness at risk.

## Misumi's Move for Business Reforms and Globalization

Based on the two frameworks explained in this chapter, Saegusa decided the basic direction of organizational reforms for Misumi. He began to move quickly along the line from Stage B to C.

- He abandoned the past new business ventures policy, decided to liquidate the internal ventures, and shifted back to the core business of industrial parts (Chapter 1).
- Strategic concepts and skills were instilled into the FA Division (Chapter 2), and the other divisions followed similar reforms.
- International strategy was commenced starting with a focus on China (Chapter 4).
- The company ended its 40-year history as a trading company, and began manufacturing operations through the acquisition of Suruga (Chapter 5).
- Production Kaizen efforts using the Toyota Production System made it possible to make and ship any of 80 sextillion ($10^{21}$) production items in two days in Japan (Chapter 6).

- Customer centers were revamped through a few years of trial-and-error reforms (Chapter 7).
- Not covered in this book, but major reform projects were also carried out in the areas of information systems, logistics, accounting (including activity based costing in Chapter 3), human resource management, and others.
- Opening new sites internationally each entailed major reform projects. Globally including Japan, Misumi now has 66 sales offices, 17 logistics centers and 22 manufacturing plants as of the publication of this English edition.

## Organizational Reforms

You may wonder how a company with only 340 employees could carry out so many heavy reform projects in parallel, eventually growing the company to more than 10,000 employees today.

Of course, there were various programs to support the organizational aspects of the reforms.

1. Reinforcing the Top Management Team
   To be explained in the Epilogue.

2. The CEO's Policy for Developing Management Talent
   Under the founder's system then in place, people who failed in business were shown the door, unusual for Japanese culture then. In contrast, Saegusa firmly believed that people who failed were important assets to the company. He had made many mistakes and failures in his 40-year-plus executive tenure, and he attributed some of his greatest achievements to the experience of his own failures.

## Riddle-solving for Business Leaders (45):
## Failure as an Asset

A company stands to lose a lot if a person who experiences a failure leaves. The money invested in that person is wasted. What's more, the experience of failure—an invaluable asset—is ceded to that person's next employer.

Of course, people who fail must be given a stern lecture without delay. It would be a mistake to go easy on them. But as long as that person shows an appropriate degree of remorse and a positive posture for the next challenge, let that be the end of it. Forgive the person and move forward.

## Riddle-solving for Business Leaders (46):
## A Stern Lecture

The strength of a company is influenced by whether there is an organizational culture that sternly lectures its people for their failures. Japanese companies reprimand their employees less today than they used to. A company that only timidly admonishes its people holds back the growth of the organization and its people. Business leaders need to accumulate frameworks on how to properly lecture their people.

3. Misumi Strategy School

The founder took the stance that people grow on their own. So, the company provided no training system. Saegusa believed that many leadership qualities are innate, but management literacy can be learned.

He started to open day-long strategy-training sessions. Officers, division general managers and team directors were divided into groups of about 30 to a maximum of 50 people, and day-long strategy-training sessions took place.

The CEO was prepared to teach strategy himself. Fortunately, he had enough energy and motivation to take on the work, although it exceeded a normal CEO's workload. He called himself a "strategy missionary" and intended to hand over all the frameworks he had accumulated over his executive career.

He spent the eight hours on his feet teaching the class, drilling the participants with many slides and questions. Since the professor was their own CEO, participants had no place to nod off or cut corners.

He has held the all-day strategy sessions 6 or 7 times a year, for a total of 120 times in 18 years (with a one-year break twice). These seminars continue today, and recently some sessions were held open to the executives outside Misumi.

4. Business Plan System
   Training alone would produce a bunch of book-smart people, a problem that plagues some large corporations. That is where Misumi's Business Plan System comes in to play, as detailed in Saegusa's Management Note 6. Business plans are the hinges that integrate organizational and strategic theories at Misumi.

   For several years after taking the reins, Saegusa personally oversaw business plan reviews for all business teams, serving as chair alongside the business division general manager. The reality of his hands-on approach was this: As he was providing guidance to the business plan presenter, the real lessons were to be absorbed by his co-chair, the general manager sitting next to him.

5. Sharing Strategic Thinking with Management Personnel
   Saegusa introduced an executive meeting named the Management Forum as a structure to bolster strategic thinking among key staffers. Executives and division general managers attended the monthly meetings, which Saegusa chaired.

He and other executives gave presentations on difficult projects or management challenges, followed by discussion. Attendees were required to submit reports or letters of opinion.

As you might expect, many of the reports were thinly veiled attempts to curry favor with him. Fine. It was still a valuable exercise to have them write the reports, to help ingrain the lessons in their minds.

If someone wrote something interesting, he might call the person into his office for a talk. It was an opportunity to interface with younger talent. And it might reveal the next candidate for future management development.

6. Communicating with Personnel
He also held a large meeting named the Open Forum for all personnel. They were two-hours sessions, completely unscripted. Anyone could ask him about anything. It was held twice a year.

7. CEO's Management Essay to Staffers
Saegusa wrote a series of CEO's essays titled, "What is Management Thinking". It was distributed by email company-wide to create a common lexicon in the organization. Themes ranged broadly, from strategic thinking, business-performance, tackling business plans and executive compensation to a eulogy he delivered for a famous figure, employee attire and so on.

8. KJKJ: Personal Letters of Advice from the CEO
Additionally, about a year after becoming CEO, Saegusa began sending out personalized emails to select executives, encouraging them to hone their skills as management talent. These one-on-one communiques were kept confidential, a means to customize guidance for individual executives.

You may wonder: What does KJKJ stand for? It's an acronym from the Japanese, meaning "letter of advice for executive talent."

The emails were sent to people considered candidates for the management track. The hope was that they would be taken as constructive advice, rather than as critiques.

Remember K. Kagami from the launch of the China business in Chapter 4? He was the first recipient of a KJKJ letter. Over the following 12 years, Saegusa issued about 200 of these letters in all.

Saegusa wrote the emails late at night, early in the morning, or over the weekend, whenever he had some time to think quietly. Even today, the emails' addressees remain secret, unless the recipient let it be known. Word of their existence has leaked out, however. Apparently at least once, when managers got together for drinks, one started to talk about the letter he received, and others lamented not having received one, jokingly taking it to mean they were not considered management talent.

9. Cell Splits of Teams
   Misumi grew rapidly after Saegusa took the reins.

It took 40 years for the company to reach $500 million in sales when Saegusa assumed CEO. In only four years, it added another $500 million and topped $1 billion, growing at a compound average of 19% per annum.

Perennially short-staffed, the company needed to expand, too.

Following Saegusa's organizational design, what he named *cell splits* occurred frequently. For example, recall the FA Business Division, led by Nagao, who was featured in Chapter 2. The division comprised only 2 business teams when Saegusa arrived. Four years later, it had 11 of them.

Across the company as a whole, there were 20 teams when Saegusa arrived. Four years later that had doubled to 38.

The following year, the number had reached 57 globally. A threefold increase.

## 10. Forming Internal Companies

In Saegusa's sixth year, shortly before the global financial crisis struck, sales topped $1.2 billion. In six years, sales grew 2.5 times, an average 16% per annum. Meanwhile, over the same period the Japanese economy saw only tepid growth.

As sales grew, the organization continued to grow, too. Personnel shortages forced officers and managers to fill multiple roles, hampering the deployment of a global strategy. It was a tough time, with the organization stretched thin.

In the beginning, seven subordinates, including officers and division general managers, reported directly to CEO. It was a standard he set based on his past experience that he should not have more than 10 subordinates to provide sufficient review and guidance. He heard GE's Jack Welch had set 13 for himself.

In reality, after only four years at the helm, the organization grew to the point where he had 20 subordinates reporting directly to him. His jam-packed calendar made it difficult to schedule appointments. Some under-performing subordinates took advantage of the situation and successfully hid away for three months or so making no contact with the CEO, causing Saegusa to lose sight into their divisions.

It was unsustainable. The Misumi Organizational Model needed an additional concept. Rapid growth had lent urgency to something that otherwise could have gone untouched for a few years. Success creates new challenges.

To Saegusa, the easiest solution was to add one more management layer at the executive level above the divisions.

Eventually, Saegusa invented a different organizational model, a "Misumi internal company". It resembled a subsidiary company in functions, but still stayed inside the Misumi's corporate organization. An Internal company has two or three divisions under it and has its own board meeting for its own management issues.

Saegusa envisioned that internal companies would have a position called president at its head. It would provide opportunities for young management to gain experience running a company. The other merit was about the fact that the Japanese tax law in those days did not allow consolidating profit and loss of subsidiaries and therefore Saegusa's idea was better for tax purposes to absorb losses incurred by new business challenges.

The internal company structure launched in July of Saegusa's fifth year. For the first time since its founding, the company jettisoned its centralized organization with all authority vested in the CEO.

## The Organization Continues to Evolve

A stagnant organizational structure dampens a company's vitality. Even changes that appear at first glance to cut across the grain of existing organizational philosophies may fit the strategy when viewed from a new vantage point.

Again, dynamism is built into the Misumi Organization Frameworks. Therefore, the organization changes as the company does. The Misumi Organizational Model is a dynamic model that continues to evolve.

Over 14 years, Misumi's organization underwent three major transformations, from Taguchi's team structure to Saegusa's organizational theory for balancing energized teams and strategic alignment, and finally, decentralized authority.

# Epilogue

## Calling All Aspiring Managers

This concludes the story of a corporate transformation at Misumi. I will conclude this book in the first person.

The story took you through the process of deploying a global strategy, production innovations and operational reforms. Each reform incorporated time-based strategies. As the reforms dovetailed with each other, the Misumi business model gradually became sophisticated enough to compete against the megatrends in business innovations that began in the West (Saegusa Management Note 5: The International Megatrend in Business Innovations). Over the span of 12 years, the company underwent an astounding transformation.

Executive recruiting ads appeared in major Japanese newspaper. "The CEO of Misumi calls on you to step forward if you aspire to become a top executive in the future"

I strove to cultivate management talent throughout my time at the helm. About three months after becoming CEO, we canvassed all job-search media with my philosophy and put recruitment ads in a major newspaper, calling on recruits to, "Apply here if you aspire to become an executive leader," and, "Put your strength to the test with us."

The message was simple. If you desire the stable career of a salaryman, there is nothing wrong with that, Saegusa would say. But if you aspire to become a strong business leader, free yourself from being tied down in a conservative environment and give Misumi a try.

I envisaged handing over the reins to a management team in their 40s. I set out to build an organization that would make that possible and, ultimately, that is what happened.

But the idea of running a one-man show until I became decrepit with old age ran counter to my commitment to cultivate management talent. Therefore, my aim was to step down once I had groomed my successor.

So, I counted backward. If I wanted to hand over the reins to a team in their 40s, what age would they need to be today? I came up with an age range of 36 to 44 years old. I assembled a pool of talent and gave them challenging assignments to help them grow into a management role.

When I arrived, I ordered a customized license plate for my company car. The plate bore a four-digit number—the first two digits for the year I became CEO and the next two digits for my age at the time. It served as a reminder of how many years had passed since I had arrived and to think about the timing of my retirement every day.

## Chasing Our Tails

Over time, I realized my decision to narrow the pool of talent by age range would not work.

At Misumi, these candidates were given opportunities they would not have seen for another 10 or 20 years at other companies. They were top-tier talent among equal-age peers and came here of their own accord, in search of opportunity. But once here, they had to learn how to grow to fill a bigger pair of shoes. Like over-inflated balloons, they were stretched too thin and they struggled to grow into their new role.

They all kept their chins up and went about their work with tremendous devotion and passion. But they did not develop quickly as management talent.

When I turned 40, I had already worked as a strategy consultant, led two business companies and a venture investment company, all three as the president. I knew I could not expect them to follow in my footsteps. Nevertheless, the management skills of this pool of roughly 40-year-old Japanese were much weaker than expected.

Most were unaccustomed to having people report to them. Some of them lacked a senior executive's common sense for numbers and failed to exhibit a drive to make money. They could talk the talk, but they could not put together a strategy. And when it came time to walk the walk, many were too weak to stay grounded and exhibit enough leadership to unify their team.

I gave them basic guidance, trying to correct their salaryman-like habits, but that took a lot of time and patience.

Our expansion overseas fueled tremendous growth, and the pool of leadership talent was already stretched thin. We reaped the benefits of reforms sooner than expected.

The situation developed so quickly that by the time they achieved some personal growth, they already needed even more management skills to manage it, as if they were chasing their own tails.

## Crisis in the Growth

If I put someone with potential into a higher position, and they were clearly in over their head, I gave them about two to four years to let them work it out—unless and until the situation became dire—all the while providing close guidance.

It was exhausting and time-consuming to teach and direct them. At times, I felt like a grade-school teacher.

While I was trying to give them the training they needed, some lost motivation. Others were too proud, unable to recognize their own failings. It all falls on deaf ears if the person lacks self-awareness.

With rapid growth, the workload intensified. In the beginning, I tried to take one-week breaks off from work twice a year. That gradually became difficult. As an officer, the higher your compensation the greater your contribution should be. Otherwise, you are doing a disservice to your employees. I have maintained that philosophy since my 30s, when I first led a company.

But you can't overwork yourself. Leaders need to maintain a proper reserve of physical and mental energy to make sound decisions. Employee development and hiring chronically fell behind the company's growth, forcing many to cover multiple roles. I even filled in for division general managers at times. We all worked hard.

## Alternative Way to Ease the Pain

Now I can speak frankly. There were times when I questioned my own commitment to developing management talent in Japan. Many times, I considered taking a shortcut—to replace people instead of spending the time and effort it would take to teach them.

But what if I had abandoned my pledge to attract and develop young talent in the face of rapid business growth? What other options would I have had?

Obviously, I could have targeted a more-experienced group—people in their 50s, say. That would have made things easier for me as we sought to keep pace with rapid growth.

But there was no guarantee such a generation would have produced a sufficiently talented pool. Many of those I interviewed were hardcore management-level salarymen—they make their junior employees do all the work while they sit back and relax. Even so, it was tempting to consider going in that direction to develop management talent, given the pressing need to keep up with the business.

Ultimately, I decided to stick it out. Otherwise, the young hires would see officer recruits would come in above them and they would have to wait another 10 years or more before they could climb the ranks to the top tiers of management. Some might question why they came to Misumi in the first place. And it would end my dream of handing over the reins to a team in their 40s. We would become just a run-of-the-mill company. The younger tiers of employees would also be negatively impacted.

To avoid that fate, I stayed the original course. Meanwhile, I kept my struggle to myself. It was my fight to fight.

Today, Misumi's management team is made up of people in their 40s or slightly above. That makes it unique for a company with over $3 billion in sales. I wouldn't be able to say that if I had changed direction back then. Looking back, I am glad I stuck it out and groomed a generation of management talent.

## The Difficulty of Developing Talent

Many left the company after failing to grow into the bigger roles I assigned them. Fortunately, many more stayed and grew. The strong leaders featured in each chapter of this book, who overcame setbacks to achieve breakthroughs and tremendous success, all distinguished themselves by meeting the challenge head-on. Even if they were to leave the company someday, they would make exemplary graduates.

Did I eventually succeed in my goal to develop management talent? Did Misumi prove successful as a testing ground for a new model of Japanese management?

During my tenure as CEO, I was constantly reminded of the difficulty of developing talent. It takes decades to groom management candidates, so I doubled the pace, trying to achieve in 10 years what might take 20 years elsewhere.

At least I succeeded in my goal to hand over the helm to a team of managers in their 40s. But it will take another decade before we truly know whether my drive to mold talent in Japan was a success.

I taught them to fish. Will they go on to teach others? Will the chain remain unbroken? Will today's middle-management ranks rise to upper-management tiers? How many of today's employees in their 20s and 30s will blossom into future leaders for Japan?

Misumi is blessed with an unusually high concentration of ambitious people. But they will need to gain more experience overcoming challenges to improve their management skills and take the lead in Japan's business world.

I hope that those who have moved on to other opportunities will find that their experiences here prove valuable as they step into future roles that leverage their management capabilities, in Japan and internationally.

## A Company is a Living Organism

After 12 years as CEO and 4 years as the Chairman of the Board, altogether 16 years on the management of Misumi, I retired. Over that time, sales grew from $500 million to over $3 billion. Employee head count grew from 340 to over 10,000 globally.

Today, as Senior Chairman, I carry no executive responsibilities, but my remaining role is to teach management frameworks and strategic thinking at the Misumi Strategy School and to give advice to the board from time to time as requested.

Companies are living beings, their fates decided by the people there at any given time. Will Misumi continue to grow, will it settle into mediocrity, or might it sputter and crash? The company's fate is in the hands of the current CEO and the management team.

The fate of a company is determined by the entrepreneurs who pour their passion into it, and the business leaders who identify with their vision. That is the beginning of a business. It requires strategy and zeal.

I hope this book provides suggestions for those of you who aspire to enhance your management skills and rise to the level of a professional business leader.

# ABOUT THE AUTHOR

## Tadashi Saegusa

Senior Chairman & the Second-Era Founder,
MISUMI Group, Inc.

Tadashi Saegusa graduated from Hitotsubashi University in Tokyo and later earned an MBA from Stanford University. He was the first Japanese consultant with the Boston Consulting Group hired in Japan.

He spent his business life breaking with convention in Japan—a nation that rewards conformity. In his 30's, he had headed two companies in turnaround situations and engaged in venture capital investment, each as the president. In his 40's, he pursued a trailblazing career as a turnaround specialist for troubled businesses, amid the collapse of Japan's economy after the bubble burst. Through his extensive experience, he developed unique management frameworks designed to revive underperforming companies.

After taking the helm at Misumi, guided by an aspiration to forge a new corporate model for Japan, he implemented a far-reaching chain of reforms. The 40-year-old company with $500 million in sales doubled to $1 billion in four short years. During his tenure Misumi grew to a $3 billion company. This book follows the pursuit of a new style of entrepreneurship and corporate transformation in global management.

*Books by Tadashi Saegusa*

---

| | Japanese Titles |
|---|---|
| *Professional Strategist** | 「戦略プロフェッショナル」 |
| *A Crisis in Japanese Corporate Management** | 「経営パワーの危機」 |
| *Turnaround Task Force** | 「Ｖ字回復の経営」 |
| *It's all about Time* | 「ザ・会社改造」 |

*Currently only available in Japanese, Korean and Chinese